meditation
the complete guide

meditation
the complete guide

More than **35** practices
for everyone from
the beginner to
the healing professional

_jump right
in to the
the "Review Tips"_

Patricia Monaghan & Eleanor G. Viereck

New World Library
Novato, California

New World Library
14 Pamaron Way
Novato, CA 94949

Cover design: Peri Palone
Text design: Mary Ann Calser
Editorial: Becky Benenate and Chris Cone

Library of Congress Cataloging-in-Publication Data

Monaghan, Patricia.
Meditation — the complete guide / by Patricia Monaghan and
Eleanor G. Viereck.
p.   cm.
Includes bibliographical references and index.
ISBN 1-57731-088-8 (alk. paper)
I. Meditation.   I. Viereck, Eleanor.   II. Title.
BL627.M655   1999
158.1'2 — dc21   99-34298
                                                        CIP

First printing, September 1999
ISBN 1-57731-088-8
Printed in Canada on acid-free paper
Distributed to the trade by Publishers Group West

10 9 8 7 6 5 4 3 2

The truth waits for eyes unclouded by longing.

— *Tao Te Ching*

Contents

INTRODUCTION • WHAT IS MEDITATION? • xvii

Why Practice Meditation?   xviii
    How Does Meditation Enhance Performance?   xix
    How Does Meditation Promote Well-Being?   xix
    What Is the Spiritual Goal of Meditation?   xx
How Is Meditation Different from Relaxation or Self-Hypnosis?   xxi
How Is Meditation Different from Thinking?   xxi
How Can I Choose the Meditation Technique That Is Right for Me?   xxi
Is There Any Religious Affiliation with Meditation?   xxii
What You Need to Meditate   xxii
How Do You Acquire the Discipline to Meditate?   xxiii
Frequently Asked Questions   xxiii
Resources   xxiv

CHAPTER 1: WHAT KIND OF MEDITATOR ARE YOU? • 1
Reasons for Meditating   2
Religion and Philosophy   3
Lifestyle, Health, and Habits   3
Scoring the Self-Test   5
Prerequisites and Obstacles   5
    Prerequisites   5
    Obstacles   6
    What to Do in an Emergency   8
Resources   9

Part 1: Shamanism

INTRODUCTION • SHAMANISM • 13
Shamanism and Women   14
Trance and Meditation   15
Shamanic Techniques   16

CHAPTER 2: TRANCE DANCING • 19

    Contemporary Uses   21
    How to Begin   22
    Review Tips   23
    Resources   24

CHAPTER 3: DRUMMING • 25

    Contemporary Uses   26
    How to Begin   27
    Review Tips   31
    Resources   32

CHAPTER 4: ECSTATIC POSTURES • 33

    Contemporary Uses   34
    How to Begin   35
    Review Tips   36
    Resources   37

CHAPTER 5: SHAMANIC JOURNEYING • 39

    Contemporary Uses   40
    How to Begin   41
    Review Tips   43
    Resources   43

Part 2: Yoga

INTRODUCTION • YOGA • 47

    Resources   48

CHAPTER 6: YOGA ASANAS • 49

    Contemporary Uses   49
    How to Begin   50
        Hints and Cautions   51
    The Postures of Asanas   53
        Standing   54
        Standing Exercise   55
    Review Tips   58
        Sitting   59
        Sitting Exercise   61
    Review Tips   62
        Lying   62

Lying Exercise   64
Review Tips   65
Warrior Pose   65
Warrior Pose Exercise   65
Review Tips   66
Resources   66

CHAPTER 7: YOGA BREATHING • 67

Contemporary Uses   68
How to Begin   70
Observe the Breath While Lying   70
Practice in a Sitting Posture   71
Review Tips   72
Resources   73

CHAPTER 8: YOGA MEDITATION • 75

Pratyahara   75
Dharana   76
Dhyana   77
Samadhi   77
How to Begin   78
Meditation Exercise   78
Review Tips   79
Resources   79

CHAPTER 9: MANTRA • 81

Contemporary Uses   83
How to Begin   84
Review Tips   85
Resources   85

Part 3: Buddhism

INTRODUCTION • BUDDHISM • 89

Resources   91

CHAPTER 10: MINDFULNESS • 93

Contemporary Uses   94
How to Begin   96

Review Tips   97
Resources   97

CHAPTER 11: LOVINGKINDNESS • 99

Contemporary Uses   99
How to Begin   100
   Traditional *Metta* Practice   101
   The Practice of *Tonglen*   102
   Lovingkindness and Guilt   103
Review Tips   103
Resources   104

CHAPTER 12: *VIPASSANĀ* • 105

Contemporary Uses   105
How to Begin   107
   Sitting Meditation for Beginners   107
   The Posture of Meditation   108
   Posture Exercise   109
Review Tips   109
Resources   109

CHAPTER 13: *ZA-ZEN* • 113

Contemporary Uses   115
How to Begin   116
Review Tips   119
Resources   119

CHAPTER 14: ZEN IN ACTION • 121

Contemporary Uses   123
How to Begin   123
Review Tips   125
Resources   126

CHAPTER 15: TANTRISM • 127

Contemporary Uses   129
How to Begin   130
Review Tips   131
Resources   132

Part 4: Taoism

INTRODUCTION • TAOISM • 135

Philosophical Concepts of Taoism 137
Traditions of Taoism 138

CHAPTER 16: T'AI CHI • 141

Contemporary Uses 142
How to Begin 143
  T'ai Chi Chih 143
Review Tips 145
Resources 146

CHAPTER 17: QIGONG • 147

Contemporary Uses 148
How to Begin 149
Review Tips 151
Resources 152

Part 5: Islam

INTRODUCTION • ISLAM • 157

The Importance of the Koran 159
The Five Pillars of Islam 161
The Sufi Movement 161

CHAPTER 18: SUFI BREATHING • 163

Contemporary Uses 165
How to Begin 165
Review Tips 167
Resources 167

CHAPTER 19: SUFI DANCING • 169

Contemporary Uses 170
How to Begin 171
Review Tips 172
Resources 172

Part 6: Western Traditions

INTRODUCTION • WESTERN TRADITIONS • 177

Western Mysticism   178
Recent Expansions of the Western Tradition   179

CHAPTER 20: CONTEMPLATIVE PRAYER • 181

Contemporary Uses   183
How to Begin   184
Review Tips   185
Resources   185

CHAPTER 21: CANDLE MEDITATION • 187

Contemporary Uses   188
How to Begin   189
Review Tips   191
Resources   191

CHAPTER 22: INSPIRATIONAL READING • 193

Contemporary Uses   194
How to Begin   195
Review Tips   197
Resources   197

CHAPTER 23: FREE-FORM MEDITATION GROUPS • 199

Contemporary Uses   200
How to Begin   201
Review Tips   203
Resources   204

CHAPTER 24: QUAKER WORSHIP • 205

Contemporary Uses   207
How to Begin   209
Review Tips   211
Resources   211

CHAPTER 25: LABYRINTH WALKING • 213

Walking Meditations   214
Labyrinths and Mazes   215

Mythical Background 216
Contemporary Uses 217
How to Begin 217
Review Tips 218
Resources 219

CHAPTER 26: BIOFEEDBACK • 221

Contemporary Uses 221
How to Begin 222
Review Tips 224
Resources 224

Part 7: Creative Meditations

INTRODUCTION • CREATIVE MEDITATIONS • 227

Creation As Brain State Alteration 228
Brain States, Meditation, and Art 230

CHAPTER 27: SKETCHING FROM NATURE • 233

Contemporary Uses 234
How to Begin 236
Review Tips 237
Resources 237

CHAPTER 28: NEEDLE CRAFTS • 239

Contemporary Uses 240
How to Begin 241
Review Tips 243
Resources 244

CHAPTER 29: HAIKU • 245

Contemporary Uses 246
How to Begin 247
Review Tips 249
Resources 250

CHAPTER 30: THE BODY SCAN • 253

Contemporary Uses 254
How to Begin 254

Body Scan Exercise   255
The Body Scan Litany   257
Review Tips   259
Resources   259

Part 8: Meditations in Life

INTRODUCTION • MEDITATIONS IN LIFE • 263

CHAPTER 31: SPORTS AS MEDITATION • 265

Contemporary Uses   267
    In the Zone   268
How to Begin   270
Review Tips   271
Resources   272

CHAPTER 32: GARDENING • 273

Contemporary Uses   274
How to Begin   275
Review Tips   276
Resources   277

CHAPTER 33: PILGRIMAGE • 279

Contemporary Uses   280
How to Begin   282
Review Tips   284
Resources   284

CHAPTER 34: NATURE • 287

Contemporary Uses   288
How to Begin   290
    Cosmic Ceremonies   290
    The Shambhala Warriors: A Prophecy   292
Review Tips   293
Resources   293

CHAPTER 35: MEDITATIONS FOR PAIN AND GRIEF • 295

Contemporary Uses   295
How to Begin   296

Physical Pain   297
Shower of Relaxation Exercise   297
Emotional Pain   298
Meditating on Emotions   299
Resolving Emotions Exercise   299
Meditating with Someone Who Is Dying   301
Meditating When Someone Criticizes You   302
Review Tips   303
Resources   304

CHAPTER 36: LISTENING • 305
Contemporary Uses   306
How to Begin   307
Listen to the Small Sounds   308
Review Tips   308
Resources   309

Part 9: Active Imagination

INTRODUCTION • ACTIVE IMAGINATION • 313
Resources   314

CHAPTER 37: DIALOGUES WITH SELF • 315
Contemporary Uses   316
How to Begin   316
Active Imagination Exercise   317
Review Tips   319
Resources   319

CHAPTER 38: VISUALIZATION • 321
Contemporary Uses   323
How to Begin   324
Visualization Exercise   324
Relaxation Technique   325
Affirmations   326
Visualization and Anxiety   326
Types of Images   327
Review Tips   329
Resources   329

CHAPTER 39: KINESTHETIC MEDITATIONS • 331

Contemporary Uses   332
How to Begin   334
    Kinesthetic Exercise   335
Review Tips   337
Resources   337

CONCLUSION • A MEDITATION ON MEDITATION • 339

INDEX • 341

ABOUT THE AUTHORS • 353

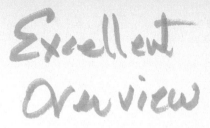
Excellent
Overview

Introduction • What Is Meditation?

*When we begin to allow the embodied current to pass through
the body freely, we effortlessly are drawn into a feeling tone
that, for lack of a better word, we call love.*

— Will Johnson

Meditation does not require faith or belief, although confidence in the efficacy of the practice does help to motivate the practitioner. The benefits of meditation practice include the creation of new levels of organization in the mind. Meditation involves choice. You are choosing to be present — now, now, now, and now. It is a practice of training your attention by focusing it on something. The focus of your attention can be on something in the present moment such as a flower, a candle, a sound, or your own breath. Through the practice the mind settles down. However, the practice is not the same as meditation; it is only a practice. In one sense of the word, meditation is not something that you do — meditation happens like a gift of grace, often as a result of practice.

Meditation is not a religion. Meditation is not a doctrine. Meditation is not another "good" that you acquire. Meditation can be objectless and consist of just sitting. Meditation should not become a career; it should be more like a hobby, something you do because of its own aesthetic pleasure. Think of it as play rather than work. While you are playing, your mind is more open. So long as the practice has a lightness of approach, there is a quality of freedom from desire and ambition. When we meditate for something we only become further trapped in the noose of acquisitiveness.

xvii

Meditation is the path, not the goal. If one needs consolation, one can find practices that tend to heal and promote comfort. But if one is prepared for a challenge, then meditative practices are available that are designed to promote awakening. Meditation does not necessarily mean sitting cross-legged and chanting a mantra, although that may work for some. This book describes many ways of meditating in the midst of other activities.

You are wise to begin by developing your own regular formal sitting or walking practices. Meditation is like the ringing of a bell. The afterglow of the experience is like the sound of the bell as it dies. You need to meditate again before the afterglow fades in order to maintain and amplify the effect. No matter what method you use, meditation can help you penetrate the illusion of separateness.

WHY PRACTICE MEDITATION?

Meditation teaches you to know where you are in life; to know how to respond with appropriate spontaneity to any situation, when to allow your emotions to flow, when to suppress them; and to know the condition of your body. Your goals for meditation will probably change throughout your life. At first you may have a goal such as healing a specific malady that is stress related. Later, according to your personal spiritual metaphors, you may enlarge your goals to include such concepts as wisdom, enlightenment, grace, recovering a lost primary experience, discovering the ground of being, or even the goal of not having a goal. (There is something to be said for the practice of wandering through inner space or outer space without an agenda.) You might adopt the goal of aligning yourself with the forces of the universe, which is fine; but then you have to figure out what those forces are.

During ordinary life our senses are constantly bombarded and our thoughts are active. Without being aware of it we are the star in "The Drama of Me." When we meditate, we become aware of our personal melodrama. Our thoughts become more calm and clear, and our ability to direct our attention to the object of our choice improves. It is essential that we develop our inner resources both for our sanity and to give us the perspective to act wisely in the world.

Three good goals to have for the practice of meditation are martial, medical, and spiritual.

How Does Meditation Enhance Performance?

The first goal is called "martial," which means the enhancement of performance. This goal can be achieved through the practice of the martial arts, in which meditation is included as a part of many traditional training programs. The martial category includes sports. Sports psychologists are using imagery and relaxation techniques in training programs for all kinds of athletes from professional to the everyday fitness walker. Chapter 31, Sports As Meditation, discusses and describes some of these practices.

Other kinds of performance can benefit from meditation as well because it enhances all types of creativity. Musicians, actors, and dancers meditate in order to improve their skill in performance. Students use meditation techniques to improve their performance on tests and in report writing. The enhanced sensitivity that results from meditation will also enhance one's ability to parent and create loving relationships. Business persons, government and commercial employees, and entrepreneurs are all learning that relaxation techniques help them make better decisions, enjoy more energy, and bring more insight to the workplace.

How Does Meditation Promote Well-Being?

Medical reasons for meditating include all manner of healing, therapy, wellness, and health-maintenance goals. Meditators live longer and suffer fewer degenerative diseases. Specific meditations for pain relief and self-healing are presented in chapter 35, Meditations for Pain and Grief, and will give you some idea of how these practices can be used. A Hindu nun who worked with dying patients in a hospital in San Francisco managed to keep a marvelous sense of equanimity in the face of the tragedies surrounding her. When someone asked her, "How do you deal with your own fear of dying?" she described the daily morning meditation practice she led for the ward staff. The entire staff participated even though they did not share the same religious beliefs or spiritual metaphor. The simple act of performing a daily meditation practice served their needs for personal fortitude, patience, wisdom, and the courage to be caregivers in the terminal cancer ward.

Meditation throws the light of awareness on the personal unconscious, which contains all that you would like to forget and all that you do not wish to admit to yourself or to anyone else. So if you have always avoided your shadow side and covered up your dark corners, this illumination may reveal some scary and difficult feelings. Some persons with addictions or other psychological disorders might benefit more from psychotherapy or counseling than they would from a private meditation practice. Many Westerners have a fear of the personal unconscious; some even think it is morbid. The Western tradition that most closely resembles meditation in its pursuit of understanding the unconscious is the psychology of the unconscious or depth psychology as codified by Carl Jung.

The healing process is enhanced by meditation in the case of physical ailments that are psychosomatic in origin. Psychosomatic illnesses are physical disorders that have an emotional or psychological cause. Meditation can have a beneficial influence on emotional balance, and it can promote physical healing in cases where disease is aggravated by emotional imbalance. Stress-related diseases and disorders seem to respond to the therapeutic effect of a meditation practice. Herbert Benson, M.D., director of the Mind/Body Center at Harvard University, studied the physiology of meditators and found decreases in their heart rate, breathing rate, metabolism, and blood lactate level, and their blood pressure is lower than the "normal" population. There is also an increase in alpha waves in the brain, and brain activity moves from the left hemisphere to the right hemisphere of the brain during meditation.

WHAT IS THE SPIRITUAL GOAL OF MEDITATION?

The third goal of meditation is spiritual. To determine what we mean by the spiritual dimension of meditation, we need to ask what we mean by spirituality. Spirituality is aliveness, according to Joseph Campbell, foremost interpreter of myth of our time. The word *spirit*, meaning life, comes from the same root as the word *inspire*. The opposite of inspire is expire, which also means death. *The Random House College Dictionary* defines spiritual as: "The incorporeal part of man in general or of an individual, or an aspect of this, such as the mind or the soul." Just as in many spiritual traditions, the goal of meditation is to create a balance between mind, heart, and body — or body and soul.

How Is Meditation Different from Relaxation or Self-Hypnosis?

Relaxation is a passive process. Although you need to relax to practice many forms of meditation, and even though meditation allows your body and mind to relax, meditation is an active process. The meditator consciously directs his or her attention to the object of meditation, or to the process of just sitting. Self-hypnosis, like meditation, involves a period of time when you concentrate your attention on an object. However, in self-hypnosis you enter a sort of semiconscious trance state. In meditation you remain conscious the entire time.

How Is Meditation Different from Thinking?

Meditation attempts to transcend the kind of thinking in which you identify with your thoughts or you are lost in your thoughts. The practice of meditation gives you the ability to observe your thoughts, just as you can observe all other experiences. Without the precise awareness developed in meditation, the subject of your thoughts usually dominates your attention and distracts you from the condition of your moment-to-moment mental state. Through meditation you become detached from the thoughts and emotions, and you reside in a "witness" consciousness. You observe thoughts and you develop the skill of allowing them to subside at will. This process is extremely restorative after a normal day of activity.

How Can I Choose the Meditation Technique That Is Right for Me?

The self-test in chapter 1 will help guide you in selecting a meditation technique. There is no one meditation technique that is right for everybody; the very question of right and wrong connotes a judgmental attitude. The important thing is to find one that works for you. You can read about the techniques in this book and try the ones that feel appropriate or possible. Don't worry about doing it right. Just practice every day and take note of the consequences in your life. Let your intuition and insight guide you. Nobody knows you as well as you do.

Although this book presents dozens of different meditation techniques, it would be a mistake to learn them all, as if knowing many different styles would make you a morally superior person. Quite the contrary. Chyogyam Trungpa, a Tibetan Buddhist master who founded the Naropa Institute for Buddhist Studies in Boulder, Colorado, says this assumption is a form of spiritual pride, which he calls *spiritual materialism.* The way to prevent this conceit is to approach meditation with a simple, uncomplicated attitude. The various techniques presented here are part of a whole tapestry. When you see the whole, you do not need to keep adding new strategies.

IS THERE ANY RELIGIOUS AFFILIATION WITH MEDITATION?

Meditation deals with something that is within us. It can lead us to a state of grace. The term *grace* comes from the Christian tradition, but the experience is common to all spiritual traditions. Grace is a gift. It can heal us and guide us and give us a sense of meaning. Whether you call the source of this gift God or soul is not important. You may call it the higher self, inner wisdom, theta-wave activity, peace, the inner ground of Being, Goddess, or natural law, if you are scientifically inclined. Whatever you call it, you can benefit from coming into harmony with it.

WHAT YOU NEED TO MEDITATE

You need three things to meditate: a quiet place, an upright and relaxed posture, and a meditative practice. If you are a beginner, the quiet place helps protect you from disturbances and distractions. An advanced meditator can sit in absorption in more challenging locations. The posture of meditation will be described in great detail in the section on sitting in chapter 6. Meditation practice includes focused concentration. It requires that you direct your attention to some thing and leave it there. It requires rigor, but not effort. In Chinese martial arts such as T'ai Chi, this non-effort is called *wu wei.* The quality of rigor is a strict, not stiff, perseverance. It includes a kind of loving devotion, but not obsession. It is not a strict discipline involving a lot of fear or effort; instead, one becomes absorbed in the object of meditation.

How Do You Acquire the Discipline to Meditate?

One way to motivate yourself to maintain a regular practice of meditation is to find a spiritual master, "fall in love" with him or her, and use this attraction to lead you to emulate the teacher. Remain discerning in selecting a spiritual master and keep your common sense. If you choose this route, be sure to read about some of the hazards in chapter I.

Another way to motivate yourself is to learn a meditation from a book or a teacher. Try it for a short time and see if you notice an improvement in your energy, your sensitivity, your equanimity, or your reaction to stress.

Most people can practice aerobics or body building without understanding much about human anatomy and physiology. This is not true for meditation. Applying meditation techniques in a cookbook style without an understanding of the fundamentals may be either dangerous or merely superficial. There is a paradox here because the most subtle and sophisticated meditator actually approaches the process very much like a beginner, bringing few expectations and assumptions.

The mind is like a crazy monkey jumping from one thing to another, endlessly distracted and dispersed. The first thing that you discover when you begin to meditate is that you cannot keep the mind still. Do not give up. This observation that the mind is restless is the first step. Instead of berating yourself for failing to succeed on the first try, take delight in the opportunity to begin to learn about your mind.

When you are training yourself in meditation, the most important rule is not to force the mind to stay focused. The more you try to force the mind to concentrate on one object, the more it will jump. If you get angry with this continuous mental jumping, your anger will only increase the mind's tendency to scatter and be distracted. The ideal state of meditation occurs when your attention is completely focused, even for a short period of time, without using any force or mental tension.

Frequently Asked Questions

Isn't it selfish to forget about the world and indulge in navel gazing? The answer to this question depends on your intent and your motive. If you want to inflate yourself and expand your ego, then you are indulging in negative narcissism. If, on the other hand, your purpose is to come to your meditation to gain more skill in living a good ordinary life, then your practice will contribute to your own well-being and the well-being of others.

Isn't it insensitive to remain happy and peaceful when confronted with the suffering of others? To feel compassion toward the suffering of others is not the same as feeling sad yourself. You will only increase the unhappiness in the world if you dwell in a sentimental sort of pity. But if you can remain calm and quiet, you will be better able to alleviate the suffering of others. So, often, the best thing you can do for others is the inner work that you do for yourself.

How do I know if I am making progress? If you are developing equanimity you have made progress. You cannot create or prevent thoughts from arising, but you can break the habit of reacting to them with likes and dislikes. The wise person is one who has few preferences.

How can I meditate with a child? Children remind us how wonderful life is. To meditate with a child, take the child by the hand and walk, and as you walk, teach them to silently say *yes, yes, yes* as they breathe in and say *thank you, thank you, thank you* as they breathe out.

Resources

Batchelor, Steven. *Buddhism without Beliefs.* New York: Riverhead Press, 1997.

Benson, Herbert, and Marian Klipper. *The Relaxation Response.* New York: Avon, 1990.

Jung, C. G. *Psychology and the East.* Bollingen Series XX. Princeton, N.J.: Princeton University Press, 1978.

Kabat-Zinn, Jon. *Wherever You Go There You Are.* New York: Hyperion, 1994.

Kriyananda, Goswami. *Beginner's Guide to Meditation.* Chicago: The Temple of Kriya Yoga, 1990.

Miller, Barbara Stoller. *Yoga: Discipline of Freedom. The Yoga Sutras Attributed to Patanjali.* New York: Bantam Books, 1998.

Ornstein, Robert. *The Right Mind: Making Sense of the Hemispheres.* New York: Harcourt Brace, 1997.

Stendl-Rast, Br. David. *The Spiritual Message of Joseph Campbell.* Audiocassette. Boulder, Colo.: Sounds True, 1997.

Trungpa, Chyogyam. *Cutting Through Spiritual Materialism.* Boston, Mass.: Shambhala, 1987.

Chapter 1 • What Kind of Meditator Are You?

It's not about having any particular experience.
The practice is about opening to whatever presents itself.
— Joseph Goldstein

Not all kinds of meditation are appropriate for every individual. Philosophical and religious beliefs, lifestyles, talents, fears, doubts, and even financial considerations come into play when deciding what kind of meditative techniques to employ. While you are unlikely to be hurt or damaged by the gentle practices described in this book, if you select a meditative style that is inappropriate for you, you may find the practice difficult to continue, experience discouragement, and eventually stop meditating.

You are reading this book because you want something from meditation. Whatever your goal in meditating, you won't achieve it if you don't practice. If you choose an inappropriate style, you won't reap its benefits — because you'll give up. You may resort to medicine for high blood pressure, resume addictive habits to deal with stress, or find yourself still disconnected from your spiritual source. Finding the right meditation style can assist you in meeting your goals more effectively.

The following self-test will provide you with information about which types of meditation are most appropriate for you. To take this test, answer each question as accurately as you are able, taking into consideration all relevant aspects of your current life and health. Should you encounter a question that is not applicable to you, simply leave it unanswered. Then turn to

1

the scoring page to discover which meditations are most suitable to you. As with any test, there may be specific aspects of your life not included in these general questions that make a style of meditation other than what this test reveals more suitable. In addition, you may find that the challenge of a style that is not immediately comfortable to you keeps you motivated to continue practicing. Use this test the way you would any other tool: as a means to self-discovery, rather than as a limitation on self-knowledge.

Reasons for Meditating

1. *Are you meditating to deal with stress?* If so, you may find the following especially beneficial: drumming, yoga postures, yogic meditation, yogic breathing, chanting, Za-zen, meditation on sacred images, Qigong, T'ai Chi, biofeedback, needle crafts, journaling, gardening, sports.

✓2. *Are you meditating to become better attuned to the spiritual essence of life?* If you are, try the following: lovingkindness, mindfulness, or insight meditation; inspirational readings; Zen practice; Quakerism; gardening; pilgrimage; nature; dialogues with self; contemplative prayer.

3. *Are you meditating to become better attuned to others and the needs of society?* The following lead in that direction: lovingkindness meditation, Zen practice, inspirational readings, meditation in groups, pilgrimage, conflict negotiation.

✓4. *Are you interested in attaining an altered state of consciousness or light trance?* If you are, try the following: trance dancing, drumming, ecstatic postures, shamanic journeying, Tantra, Sufi dancing, labyrinth walking, guided meditations.

    If you are fearful of light trance, you may find these meditations challenging or even upsetting, especially those based in shamanic traditions.

✓5. *Are you meditating to become more deeply conscious of the natural world?* If so, you will find sketching from nature, gardening, and nature meditations appropriate.

6. *Are you meditating to deal with chronic pain?* If so, you may find the following beneficial: Qigong, yogic postures, T'ai Chi, biofeedback.

↜ 7. *Are you meditating to enhance your creative abilities or connect to the unconscious?* If so, you will find the section on creative meditations especially useful.

RELIGION AND PHILOSOPHY

1. *Do you practice a specific religion?* Those who practice a specific religion often find it best to follow, or at least to begin, with a meditative practice that reflects their beliefs. The following belief systems are represented in this book: Hinduism (see yoga), Buddhism, Taoism, Islam, Christianity (see contemplative prayer, inspirational reading, Quakerism), neopaganism (see candle meditation).

2. *If you practice a specific religion, does it discourage you from joining in the practice of another religion?* If you are discouraged from practicing the rituals of another faith, you may want to try one of the following meditations, none of which are faith-based: meditation in groups, biofeedback, sketching from nature, needle crafts, journaling, gardening, sports, pilgrimage, nature meditation, dialogues with self, guided meditations, listening.

3. *Are you uncomfortable with religious language and imagery?* If yes, you will find the non–faith-based meditations listed above to be appropriate.

LIFESTYLE, HEALTH, AND HABITS

1. *Are you able to meditate daily?* If you are not able to meditate at specific times each day, you may wish to consider the following forms of meditation: shamanic meditations (all), mindfulness meditation, lovingkindness meditation, Zen practice, inspirational reading, labyrinth walking, biofeedback, sketching from nature, needle crafts, gardening, pilgrimage, nature meditations, dialogues with self, listening.

2. *Are you distracted by the presence of others in meditation?* Those who need privacy for meditation will find the following well-suited to their needs: yogic postures, yogic breathing, meditation on sacred images, Sufi breathing, inspirational reading, contemplative prayer, candle meditation, sketching from nature, journaling, haiku, nature meditations, dialogues with self, listening.

3. *Do you find you fall asleep or drift into daydreaming when just sitting still?*

If so, to stay alert use active meditations such as the following: drumming, trance dancing, yogic postures, Qigong, T'ai Chi, Sufi dancing, labyrinth walking, all creative meditations, all meditations in life.

4. *Do you define yourself as creative?* If you have been discouraged from seeing yourself as creative, you may gain a great deal from exploring the creative meditations (see Part 7, Creative Meditations). They are low risk, enjoyable, and effective.

If you already define yourself as creative, less-structured meditations may be especially appealing to you; these include meditations in the shamanic, creative, meditation in life, and active imagination chapters.

✓ 5. *Are you interested in the psychological ramifications of the inner search?* The meditations listed in the active imagination chapter are especially profound in this regard, being based predominantly on the work of Carl Jung.

6. *Do you want to learn to quiet your mind once, and never have to do it again?* Biofeedback will teach you to control your inner responses to outer events. Once learned, the results are said to be relatively permanent. Other meditative techniques demand an ongoing commitment.

7. *Are you fearful of sexual feelings being aroused during meditation?* If so, avoid trance dancing, drumming, and Tantra.

8. *Do you suffer any physical handicaps?* Even meditative styles that require movement can usually be adapted for those with limited mobility; Qigong is especially effective for such people who are seeking a movement meditation. Physical limitations should not limit your meditative options.

9. *Do you suffer from an emotional or mental disorder?* Most meditative styles enhance, rather than detract from, the lives of those with mental or emotional disorders. However, certain shamanic techniques can be difficult for such individuals; these include trance dancing and ecstatic postures. Tantra is not usually a good option in such cases; pilgrimage, with the intense strains that travel can present, could also be a special challenge to such individuals. For those with anxiety or depressive disorders, who are seeking relief through meditation, biofeedback is an especially good option.

10. *Do you have epilepsy?* If so, avoid trance dancing.

Scoring the Self-Test

Most people will find that several forms of meditation are suitable to them. Looking through your answers, you will notice that some meditative forms occur frequently. Select one or more with which to start your practice. Choosing well at the beginning of your journey will contribute to a positive experience.

You may also discover there is a practice in which you are engaging — or more than one — without being aware of its meditative possibilities. Making those aspects of such activities as needlework and gardening more conscious may be all you need to enhance your life. Conversely, you may decide that you need to expand your repertoire of meditative options. There is no limit to the number of meditative styles a single person can practice. These meditations are not, in general, mutually exclusive (although some faith-based disciplines require you to refrain from using practices from other faiths). Your meditative needs may change with time and age, or with life's particular challenges; what worked for you as a young mother may no longer work in retirement.

Use this book as you would a map to a new country you are eager to explore. Let its chapters offer openings to ideas and practices and concepts that can enhance your life immeasurably. But the map is never the territory. Only by practicing these meditative forms yourself will you find the answers you seek — answers which, inevitably, lie within.

Prerequisites and Obstacles

Prerequisites

The major religious and philosophical traditions of the world each have a set of moral precepts and ethical guidelines they follow. You are probably familiar with the Ten Commandments of the Judeo-Christian tradition. Similar advice to avoid killing, stealing, lying, and harming others is contained in Buddhism, Hinduism, Confucianism, and indigenous traditions around the world. These social rules serve the good of society. The practitioner who abides by them is prepared to meditate. If you have just robbed a bank or murdered someone your meditation will be agitated, to say the least, and your meditation may also be agitated if you have pilfered, lied, coveted, or committed other sins.

OBSTACLES

The traditional meditation practices also have warnings about the dangers and stumbling blocks along the path of life. These difficulties arise in persons of all ages and in all types of meditative practice. The five obstacles from the Eastern traditions are: aversion, attachment, restlessness, ignorance, and sleepiness. Even if you have managed to abide by the various commandments of ethical and moral behavior, your meditation may be plagued by some of these obstacles.

People with different types of temperaments and personalities will experience different obstacles. Greedy types will be grasping for spiritual experiences and probably suffer more from the obstacle of attachment. Any feeling of desire or longing can be an obstacle in this category. Angry types are likely to judge others and to suffer feelings of opposition and recalcitrance. Anger is a powerful type of aversion.

Aversion can be mental or it can take the form of physical pain. Please note, however, that some pain is dangerous and is a signal that you are sitting in the wrong position and need to find a comfortable way of sitting. Some meditators have done permanent damage to their knees by ignoring this kind of pain. Pain caused by aversion is a different kind of physical pain that signals deep patterns of tension are coming into awareness. This is a good pain because it releases old stuck pain. If you ignore the dangerous pain you may harm yourself, but if you ignore the good pain, you may prevent yourself from working your way to a place where you have greater perspective and insight. How to tell the difference between the two is a subtle and important process.

The obstacle of restlessness promotes too much excitement and nervousness. Many types of disquieting feelings may arise during meditation and they can serve as obstacles. Ignorance of practice techniques can be dispelled by study, and sleepiness can be countered by standing, walking, or meditating outside. Getting more sleep sometimes helps to prevent sleepiness during meditation.

Every spiritual tradition has its own model. The practice of meditation can gently bring you a little more ease and quiet happiness and help you cultivate more calmness and lovingkindness. But the human psyche contains demonic, shadowy, and negative elements that must be faced sooner or later in order to integrate them and attain the greatest freedom.

So one has to face the whole inner world, pleasure and pain equally.

One kind of pain may be described by the metaphor of *kundalini.* In the Hindu tradition, *kundalini* is seen as an energy that usually remains "asleep" at the base of the spine. When this energy is awakened, it rises slowly up the spinal canal all the way to the head. This awakening may mark the beginning of the process of enlightenment. During its rise the *kundalini* encounters blocks or stress points that can cause pain. Once the block is removed, the *kundalini* energy moves upward and continues to awaken consciousness.

It is a balancing process. During meditation there may be sensations of heat or vibration. The sensations may be pleasant or frightening. One may even experience rapture. There may be trembling, shaking, or wild movement. There may be very pleasant thrills, vibrations, tingling, or prickles. You may feel as if your spine is on fire. You may see many lights, or a white light, or your entire body may dissolve into light. Other sensations of *kundalini* rising are not pleasant at all. They include pain and distressing visions or emotional upheavals. This process can go on for years as the body opens up and balances its energy systems.

Meditation can produce many kinds of altered states including strong emotional swings. Some of these states may be delightful, but they are not the goal. The real work is to let go of *whatever* is present. The work is to experience the entire world of phenomena, to see, hear, smell, taste, touch, and think — and to find our freedom in spite of the storm rather than insisting that the phenomena suit our preferences.

Meditative practices are powerful and potentially dangerous. If you are working alone and have a feeling that it is not safe to do this thing, please protect yourself. This "not safe" feeling might include extreme fear, or depression, or confusion, or even physical symptoms. If something like this happens to you, stop, and consult with a teacher, counselor, or expert who can advise you about the practice. Meditation is certainly not a panacea. In fact, Krishnamurti, when asked "What good does all this meditation do?" answered "It is no use at all." It is not guaranteed to make you rich, beautiful, or famous. It is a paradox. You do want to achieve your goal, but in your meditation practice you need to let go of the goal-oriented, overachieving, task-centered mode of doing and reside in the mode of being that helps to integrate your mind and body. It is the paradox of the Zen instruction, "Try not to try."

What to Do in an Emergency

The guidance of a skilled teacher is often necessary. There is a Spiritual Emergency Network that helps guide persons who are suffering a spiritual emergency and helps professional counselors and physicians to distinguish between a spiritual emergency and a psychotic breakdown. One way to tell the difference is that the person who sees visions knows that they are visions in a spiritual emergency, whereas in a psychotic situation the person believes the hallucinations are real. But if the sensations are too unpleasant and there is no teacher, simply stop the practice and focus on simple earthy things to ground yourself. Dig in the garden, walk or jog outside, get a massage, take a bath or shower, eat heavier foods. Slow down your spiritual awakening if you feel that it is threatening you.

Meditating for spiritual reasons does not require that you adhere to a particular religion. Despite the fact that the leaders of some fundamentalist religions disapprove of meditation because they want you to pray only in their way, one might argue that there are many paths to the same summit, and that all the traditions of the world's spiritual seekers have validity.

This brings up the issue of cults and brainwashing. A lot of cult leaders will promise to show you their truth, which they claim is the *only* truth, and they often threaten dire consequences if you listen to any other teacher. If you are looking for a teacher, you need to be aware of the dangers of and know how to identify a cult. A cult may support you, but it will also repress and limit you. Be wary if there are no graduates, and the followers remain forever dependent. Be wary if you are not permitted to ask questions or if the answer is "because the leader says so." Be wary if family members are regarded with paranoia. Be wary if the teacher insists that you surrender your will and your pocketbook, even if the word used is *loving* rather than *surrender.* Be wary if the group keeps secrets, especially about sex and money.

In meditation you develop the ability to witness with passive attention, to observe. This makes you vulnerable. So, it is important to choose a safe environment in which to meditate. In everyday life you constantly make choices and decisions. After practicing meditation with its choiceless awareness, you need to reenter your real-time life with some care; and you may find yourself reexamining your choices about money, relationships, and society. After you have given up your preferences and entered a timeless bliss, you may have to redevelop your everyday judgment skills. Some people lose interest in worldly things. However, meditation is a process of integrating the various ways of knowing and being, not an escape from ordinary reality. Meditation time provides a temporary respite from some aspects of ordinary reality.

After a meditation retreat or powerful inner practice, you may experience some difficulty reentering a challenging situation that you have escaped during meditation. It is much easier to find balance when you do not have to deal with an angry spouse or boss. Going back to them can cause a kind of culture shock. You may find yourself making new decisions about your relationships.

Meditation can be used as an escape or a way to deny difficulties, as a way to avoid feeling certain emotions, or as a way to dodge one's own shadow. We may imitate a spiritual practice to bolster our ego or seek security from change. As we mature in our practice we can find more freedom by facing the ways in which we have tried to escape or imitate or hide. The price for not facing our self-sabotaging behavior is to become stuck and depressed.

We cultivate compassion, but sometimes pity masquerades as compassion. Pity is more sentimental. We cultivate equanimity but sometimes indifference masquerades as equanimity. We cultivate lovingkindness but sometimes attachment masquerades as lovingkindness. These enemies arise from ignorance or fear. The way to protect against these enemies is to use our powers of discrimination to distinguish between the real and false values.

RESOURCES

Grof, Stanislav, M.D., and Christina Grof, eds. *Spiritual Emergency.* New York: Putnam, 1989.

Salzberg, Sharon, and Joseph Goldstein. *Insight Meditation: Correspondence Course Workbook.* Boulder, Colo.: Sounds True, 1996.

Spiritual Emergency Network, Institute of Transpersonal Psychology, 250 Oak Grove Ave., Menlo Park, CA 94025; (415) 327-2776

part 1
shamanism

Introduction • Shamanism

Those we call the ancients were really new in everything.
— Blaise Pascal

Deep in the recesses of European caves, great horses leap and gallop, bison rear and charge, and antelope graze and run. Painted or incised upon rock, these are vestiges of the earliest human culture of which we have record. They show that the spiritual impulse can be traced to the dawn of humanity, for the placement of these paintings, as well as their surrounding motifs and figures, suggest that the caves were not galleries or museums, but rather were ancient churches.

Little remains to tell us the specifics of the worship of those who painted and carved their visions in the vaulting caves some twenty-five to thirty thousand years ago. The caves may have been used for initiation rituals, for they do not seem to have been in regular use but rather to have been the location for occasional and important ceremonies. They are often located in inaccessible and even dangerous places, suggesting a spiritual journey preceded the revelation of their glories.

One of the most telling finds is a simple trace that could have been easily overlooked: the pattern of footprints, made in soft mud many thousands of years ago, then hardened by the same rocky glaze that forms stalactites and stalagmites. These footprints show someone moving in a circle, many

13

times, landing with each step hard on the heel. It is the record, scholars believe, of an ancient ritual dance.

On the cave walls dating to the Old Stone Age or Paleolithic period, we occasionally find human figures. One of these, the famous "sorcerer" image, has staring eyes and a rigid body that has apparently been punctured by many arrows. The body is half-standing, not lying down as a dead person would be. And its erect sexual organ further suggests that the figure is alive.

What could this strange position indicate? Scholars of shamanism believe the image represents the initiation of a shaman, for accounts from shamans in the last century show a remarkable similarity in imagery despite their wide geographical dispersion. Whether in Siberia or Australia, shamans describe their initiation as being torn apart or punctured with sharp objects such as spears or arrows. This psychic dismemberment is followed by recreation as a new being, one who has access to spirit realms not available to the uninitiated.

After initiation, it was the shaman's duty to enter into trance and, while in that altered state, to effect changes in the material world. Sometimes the shaman traveled to a distant realm where spirits of animals dwelled, and there begged for a more successful hunt. Sometimes the shaman went to the land of the dead, finding there the soul of someone who had died but whose spirit haunted survivors. The shamanic trance was not entered lightly, for the realms that the shaman traversed could be dangerous. The visions that shamans describe are frequently terrifying, involving spirit beings of great power and occasional malevolence. Thus the shaman had an arsenal of psychic practices to defend against their power, what the great scholar Mirca Eliade called "archaic techniques of ecstasy."

Shamanism and Women

While there is an increasing number of scholarly as well as popular works on shamanism, many of them imply, or even directly state, that shamanism is entirely or almost exclusively a male prerogative. Nothing could be further from the truth. In many male-dominated shamanic cultures, shamans must wear female attire when they practice, which suggests that female domination of this religious way may have been common in the past.

In other areas, shamanism is specifically a feminine role. Indeed, one taunting song from medieval Japan refers in derogatory fashion to a region as so deprived that "they even have male shamans there." In Japan and Korea, shamanism even today remains part of the religious sphere of women. In Siberia, frequently described as the ancient birthplace of shamanism, practitioners were as often female as male. Throughout the Americas, women as well as men practiced this important skill. In Scandinavian lands, the prophetic *voluspa* was the shaman of her society. Female shamans have been an important part of most if not all societies that practiced this religion.

It is possible that political changes resulted in the obliteration of the female shaman. This was certainly true in China, where there are records of widespread persecution of women shamans, so severe that ultimately all female practitioners were martyred. In Korea, too, women shamans or *mudang* were persecuted, although the religions survived underground for more than fifteen hundred years to reemerge in recent years.

The techniques that ancient shamans used are accessible to both men and women. Thus any source that suggests the role of shaman is restricted to men should be recognized as limited or inaccurate.

TRANCE AND MEDITATION

Shamanism's "archaic techniques of ecstasy" are humanity's most ancient reservoir of information about the way body, mind, and spirit interact. Although there is some evidence that shamanic practices may extend even to the precursor of our species, the Neanderthal race, it is clear that since the rise of *Homo sapiens* with the Cro-Magnon people our bodies and minds have not significantly changed or evolved. What worked for our most ancient relatives will still work for us: drumming and dancing will change our consciousness.

Many scholars find, in this most ancient of religions, the basis of later meditative disciplines such as yoga or the martial arts. Others contend that the intention of such disciplines is to attain a state of consciousness that, while different from that of ordinary life, nonetheless stops short of the visionary trance common to shamanism. Yet the shaman, rigid in body while the soul flies to another realm, seems physiologically little different from the yogi absorbed in deep meditation. What differs is the epic adventure reported by the shaman after returning from that altered state, an adventure that seems to have little in common with the mindless awareness of, for instance, the Zen practitioner.

Trance is, however, a common human experience. Studies of people who are asked to trace their thoughts while awake reveal that we engage in constant momentary forays into a dreamlike state. What we call consciousness is not, in fact, a steady state of crisply lucid awareness, but a fluidly shifting one. To enter into trance is to accept and embrace the more visionary or dreamlike moments, to enter that river of images with the confidence that it is possible to return. Trance is an extraordinarily variable experience, ranging from a light daydream to an intense transformative experience. It is a common human experience that offers benefits similar to what is more conventionally called meditation: it relaxes and refreshes, lowering blood pressure and heightening sensory awareness, pulling the mind away from limiting patterns and opening new doors of perception.

Some individuals seem to enter into trance more readily than others. For such a person, any meditative practice can bring on a trancelike experience in which the mind is flooded with vivid images and one experiences a sense of exhilaration tinged with danger. Often such people have vivid dreams as well, whether they can recall them in the waking state or not. For the unprepared, the trance state can be surprising and sometimes frightening. If one is not expecting to encounter dreamlike beings and narratives, even a light trance can feel dangerously out of control. Learning the techniques of shamanism can be either rewarding in itself or can assist the practitioner of other meditative disciplines by offering control over the natural trance state.

SHAMANIC TECHNIQUES

Shamanic techniques vary surprisingly little over the great span of this religion's domain. Two of the most important techniques, drumming and dancing, form the basis for the shamanically-oriented meditative techniques used today. Another, more controversial one, is the use of psychotropic or mind-altering substances. There is significant literature that maintains that shamans often employed vegetative concoctions: mushrooms, ergot from rye or wheat, even alcohol. Those who have struggled with addictive behaviors involving drugs or alcohol may benefit from learning shamanic consciousness alteration techniques, for their original soul intention in using addictive substances may have been to achieve the trance state or ecstasy.

The drum is, to the shaman, the main tool for altering consciousness, and is described by the shaman as creating a rope that both leads to the spheres beyond this one and provides a means to travel back to ordinary reality. Shamanic drumming is repetitive rather than complex and creates measurable physiological changes in both the drummer and the listener. Specifically, both the heartbeat and breath will "entrain" or synchronize with the drum, so that groups of individuals will find themselves literally embodying the rhythm.

Dancing, too, has the effect of changing consciousness. Even ballroom dance can create an ebullient mood of release and refreshment, but trance is induced either by repetitive dancing, as in many Native American pow-wow dances, or by expressive dance that follows only the body's promptings rather than choreographed steps (see chapter 39, Kinesthetic Meditation). The combination of drumming and dancing is found throughout the world and represents one of the most intense techniques for achieving the trance state upon which shamanism relies.

In shamanic tradition, extensive training was necessary to learn to employ these techniques. Called to shamanic practice by an inner experience, the novice shaman went through rigorous training. This included learning the myths and figures that explained the universe of images that emerge in trance. These images have an archetypal resonance that transcends culture, but each shamanic region developed its own mythic vocabulary. The name and attributes of the Great Goddess might vary, from the sun goddess of Australia to the great undersea divinity of the Inuit, but her presence is found in all shamanic religions.

Today, it is likely that someone interested in shamanism will not have the support of a community grounded in a millennia of practice, nor a shared vocabulary that names aspects of the experience. Nonetheless, increasing public awareness of and interest in this practice has led to the production of many weekend workshops that purport to teach shamanism. Given our cultural unfamiliarity with the trance state, such workshops can be a safe haven for those who wish to learn to navigate it. However, it is important to ascertain that the leaders are both skilled and ethical, for those in the trance state are very susceptible to suggestion.

Trance is such a natural human experience, however, that it is not necessary to attend a workshop to learn how to enter and return. Through dancing or drumming, you can begin to explore trance. Be aware that images and emotions will arise that may take some processing to understand. At times these can be perplexing, even disturbing images, just as dreams can sometimes be nightmares. They are no more or less real than dreams; they contain valuable information that, decoded, can help you live more fully and authentically. If you decide to explore the trance state on your own, it is useful to have some kind of support system, whether that be a friend who knows you well or a teacher of comparative religions with whom you can discuss your adventures.

Shamanism is not the property of any specific culture; it is a worldwide religious technique. However, the vocabularies and rituals vary from region to region. No one system is more real or true than any other. However, study and work within a certain system can be more appropriate for individual seekers. For instance, some American Indian people believe it is important to refrain from teaching their nation's shamanic techniques to outsiders; others feel differently and are willing to share this information. Any teacher of integrity can be respected, even if his or her view is at odds with that of others. Anyone charging enormous sums for little information, whether the subject be shamanism or anything else, is probably not the best choice for a teacher. Let good sense and an attitude of respect for the traditions be your guide, and you are unlikely to be led astray.

Chapter 2 • Trance Dancing

When your body dances, your soul travels and remembers,
free of the limits of this life,
free of the limitations of time and space.

— Frank Natale

Dance is not just a human activity. The dance of bees, which conveys to the hive's workers the location of a particularly abundant nectar source, is widely known. Sandhill cranes bend and sway in complex patterns when they perform their spectacular mating dances. Chimpanzees have been known to dance in circles, spontaneously and with great formality, sometimes even costuming themselves with vines. The dances of the animal world suggest that the human desire to move rhythmically has roots deep in our limbic system, referred to as the "lizard brain," which is the oldest part of our complex brain.

Dance, especially rhythmic and repetitive dance, connects us with the deepest part of our animal selves, moving us past the chattering of our more developed brains. As such, it has been employed for religious and meditative purposes for eons, perhaps since the beginning of human civilization. Petrified footsteps in the Paleolithic cave of Tuc d'Audoubert in France suggest a performance in which the dancer stepped heavily on the heel, circling round and round before a clay sculpture of mating bison. Such circle dances are found all around the globe and are often associated with shamanic healing ceremonies.

Animal movements are acknowledged, in legend, as the sources for some human dances. The ancient Minoans danced the stately "crane dance" in their religious rituals, imitating the crane's elaborate mating movements and giving rise to folk dances that are still part of Mediterranean culture. The same animal dances gave rise, in Africa, to the Watusi dance performed by girls ready for marriage. The Chinese meditative and martial art of T'ai Chi was inspired, legend has it, by observing a snake and a crane fighting to the death; movements in that art, such as "white crane flying" and "repulse monkey," still bear animal names. The Iowa people of the Americas claimed their circle dances were inspired by turtles, while the Dogon of Mali learned to dance from Yurugu the fox, who also provided information about how to use the dance as a divination tool.

Mythically, dance is connected with both creation and destruction. In the Hindu religion, the goddess of matter, Maya, creates the world through her dance; but the great death-goddess Kali will destroy the world the same way. Kali, the myths tell us, one day became so entranced with her own dancing that she was shaking the very foundations of the universe. Her consort, Shiva, lay down before her to try to stop her. She, oblivious, continued to dance until the great god was almost dead. Then she awakened from her oblivion, just in time to spare his life. One day, however, she will begin dancing again, and this next time her dance will be unstoppable. Shiva himself is called the Lord of the Dance, and sculptures of him performing the creative/destructive dance of life are among the treasures of India.

Similarly, in Greek mythology, the goddess Erynome created the world by dancing with her self-created partner, the snake god of the winds. Also among the Greeks, we find the mysterious tales of the maenads, female followers of the god of ecstasy, Dionysos, who became so intoxicated by their dancing that they sometimes tore living creatures apart with their bare hands. Usually these creatures were wild beasts, but occasionally the maenads would mistake a human child for an animal and rend it to pieces. The maenads were said to dance barefoot in the snow on sacred Mount Parnassus, so entranced that they did not notice the pain of the cold.

In Haitian *voudoun*, too, dancing is an important part of religious experience. There, ecstatic states occur when a dancer is "ridden" or possessed of a specific *orisha* or divinity. Each orisha has a specific way of moving in the dance, so when they appear, they are acknowledged and greeted by the other worshipers. In Korea, too, women called *mudang* or *manshin* use dance as a means of altering their consciousness, in this case not to invite divine possession but to travel to otherworldly realms.

CONTEMPORARY USES

In the <u>mosh pits and rave halls</u> of today's urban centers, we can find people seeking and experiencing the same kinds of ecstatic experiences that earlier peoples found in their religious dancing. But the setting is not necessarily a comfortable one for those seeking to use dance meditatively. Such events are organized for secular, usually commercial, reasons. <u>They provide an opportunity for alteration of consciousness through dancing, but they may not always provide an emotionally and psychically safe space</u> for doing so.

There are, however, other options. The ceremonies of those who use dancing as a part of religion are still being performed throughout the world.

For those whose roots are in Native America, powwow dancing is a powerful route to the spirit; even those without such a heritage can, in a limited way, participate. In the United States, powwows are often open to non-Indian people, who can join in the "intertribal" circle dances. It is important for non-Indians attending a powwow to ascertain what is polite and what is intrusive. Some powwows restrict dancers to those who have Indian blood or who are following a specific tradition; sundances, for instance, are not typically open to any drop-in participants. But at large public powwows, there are usually times when strangers are welcome in the dance circle.

The basic step is simple enough to learn: lift the foot, touch the floor with the ball of that foot, then step forward. This one-two rhythm is relatively easy, but one can just walk rhythmically to the sound of the drum. Once the dance is over, leave the dance floor until you have determined whether the next dance is an intertribal one.

Similarly, African Americans may locate practitioners of *voudoun* or *orisha* religions who are willing to teach the religious underpinnings as well as the dances of the religions. Occasionally, those not rooted in that heritage can similarly find instruction and initiation. The religious rituals of these traditions are not usually publicly advertised.

In addition to these traditional dance religions, there is also something that could be called nondenominational trance dancing. Instructors who are not connected to a specific tradition develop their own movement styles, which they then teach in New Age or healing centers; often these are described as "shamanic dancing" or "movement meditation." Some instructors employ movements from Asian martial arts; others stress a completely free-form movement. Most use drums, often with live drummers, although some use recorded music.

How to Begin

Trance dancing is a kind of meditation that creates a euphoric, sometimes ecstatic state of altered consciousness. There are those for whom the definition of meditation is limited to the attainment of a serene, contemplative state. For such seekers, trance dancing may be disturbingly exciting. Commonly, too, trance dancers experience an intensifying of emotion, sometimes including sexual passion; again, this is disturbing to some, while others can appreciate and learn from the information provided by our emotional selves in the meditative experience.

Similarly, there are some physical challenges that may indicate that trance dancing is not a suitable choice of meditative style. Those with epilepsy should be especially careful of this activity, as there is some possibility of seizures occurring as a result of the dancing. Similarly, those who have severe cardiovascular difficulties may find this form of meditation too strenuous; however, it is not necessary to dance as vigorously as possible, for continually repeating small movements or steps can be sufficient to bring on the meditative state.

Trance dancing can be performed solo, or in a group setting. Most newcomers will find that the group setting heightens their experience. However, with a little practice it is possible to use dance meditatively without others. Find a time when you are not likely to be disturbed for at least a half-hour. If using recorded music, select something with a sturdy beat and with long rather than short selections; simple drum music is often sufficient.

Begin by moving spontaneously to the music. You will soon find yourself falling into several repetitive movement patterns. Move into the repetition, rather than changing the motions; repetitive movement is more trance-provoking than continual change. As you move, concentrate on the music; feel it flow through you; move past any thoughts of how you appear or whether you are "doing it right." There is no "right way" to dance; there is only the way your body wishes to move. Listen to it, and follow its lead.

To practice trance dancing in groups, you can simply ask friends over and dance with them. For more structured experiences, look for workshops or classes. At these gatherings you will sometimes be offered a blindfold or padded eye cover, which cuts out your awareness of the others in the group and permits you to concentrate on the messages coming from your body. You will often be less self-conscious with such a blindfold. Surprisingly, you won't crash into others as often as you might expect, for senses other than sight will usually warn you of another's nearby presence.

Finally, pay attention to any negative feelings that might arise in you when you interview a trance-dance teacher or attend a workshop. When you are in a light trance, you are very suggestible; unscrupulous people may use this state to encourage you into relationships or activities with which you are not comfortable. Never remain in a class or workshop where you feel the slightest discomfort or confusion about the leader's intentions. Trance dancing is a powerful opener of the soul. It is better to dance at home than to risk opening up in an unsafe space.

REVIEW TIPS

- Select a style of trance dancing to explore. If you have a religious or ethnic heritage that includes a dancing tradition, consider exploring that.
- If you are considering exploring a traditional indigenous religion to which you are not connected by heritage, ask whether you are welcome rather than assuming you are.
- Dancing at home is a good way to enjoy the benefits of trance dancing. Make sure you will be uninterrupted for at least a half-hour; use music that is repetitive and strong in beat; let your movements arise from your body's sensations rather than from a choreographed set of steps.
- If you want to experience trance dancing in a group, observe a class before you join. Pay attention for any signs of inappropriate behavior by the leader. If you experience any discomfort about the leader's motivations or intentions, withdraw immediately.

RESOURCES

Andes, Karen. *A Woman's Book of Power: Using Dancing to Cultivate Energy and Health in Mind, Body, and Spirit.* New York: Perigee Books, 1995.

Andrews, Ted. *Magickal Dance: Your Body As an Instrument of Power.* Saint Paul, Minn.: Llewellyn, 1993.

De Sola, Carla, ed. *Spirit Moves: A Handbook of Dance and Prayer.* Richmond, Calif.: The Sharing Company, 1986.

Lonsdale, Steven. *Animals and the Origin of Dance.* New York: Thames & Hudson, 1981.

Natale, Frank. *Trance Dance: The Dance of Life.* Boston, Mass.: Element Books, Inc., 1995.

Roth, Gabrielle. *Maps to Ecstasy: A Healing Journey for the Untamed Spirit.* Novato, Calif.: New World Library, 1998.

Roth, Gabrielle. *Sweat Your Prayers.* New York: J. P. Tarcher, 1997.

Stewart, Iris. *Sacred Woman, Sacred Dance: Awakening Spirituality through Dance and Ritual.* Rochester, Vt.: Inner Traditions, 1998.

The Natale Institute, P.O. Box 163594, Austin TX 78716; (512) 708-8888

Chapter 3 • Drumming

Man by nature is a rhythmic being.
He walks, breathes, and sings rhythmically;
his heart beats, an internal drum.

— Steven Londsdale

The use of the drum to attain a meditative state is both ancient and widespread. Drums are found in virtually every culture and on every continent. Frame drums called *bodhrans* are played in Ireland with tiny fat sticks, while similar but much larger drums are played with long bow-like rods by the arctic Inuit. Hollow logs covered with skin form the African *ashiko* and *djembe;* ceramic and metal vases, the Arab *doumbeks,* are mounted with linen or skin or even plastic heads. Asian instruments range from the massive *taiko* drums of Japan to the small two-headed bell-rimmed drums of Korea; Native American drums are typically fashioned of hide and played with skin-covered sticks. Rattles, tambourines, bells, even parts of the human body — anything that can be struck to make a sound — form parts of the vocabulary of percussion.

Not only are percussive instruments found throughout the world; so too is the association of drumming with spiritual states. Among the Ojibwa of the north-central American forests, the drum was one of the primary civilizing gifts from divinity to humanity. In early Japan — and still today in rural Okinawa — the drum is connected to the shaman-woman called the *miko* or *noro,* as it is in Korea, where spirit summoners called *mudang* dance in flowing silk to the drum's heavy vibration. Drumming accompanied religious ceremonies in most ancient and tribal societies, such as when the Egyptian goddess Hathor was summoned with timbrels and sistras, which were considered creators of a kind of percussive prayer and were presumed to put devotees into a focused state of mind for ritual. Throughout Asia and the Americas, the pulse of the drum was the thread that shamans followed to return to their bodies after journeying in other realms. (See chapter 5, Shamanic Journeying, for more on this form of meditation.)

While the sound of the drum — the heartbeat of life — is vitally important to its religious and symbolic significance, its material and shape also hold meaning. Thus the bowl-shaped drum represents the magical essence of earth, while the hourglass-shaped drum pictures divinity pouring into the human world. On hide drums, magical symbols and representations of the celestial gods are often painted. While today the trap set may be associated with ballroom dancing and the snare drum with military drills, the ancient connection between drumming and the spirit has not been obliterated, and the use of drumming to attain meditative states is becoming increasingly popular, especially among neopagan ritualists. (See chapter 21, Candle Meditation, for more on contemporary neopaganism.)

Contemporary Uses

Drumming has never ceased to be employed in traditional religions, including those native to residents of the Americas. On any summer weekend in the Midwest, the sound of the massive tribal drum, struck rhythmically by a dozen players, powers the dancing at powwows. African *orisha* groups gather in urban areas to draw *bembe,* the power of spirits, into their midst. *Voudoun* practitioners rely upon their drummers to invoke the *loa* who will ride the dancers in ritual.

But not all drumming is practiced in the context of tribal and ethnic traditions. In the last decade, drumming has become widely recognized as a style of meditation that transcends any specific religion. Private drum groups and public drumming circles have sprung up in major cities as well as in smaller communities. A significant part of this movement has been the emergence — or reemergence, as drummer and author of *When the Drummers Were Women: A Spiritual History of Women,* Layne Redmond argues — of women's drum groups. Redmond traces the connection of women and the drum, especially the frame drum, into prehistory. Discouraged for millennia because of its association with ancient woman-empowering religions, the women's drum circle now draws both beginners and advanced drummers alike.

What makes drumming a meditation rather than — or perhaps, in addition to — an art? Like any meditation, we find distinct physiological effects resulting from drumming. The most important of these is that drummers' and listeners' heartbeats synchronize to the pulse of the drum. Not only that: they synchronize to each other in a process called "entrainment." In doing so, our bodies simply follow the laws of physics, for entrainment occurs even among inanimate objects; thus a roomful of cuckoo clocks, originally ticking in their individual and unique timings, will ultimately synchronize themselves through entrainment — with no effort on the watchmaker's part.

Rudimentary drumming takes little training, so its physiological effects can be enjoyed even by inexperienced musicians. Drum circles have recently been introduced into nursing homes where patients with Alzheimer's disease, who are otherwise unable to sustain a focus, manage to keep a steady drum rhythm; they are found to be less fretful for some hours afterwards. Similarly, drumming has been used to relieve stress among victims of trauma, including Vietnam veterans; the relief apparently occurs because disrupted brain wave patterns are regularized. In addition, drumming has been used as a way of assisting those with heart arrhythmia to establish and maintain a steady heartbeat — the drum working as a sort of external pacemaker.

In addition to the physiological effects, drummers report significant alterations in their mental and emotional states while drumming. Drumming demands an intense focus on immediate physical sensations, so intense that chronic worries and obsessive concerns are driven from the mind. While it is possible to attain these benefits drumming by oneself, or by accompanying recorded drum music, most drummers report enhanced benefits from drumming with one or more others.

How to Begin

That percussion class you took in high school or college probably did not prepare you for the kind of drumming needed to provoke a meditative state. Such classes assume the drum's employment as an accompaniment to other instruments, whereas meditative drumming generally focuses on the drum alone. While a class might help you acquire skills useful in meditative drumming, it is more likely to make you self-conscious about technique. And worrying about technique is the last thing you need to do while you meditate with the drum.

Unlike most forms of meditation, drumming requires equipment: specifically, some form of rhythm instrument. It is possible (and certainly very cheap) to use body parts — two hands, hand to thigh, and so forth. However, the percussive effect of an external instrument is more powerful than simple clapping in assisting the process of meditation, to say nothing of chafing less. Rattles, like the African *sekere* (a shell-covered gourd), or bells (including cymbals) are also possible choices and can often be easily handcrafted. For the beginner, however, a simple frame drum will be the easiest to play and will create the most effective meditative accompaniment.

The frame drum is created when the skin of an animal (usually goat, lamb, or deer) is stretched and secured over a circular wooden frame. Frame drums can be as large as the three-foot-diameter powwow drums of the Midwest, or as small as a tambourine, which is simply a jingle-rimmed handheld drum. Midsized skin drums, like the Irish *bodhran* or the Native American frame drum, are readily available in ethnic and New Age stores; such a drum is also relatively easy to make. Frame drums can be played with the hands directly or with drumsticks, either covered with hide (as in Native American drumming) or uncovered (as with the Irish *bodhran*).

Other drums to consider are the barrel-shaped drums like the African *djembe* and *ashiko,* and the vase-shaped Arabian *tabla* and *doumbek.* Made of ceramic or wood or metal, these drums have longer bodies than the frame drum and can be played by being held between the legs, if one is seated; standing drummers may find a fabric strap or similar support helpful. Most single-headed drums need to have their lower, uncovered end left open so that the sound can travel through it; so it is customary to tilt the drum slightly rather than muffling the sound by placing it directly on the floor or ground, if one plays while seated. Although such drums offer a certain flexibility of tone, they are somewhat less easy to play for novices.

Beginning drummers should be aware that their first drum is often that — the first of many. So is makes sense to purchase, as a first drum, an inexpensive one. As you become more familiar with types and sizes and suppliers of drums, you can select one or more additional drums that are adapted to your style of playing and to your body size and shape.

Once the drum has been acquired, the beginner has two choices: to drum alone or to drum with others. Drumming by oneself is difficult for most beginners. Not knowing many rhythms, or even how to hold a steady pulse, the beginner may well pound away for awhile, all the time feeling foolish and self-critical. This is hardly the meditative state you are seeking! If drumming alone is your only way to experience this meditation, find a tape of simple drum rhythms and play a simple pulse in accompaniment.

The pulse is the basic rhythm of any drum piece, the fabric on which additional rhythmic embroideries are placed. The pulse is a sound that does not vary: beat, beat, beat, beat goes the pulse. Learning to hear and keep the pulse is the first step in learning to drum meditatively. Learning the pulse is not something that occurs only in your ears; it occurs in your whole body. So learn to play the pulse by playing.

You may find your experience is enhanced by taking one or more basic drum lessons. Finding a good drum teacher can be very useful for the beginning solo drummer. Whereas twenty years ago it would have been difficult to find teachers who taught anything other than band drumming, it's now much easier to find instruction in ethnic and meditative drumming. Intensive workshops, rather than individual lessons, are often an excellent way to both experience the effects of drumming and to gain basic instruction.

Those who wish to join an ongoing drum circle may find it useful to practice holding a pulse to recorded music before drumming in public. This is especially recommended for shy people or those who suffer from performance anxiety. Drumming to recorded music can also substitute — although minimally — for a drum circle when you are ill or have a busy schedule. Beginning drummers should practice holding a steady pulse while accompanying recordings; more advanced drummers can select an appropriate rhythm from among those offered at a drum circle or class.

Drumming at home to recorded music is, however, only the palest reflection of the power of a drumming circle. If you do not know of any public drum circles in your community, try organizing one of your own. This is not, however, necessarily easy to do. Beginning drummers are often somewhat sheepish about their lack of skill, and an overly-embarrassed beginner can thwart a small group's attempt to get a drum circle rolling by talking about drumming rather than drumming. A strong leader is necessary to start the drumming and keep it moving. If everyone is a beginner, using recorded music as a focal point may be helpful for some months until the group learns to listen to each other and to relax into the experience.

A more successful strategy for beginning drummers who have the option is to attend public drum circles, workshops, and festivals. Information on regular public circles is often posted at metaphysical and women's bookstores, both of which serve as nerve centers for their respective communities; local specialty publications may also be a source of information. Stores that sell ethnic instruments often have information about such events, and neopagan festivals many times offer drum circles and workshops as part of their extensive offerings.

It is a good idea to call before attending, to ascertain whether the group employs any specific tradition of drumming and whether beginners are welcome. Some drum circles profess openness to the novice, but in fact are dominated by extremely proficient drummers who frown upon, and can sometimes mock, the beginner's efforts. While this is not typical, it can occur; should you encounter a circle of this sort, beat a hasty retreat and do not return.

Be sure to bring an instrument, at least a rattle or bell, to the circle. Often, established circles have extra drums, or there will be drummers there who bring several instruments and who don't mind strangers playing them. However, do not assume this is the case in all drum circles or with all drummers. Courtesy requires that you ask permission before using anyone's drum. Handle it with extreme care, and be certain not to wear any rings or other jewelry that could damage the head. Exploring a variety of drum sounds at a drum circle is a good way to familiarize yourself with the possibilities of percussion instruments.

Once the drumming starts, join in. Find a rhythm that is neither too slow to hold your attention, nor too fast or complicated to sustain. Your intention as a meditative drummer is to let the drum's beat become your focus. Listen to the other drummers, locate a beat that is in rhythm with theirs — it may be as simple as the pulse itself, which is usually the easiest rhythm for beginning drummers to sustain — and begin drumming.

Each round of drumming will usually last from fifteen minutes to a half-hour. During that time, there will be shifts and variations in the rhythm, although the pulse should remain consistent. Try not to let yourself speed up; drumming faster and faster and faster is a frequent temptation to beginning drummers, who can become very excited by the pounding rhythm. Meditative drumming does not require — and is often interrupted by — such showboating. If you grow tired or find yourself unable to continue holding your rhythm, stop and enjoy the other drummers; you will sustain many of the same physiological benefits, and won't disturb the group's rhythm.

Drum circles develop their own traditions, which the visitor should respect. In some circles, there is a midpoint break for announcements and refreshments. Some circles welcome intoxicating beverages, while others frown upon such usage. Don't presume you know the folkways of a drum circle just because you've attended another one. Pay attention, ask questions, and respect the circle you've entered.

An exciting way of experiencing meditative drumming is at outdoor festivals, often sponsored by neopagan or New Age organizations. Such festivals usually include drum circles — some of which may be intimidatingly professional for the novice, but others of which welcome anyone who respects the circle and can hold a basic pulse. At some festivals, such as the long-established Starwood festival in western New York, drumming goes on continually for many days; many others offer briefer drum circles and instructional workshops, often under the tutelage of an experienced ethnic or meditative drummer.

Review Tips

- Get a drum.
- Practice holding a pulse, either by yourself or to recorded music.
- Locate a drum circle or form one.
- Establish or learn the customs of the drum circle.
- Listen to the rhythm established by the circle or lead drummer.
- Find a pulse or beat that you can sustain.
- Free your mind of external concerns and concentrate on the sound.
- Should you grow tired, sit and listen to the other drummers.

RESOURCES

Blacker, Carmen. *The Catalpa Bow: A Study of Shamanistic Practices in Japan.* New York: Unwin Paperbacks, 1982.

Drake, Michael. *The Shamanic Drum: A Guide to Sacred Drumming.* Goldendale, Wash.: Talking Drum Publications, 1991.

Hart, Mickey, and Fredric Lieberman, with D. A. Sonneborn. *Drumming on the Edge of Magic.* San Francisco: HarperSanFrancisco, 1989.

Hart, Mickey, and Fredric Lieberman, with D. A. Sonneborn. *Planet Drum: A Celebration of Percussion and Rhythm.* San Francisco: HarperSanFrancisco, 1991.

Lonsdale, Steven. *Animals and the Origin of Dance.* London: Thames & Hudson, 1981.

Redmond, Layne. *When the Drummers Were Women: A Spiritual History of Rhythm.* New York: Three Rivers Press, 1997.

Rouget, Gilbert. *Music and Trance: A Theory of the Relations between Music and Possession.* Chicago: University of Chicago Press, 1986.

Starwood Festival, sponsored by the Association for Consciousness Exploration. 1643 Lee #9, Cleveland Heights, OH 44118; (800) 446-4962

Chapter 4 • Ecstatic Postures

There is nothing but the spirits of all things.
That is the real world that is behind this one,
and everything we hear is something
like a shadow from that world.

— Black Elk

In early European cave art, individuals — presumed to be shamans — are depicted in specific and unusual postures, such as lying at a 35-degree angle. Other ancient art, from many eras and cultures, similarly shows figures in postures interpreted as prayer or inner ecstasy; the hands may be over the head or held beneath the breasts, the legs may be folded beneath the body or crossed in a certain way. Some interpret these positions as indicating how humanity is envisioned in relationship to the divine. Thus the Christian tradition of kneeling in prayer with lowered eyes is described as representing humility in the face of God, while the glazed eyes and thrown-back head of the maenad who worships Dionysos is said to indicate her ecstatic communion with her god.

The interpretation that bodily postures are a means of communicating to others — reverence or ecstasy, in the above instances — may be only part of the story, however. Postures of prayer and meditation may have specific somatic or bodily effects on those who assume them. Many spiritual traditions ask that the participant assume a defined posture in order to enhance or attain a spiritual state. Yoga is perhaps the best-known of these traditions, but in other Asian forms such as Qigong and T'ai Chi, postures are also important. Shamanism, a religion practiced for millennia by people on every continent, may have similarly had postures associated with altered states and meditative trances.

33

CONTEMPORARY USES

In the mid-1970s, anthropologist Felicitas Goodman wondered whether the postures shown in ancient and tribal art might hold clues to the religious experiences of the people who made it. Were the posture and gestures of the sculpted man and woman found in a seven thousand-year-old grave in Cernavoda, Romania, intended to convey some meaning to onlookers? Or could the postures have meaning within themselves — did holding these poses create an inner experience that would transcend culture and be attainable by people today?

Goodman collected a variety of poses from the ancient art of several cultures. She then asked volunteers to assume these poses and afterward share what their experiences had been. The volunteers were not instructed about what Goodman suspected the poses meant, nor were they given other suggestions that might have affected their experience. Astonishingly, Goodman's volunteers reported that the postures themselves created a light trance — and that the visual images that came to those holding the poses were remarkably similar. Goodman dubbed this experience "posture-meditated trance" and set about refining her collection of poses. Working with many individuals over more than two decades, she has continued to find consistent reports of the effects of the poses involved.

She found the postures in the art of ancient hunter-gatherer cultures and later agriculturalists; she also found some postures that were used by the latter group but seem to have been inherited from their forebears. Goodman named the postures after the location in which the figures were found, the apparent use of the posture or the spiritual being invoked, or the experiences reported by contemporary practitioners. The basic postures include those that induce sensations of healing, divining, celebration, metamorphosis, and mythmaking.

Goodman and her colleague, Belinda Berkowitz, have conducted many workshops in this method of meditation, and have trained other teachers through the Cuyamungue Institute. While this method shares some characteristics with other posture-based activities such as yoga or T'ai Chi, it is described as resulting in trance rather than meditation. This distinction may not be relevant to those seeking a specific effect, such as attaining a less-harried frame of mind or creating an opening for a more spiritual attitude toward life, nor for those interested in exploring various meditative methods.

But there are two categories of individuals for whom trance work such as this may be uncomfortable or difficult to practice. Those who narrowly define meditation — those, for instance, who require an emptying of the mind with no visionary activity — may resist or reject the sometimes powerful images and emotions that trance work can elicit. In addition, those with rigid personal boundaries may feel endangered by the transpersonal dimensions of ecstatic states. For others, however, the exploration of ecstatic postures offers a variety of deepening spiritual experiences.

How to Begin

Like other meditations based in shamanic tradition, the drum serves as a backdrop to this meditation. Although recorded drumming is available and can be used without ill-effect, the greater sonic resonance of the live drum is more effective in assisting this meditation. The drumbeat should be two hundred beats per minute — a relatively fast rhythm — and should be a simple continuous rhythm rather than a complex one that draws attention to itself.

While it is possible to do this meditation alone, Goodman and other experts in trance recommend group work instead. In the rare instance that the practitioner finds it difficult to leave the trance, others can assist in grounding her or him into everyday reality. In addition, most people report that their experience is richer and more profound when shared with others.

To begin, eat lightly before the session, as many people report that heavy meals inhibit the trance experience. It is useful to review the posture before beginning the meditation, so that you may move smoothly into it when the time comes. Then, begin with a simple ceremony based in traditions indigenous to the Americas. Blow upon a handful of cornmeal, then hold it over the rattle or drum (or tape recorder) that will provide your rhythmic accompaniment. Gesture in the six directions: north, south, east, west, up, and down. Then call the spirits of these directions by rattling, drumming, or gesturing to each. Follow this by offering cornmeal to the spirits of these directions.

Sit for a few moments and breathe. Fifty inhalations and exhalations are suggested, to calm and focus the mind before assuming the posture. When you have completed this preliminary meditation, assume the following posture, which Goodman has named "Mayan Empowerment" and describes as good for generating healing energies. This posture was found in figures from both Mezo-America and Polynesia, and variations of it are seen in figures from Minoan Greece and Persia.

Kneeling on the floor with your buttocks resting upon your heels, spread your knees apart to a comfortable distance. Making tight fists of your hands with your thumbs facing your chest, raise your elbows to shoulder level and place your fists together, fitting the knuckles of one hand tightly into the spaces between the knuckles of the other hand. The backs of both hands should face the ceiling. Lean back your head slightly and open your mouth gently.

Hold this posture for fifteen minutes, attending to the inner sensations that arise. When the period of meditation is over, gradually uncurl from the posture and rest briefly, to readjust to normal consciousness. Should you feel any slight dizziness, drinking some water and chewing a bit of bread will usually right the senses. Sharing the experience with other members of the group is useful at this point, as is writing a record of your inner experience in a journal, or otherwise recording the event.

This is only one of the many postures that Goodman has cataloged and described. All have been found to produce a feeling of well-being, healing, and/or personal strength in practitioners. Like other shamanic meditations, this is rarely practiced on a daily basis, but rather as the inner need arises. Ecstatic posture meditation can be a useful adjunct to other practices, as well as to the psychotherapeutic journey.

REVIEW TIPS

- Locate a skilled teacher that specializes in this approach, or contact Goodman's institute for information on workshops and other training.
- Make sure you are comfortable with this approach and that you do not find the idea of being in a light trance threatening.
- If you do not have access to workshops or training, you may still learn this technique from the written works of Goodman and Berkowitz.
- If you are learning from written materials, gather with friends who are interested in learning this meditative technique. If some are willing to serve as drummers, good; otherwise, get a tape of

shamanic journey drumming, which will be at the required tempo.

• Usually only one or two postures, together with the preliminary meditation and sharing afterwards, will be sufficient for each session together. You may, however, want to spend a longer time together — a day, for instance — at the beginning of your work with a group, both to familiarize yourself with the approach and to become comfortable with each other.

• The postures that Goodman has published are those that provide healing and other positive benefits; so when executed correctly they are not in any way dangerous even to the novice practitioner. Any trance state, however, can leave some individuals disoriented afterwards. Be sure to provide enough time to center yourself in everyday reality before terminating the session.

RESOURCES

Goodman, Felicitas. *Where the Spirits Ride the Wind: Trance Journeys and Other Ecstatic Experiences.* Bloomington, Ind.: Indiana University Press, 1990.

Gore, Belinda, with Felicitas Goodman. *Ecstatic Body Postures: An Alternative Reality Workbook.* Santa Fe, N.Mex.: Bear and Company, 1995.

Kalweit, Holger, and Elisabeth Kubler-Ross. *Dreamtime and Inner Space: The World of the Shaman.* Boston, Mass.: Shambhala, 1988.

Sansonese, J. Nigro. *The Body of Myth: Mythology, Shamanic Trance, and the Sacred Geometry of the Body.* Rochester, Vt.: Inner Traditions, 1994.

The Cuyamungue Institute, Route 5 Box 358C, Santa Fe, NM 87501; (505) 455-2749

Chapter 5 • Shamanic Journeying

From the spiritual point of view,
the journey is never merely a passage through space,
but rather an expression of urgent desires for discovery and change.

— Jean Cirlot

Shamanism is one of the world's most ancient religions. Unlike Christianity, Buddhism, and Islam, shamanism is not based upon a single historical spiritual leader; nor does it have a centralized and bureaucratically organized church. Like Japanese Shinto (one of the sources of Zen Buddhism), Chinese Taoism, and Indian Hinduism, shamanism is a religion that grew out of spiritual traditions whose roots go back many thousands of years, perhaps even to Neolithic or Paleolithic sources.

Shamanism takes its name from the Siberian Tungus word *shaman*, meaning "someone who travels to the spirits." Such spiritual traveling is the basis of shamanism wherever it is found — and it is found throughout Asia, through both North and South America, in Australia, in Siberia, and Scandinavia, and perhaps among the European Celts. An individual, sophisticated in ways of altering consciousness, goes beyond this reality in order to heal an individual or community. This healing component is found in shamanism wherever it occurs. Shamans are the doctors and therapists of their communities, traveling to other dimensions to find and eliminate the sources of illness and pain in this world.

Typically, the shamanic world is pictured as having several levels, joined by a great world tree (or a rope, a snake, or other similar form). These levels are not to be construed as hierarchically organized; the upper

39

world is not heaven, the lower world is not hell. Rather, they represent different spiritual and physical realities, all of which coexist at the same time. Only the shaman has the ability to move between and among these worlds, using what the great religious scholar Mircea Eliade called "archaic techniques of ecstasy" to do so.

Primary among these techniques is drumming. In some cultures, shamans themselves drum; in other cultures, as among the Korean women shamans called *mudang,* an assistant serves as drummer while the shaman dances. The drumming is steady and insistent, often at a sharp clip but sometimes in a slow droning rhythm. The drum is described by shamans as a rope that permits climbing and descending to different levels of consciousness.

Dancing, too, is often part of the shamanic journey. Simple repetitive steps are part of the early journey, when the shaman is seeking to leave this level of reality. Later, the shaman might dance to imitate a totem or protector animal, or to elicit some curative information from a spirit.

Who becomes a shaman in traditional societies? There is no single answer to this question. In many societies, shamans are self-chosen by a process called "arctic hysteria" (so named because it is prevalent in arctic shamanism, but also found elsewhere) in which a kind of psychic illness comes upon the potential shaman; during this visionary illness, the shaman sees herself or himself dismembered and rebuilt. There is, however, another initiatory system in which a family sustains shamanic knowledge for its community, training each new generation in the rites and techniques of shamanic ritual. In such societies, shamanism is considered an inherited trait, like left-handedness or blue eyes.

CONTEMPORARY USES

In the 1970s, anthropologist Michael Harner began to explore ways of making ancient shamanic practice available to contemporary, nontribal people, as well as to examine connections between shamanic traditions that are geographically widely separated. Through his study and teaching, a new orientation toward this ancient religion has emerged, emphasizing the shamanic journey as a meditative and healing technique.

This use of shamanic techniques — even, indeed, the use of the word *shaman* — has not been without controversy. Some traditional practitioners, especially American Indians, have argued that shamanism cannot be imported into a culture where it is not naturally rooted. Charges of cultural imperialism have occasionally been leveled at those of European heritage who declare themselves shamanic practitioners. Yet those who have benefited from soul retrieval, journeying, and similar techniques argue that the ancient shamanic religion was so widespread that no one can claim the right to authorize its practice. Those engaging in shamanic studies should consider these differing opinions carefully.

There are also those who would argue that shamanic journeying is not, in fact, meditation. If meditation is defined only as emptying the mind, journeying would certainly not be meditative. But many meditative techniques, such as visualization, involve forming images within the mind with the intention of producing a healing effect and/or a release into a higher state of consciousness — the same technique and identical intention of the shamanic journey.

How to Begin

The shamanic journey was once practiced by specialists who served their communities as healers. In current shamanic practice, however, journeying is a technique that can be taught to, and learned by, virtually anyone. Journeying is an inner experience that resembles, in some ways, the guided visions of active imagination or of visualization. To the accompaniment of a drum, the journeyer travels a visionary road to seek healing images.

Journeying is a powerful tool for the alteration of consciousness. Some of the images that appear may be upsetting or even frightening. So beginners may wish to study with a shamanic practitioner before embarking upon journeying alone. While it is certainly possible to teach oneself the relatively simple techniques of journeying, the wisdom of an experienced teacher can help provide both an emotionally and spiritually safe setting for the journey and can assist in interpreting the images that emerge afterwards.

As with any spiritual discipline, it is important to be cautious in selecting a teacher. Untrained or, worse, unscrupulous individuals can be more damaging than healing. Interview a teacher or practitioner before journeying; ask for and check references; and, most importantly, rely upon your inner sense and, if anything feels uncomfortable, stop immediately.

Journeying between the worlds is not an occupation to be undertaken lightly or in bad company.

Typically, the one (or ones) intending to journey lies flat, either on a bed or couch, or on the floor. Lights are usually dimmed, to provide a restful atmosphere. Drumming then begins. Live drumming is more effective than recorded, but even recorded drumming can help create the physiological response that triggers the journeying state. The drum rhythm is quick, about ninety beats per minute. The drum need not be loud; it is the steady rhythm, not the vibrational intensity, that enhances the journey.

The shaman will then direct the journeyer to imagine an inner landscape, which represents the normal level of consciousness. This may be a real landscape, though it need not be. Then, depending upon whether healing is sought from the lower, more instinctual self or from the higher, more intuitive mind, the shaman will guide the journeyer into a visionary space below or above the first level. Something — a rope, a ladder, even a tree root — is visualized as providing the route between the worlds. In the other world, animals may be encountered; called power animals, these deeply personal images of strength are an important healing tool. Narratives may unfold, people may appear and speak, the setting may shift or change. Shamanic journeys have imagery somewhat like dreams, yet they occur in the waking state.

At the climactic point in each journey, some symbol is encountered or attained that signifies the healing sought. It may be a plant, an animal, a spoken message, or even an event. When the journeyer receives this symbol, the return to the world of normal consciousness begins. Here the drum is especially important. Usually during the journey itself, the journeyer has become unaware of the drumbeat. At the point of return, the shaman changes to a slower, then faster beat, which leads the journeyer to retrace his or her steps to the rope or other object that provides reentry to the everyday landscape. Finally, there is a period of rest and then discussion of the meaning of the journey after its conclusion.

Many students of shamanism journey by themselves, once they have become familiar with the technique and feel they can assimilate the information gained this way. Journeying is typically not undertaken as a regular discipline, in the way that Quaker meetings are regularly held on Sundays or Zen students sit in meditation daily. Rather, those who follow this path will use this technique irregularly, when called to do so by external or internal events.

REVIEW TIPS

- Be certain that you are conversant with the ethical and social questions that the practice of contemporary shamanism entails. If you feel any discomfort with the practice, do not engage in it.
- Locate a good teacher. Don't just rely on advertisements or a one-word indigenous-sounding name. Interview the practitioner; ask for references; check the references. Do not work with any-one you suspect may be unethical or unstable.
- Read about shamanism. Learn about the cultures wherein it is commonly practiced. Become conversant with the vocabulary and the principles before you begin journeying.
- Consider whether you prefer to have your first journey as part of a group workshop or in a private session. Group workshops are usually less expensive, but can make some beginners feel exposed and uncomfortable.
- For an individual session, you may request to bring along a friend, who will serve as your witness and can help you assimilate the experience afterwards.
- Allow yourself plenty of time to think about the images that emerge from the journey. Write about them, paint them, and otherwise engage with them. The deepest healing comes from the greatest commitment to the process.
- Don't try to make journeying your only meditative practice. It is best used occasionally, to meet specific needs, rather than as an everyday experience.

RESOURCES

Eliade, Mircea. *Shamanism: Archaic Techniques of Ecstasy.* New York: Pantheon Books, 1964.

Gagan, Jeannet. *Journeying: Where Shamanism and Psychology Meet.* Santa Fe, N.Mex.: Rio Chama Publications, 1998.

Hisako, Kamata. "Daughters of the Gods: Shaman Priestesses in Japan and Okinawa." *Folk Cultures of Japan and East Asia.* Malibu, Calif.: Sophia University Press, 1966.

Scully, Nicki. *The Golden Cauldron: Shamanic Journeys on the Path of Wisdom.* Santa Fe, N.Mex.: Bear & Company, 1991.

Smith, C. Michael. *Jung and Shamanism in Dialogue: Retrieving the Soul/Retrieving the Sacred.* Mahwah, N.J.: Paulist Press, 1997.

Waters, Catherine, and Ronald Havens. *An Orientation to the Trance Experience.* Audiocassette. Velpre, Ohio: Bunner/Mazel, 1989.

part 2
yoga

Introduction • Yoga

This dewdrop universe
is just a dewdrop
and yet,
and yet.

— Zen Master Izza

The origins of Yoga are lost in prehistory. Archeologists have identified Yoga postures carved as long as four thousand years ago on stone artifacts from the Indus Valley in what is now Pakistan. But the first writings that describe the path of Yoga came from about 200 B.C.E. in the form of the aphorisms or sutras of Patanjali. These sutras codified, in written form, information that had been in existence for a long time. The sutras give instructions on how to quiet the mind. Both Patanjali and Buddha, who lived about two hundred years earlier, believed that the source of suffering is the craving for permanence in a universe of impermanence. However, they differed in their belief in the existence of a permanent reality. Patanjali's Yoga holds that there is a material reality called *prakriti* in Sanskrit, and a spiritual reality called *purusha.* Buddha, who must have studied Yoga, taught that everything is impermanent.

Yoga is a rich, variegated tradition that holds appeal for people with a wide range of temperaments and aptitudes. It appeals to Westerners for reasons similar to those that attract people to Zen, Tantrism, Sufism, and Shamanism. According to Yoga, we can never escape the influence of the unconscious by mere intellectual understanding of its contents. The path of enlightenment or liberation requires more than an intellectual mode of cognition. It requires the combination of the intellect and the intuitive or other sensory modes of knowing.

47

The eight steps of yoga are called *ashtanga*. The word means "eight limbs." They describe the definite steps that must be taken before one can achieve a meditative state. The eight limbs are:

yama	the moral precepts — abstention
niyama	purifications — observance
asana	the perfection of the physical body — posture
pranayama	breath awareness
pratyahara	withdrawing consciousness
dharana	concentration
dhyana	contemplation
samadhi	no mind

The first two steps address the issue of ethical behavior — they are similar to the Ten Commandments. This book includes chapters for step three, *asana* (posture) and step four, *pranayama* (breath extension). The last four steps have to do with the states of meditation. These are described in chapter 8, Yoga Meditation. The last three steps are comparable to similar stages in Western religious traditions in which *dharana* is called *consideratio* (considering), *dhyana* is called *contemplatio* (contemplation), and the state of *samadhi* is called *raptus* (rapture). Each step, when mastered, naturally leads to the following step.

RESOURCES

Some web sites pertaining to yoga are listed below.
www.sivananda.org/index.html
www.yogagroup.org/
www.mahesh.com/india/health/yoga.html
www.ayurveda.com/yoga.htm
www.yogajournal.com
www.timages.com/
www.ashtanga.com/
www.base.com/blaise/powyoga.html
hmt.com/kundalini/xindex.html
indiasearchengine.com/

Chapter 6 • Yoga Asanas

Yoga is like music. The rhythm of the body,
the melody of the mind, and the harmony of the soul
create the symphony of life.

— B. K. S. Iyengar

Hatha yoga is a practice in which one uses one's own physical body to achieve greater awareness by moving it into postures and attending to its sensations. The postures are called asanas. There are thousands of asanas, perhaps as many as 180,000. The goal of yoga is deeper, richer, and more complex than physical fitness. It includes creating a balance in the energy of the body, an inner goal of body and mind in harmony. It is the original meaning for the word *yoga*, which comes from a word for "to yoke," that implies yoking the body to the soul, or the individual to God. Other kinds of yoga, besides hatha yoga, include: *jnani* yoga (the path of wisdom), dharma yoga (the path of service), bhakti yoga (the path of devotion), karma yoga (the path of action), and raja yoga (a combined path).

CONTEMPORARY USES

Today the Westerners who practice yoga include persons with illnesses or disabilities, pregnant women, athletes, and individuals of any age who wish to improve their balance of energy. The need for more flexibility and suppleness is common in the West since physical fitness training programs focus less attention on those aspects of the body.

With yoga training you learn to acquire a balance between power and flexibility; you develop a peaceful strength that comes from an inner vitality;

49

and you discover a flowing energy. You learn to make distinctions so that you can face the challenge of a pose that requires strength and balance while at the same time keeping your breath smooth and your eyes soft. You learn how to achieve sensitivity in the midst of challenging situations. This includes the challenging situation of a sitting meditation practice.

The practice of hatha yoga is a meditation in itself and it is also a preparation for a formal sitting meditation practice. Yoga works as meditation the same way as other body-centered meditations such as T'ai Chi, Qigong, walking meditation, and other sports or arts. It is the intention and attitude that make the difference. As in other meditative practices, the exercises of hatha yoga are intended to produce a state of "no conceptualizing while remaining fully awake," according to Robert Ornstein, author of *The Right Mind.* During the practice of asanas one objective is to become relaxed; another is to turn off the normal internal talk. It is a system for training body and mind simultaneously; and it tends to promote right brain activity.

How to Begin

Yoga is a way of moving into stillness. This goal includes the ability to stretch easily; but there is a great difference between doing a healthy stretch and trying to go further with aggression or force. Everybody reaches their edge, that is, the end of the range of movement in any stretch. Yoga is a balance of the joy of movement and an awareness of the body.

In the practice of hatha yoga you work to be capable of relaxing and letting go in all imaginable situations and positions. Each posture brings new parts of the body to your attention. As you move into a posture, you may first feel a tightness, stretch, or pressure. It is then that you practice relaxing and letting go, which are not the same as heaviness or passivity. You become tranquil and alert in the face of the intense sensation of a stretch such as the forward bend or the back bend.

If you want to know yoga you must actually practice yoga. Merely reading about it does not suffice. You will learn to ask yourself if you can see that a new form of action, a new form of noncumulative knowledge, is possible, one that will break up your habitual way of being and allow you to act differently.

The yoga postures are similar to some moves or stretches used in dance or floor gymnastics. Many sports coaches have incorporated yoga moves into their warm-up routines. You may wonder what the difference is between practicing yoga asanas and some other kind of sports or dance stretches. The difference lies in the intention. The intention in yoga is to increase your consciousness. The skills you develop in strength, flexibility, and balance are by-products. So there is a lesson here that is captured in the famous Zen paradox wherein the meditator is exhorted to "try not to try." In the practice of yoga asanas, your primary intention is to develop an awareness of *what is.* If you notice some tightness, stiffness, or weakness, you simply notice it and allow the body to slack off slightly until it feels more easy and relaxed.

An open mind and a quiet heart are both the prerequisites and the consequences of yoga practice. If you think you know a lot about yoga, this may be a hindrance because your intellectual memory and knowledge may fill up your mind so that there is no room left for learning. Wisdom is not equal to information. Wisdom is intelligence, which includes the ability to exercise discrimination, to make decisions, and to have good judgment. Intelligence is also the capacity to observe, to gather information, and to act on it. Intelligence demands doubting, questioning, and is not distracted by the enthusiasm and energy of others. Intelligence demands impersonal observation. To comprehend the whole of a human being, all his/her complexities, physical responses, emotional reactions, intellectual capacities, affectations, and travails, to perceive all that in one act — that is supreme intelligence.

In yoga practice you can aspire toward supreme intelligence even if you are not athletic. You can practice good yoga whether your body is handicapped, injured, or weakened by age. The mind can still achieve harmony and intelligence.

HINTS AND CAUTIONS

These precautions apply when you are participating in a full, vigorous yoga practice. You can always enjoy a simple stretch, relaxation, or breathing practice any time during the day. But a complete session of full-body work requires that you take heed of the following.

Food

Do not practice the postures on a full stomach. Either limit your meal to a light serving of fruit and juice, or wait an hour or so after eating before beginning your yoga practice.

Time

Early morning is a good time to practice, even though the body is stiff. Your mind is fresh and you will get more from your practice if you do it in the morning. Morning is also a good time for more vigorous asanas. Practicing in the morning helps you work better all day.

Practicing in the evening is easier because the body is warmed up. Evening practice is naturally more meditative, restorative, and mellow because you tend to be a bit more tired in the evening.

Place

The practice area does not need to be large, but it should be clean and free from distractions. It should not be excessively hot or cold. Mothers with small children have to make the best of the situation if they want to practice while their children are present. Sometimes this can be of benefit to both mother and child, but if the child is distracting the mother, then the practice should be postponed. Many mothers with small children find that practicing yoga seems to help not only their own state of mind but that of their child as well.

Cautions

You should not feel any strain in your face, ears, or chest during the practice. If you do feel pain, you need to learn to distinguish between good pain and bad pain. Good pain is temporary and may be caused by working an underused muscle. Good pain may also be experienced when you need to face and feel old stuck pain in order to loosen up. Bad pain is usually caused by overstretching a tendon or joint, and it tends to last longer.

Eyes

Practice hatha yoga with your eyes open, but with soft vision, that is, without focusing on any one thing.

Special Considerations

If you have a medical condition that might interfere with your practice, consult with a yoga teacher for advice on how to protect yourself. Pregnant women can join a regular yoga class if the teacher is prepared to give them instructions on how to modify the postures to suit their needs. All poses can be practiced during the first three months of pregnancy and during menstruation if the bleeding is not too heavy and there is no discomfort. If you are suffering cramps during menstruation, you may find that some of the therapeutic or restorative asanas afford relief. To learn what these are and how to perform them you need to go to an experienced yoga teacher. If that is not possible, consult a good manual such as B. K. S. Iyengar's *Light on Yoga*.

THE POSTURES OF ASANAS

The word *posture* comes from the Latin words *positura*, which means "a position," and *ponere*, which means "to place." It refers to how we place our body in space. The word also refers to an attitude of the mind. And the postures of the mind and body affect one another. When you study and practice asanas you are learning body awareness and you are learning to love yourself. The asana is just the path. You learn to give from your heart and express who you are, to open up and let people see you. This is an in-body experience, not an out-of-body experience. Remember, it is all right to be stiff. The asana is not a problem to be solved; it is just an experience.

There is a misconception that yoga is all about flexibility. There is an element of flexibility in the experience of the asanas, but there is much more to it than that. In your poses, if you are naturally very flexible, it is especially important for you to hold back and resist in order to balance strength with suppleness. If you do not have strength, then your body will be soft and lacking in endurance and power. However, quality yoga is not merely a question of balancing flexibility and strength. It is also an exploratory process requiring awareness and responsibility.

When you study yoga, remember that the work is a matter of learning about yourself as well as learning about the asanas or the other practices. The study of yoga poses precedes the study of breathing practices, and these are both preliminary to the practice of meditation in the path of *ashtanga* yoga. There is a good reason for this. Your body and breathing technique will enhance your meditation. In fact, having a proper sitting posture and a smooth, full automatic breathing pattern promotes a calm and meditative state of mind. You begin, as with anything, one step at a time. We tend to think there is a dividing line in a posture between weak/strong, tight/flexible, or wandering mind/focused mind. Instead of trying to emphasize just one side of each of these dualities, in your imagination replace the list of all possible dualities with a round circle and place everything inside it. Let there be space and sensitivity. Allow your body to resonate in the posture. This means that you make less of an effort and remain open to receive the information that the pose has to give you.

STANDING

Tadasana

The basic standing posture can provide an illustration of how a yoga practice works.

The mountain pose, called *tadasana* in Sanskrit, is the basic standing posture. To perform it simply come to standing in your bare feet and observe what you feel. Stand tall and stable as a mountain. Gravity is so much a part of our experience that we tend to take it for granted or to fight it. And yet, when we align ourselves with gravity, it actually supports us. In practicing the mountain pose we learn to align ourselves with gravity from within.

The image of a plant is often useful as a metaphor for standing. If we were plants, our legs would be the roots, our spine the stem, and our head the upward-growing flower or fruit. The essential experience of this image is that our roots are being drawn into the earth, without effort or action, even as the sun is pulling our flower up. The force that is generated by this duality shoots up through the spine. Feel the thrust. Through our connection with the pull of gravity, we experience the elongation of the spine that comes with each wave of the breath. If you will spend some time every day in stillness while standing and observing the details of your postural alignment, you will find that the rest of your day's activities proceed with greater ease and comfort.

Most of us have postural imbalances. The best way to correct them is not by forcing yourself to stretch tall and straight against a wall. This may work for the moment, but the minute you stop the stretch and think of something else you are likely to go back to your habit of slouching or bending forward or some sort of imbalance. It is far better to practice the mountain pose when there is time to sense and feel the tension, and to allow the tension to subside by making small postural adjustments.

Standing Exercise

1. As you stand in your bare feet, imagine you are a marionette hanging on a string that runs through your spine. Feel your pelvis, and like a pendulum, swing it from side to side slowly, allowing the amplitude of the swinging to decrease until you find the exact center. See if you can feel if your right and left sides are balanced. Think of the space above your head and imagine that your head is rising up like a balloon into that space. There should be no tension in your neck. This is not a stretch, it is a process that uses visualization to allow your body to respond.

2. Feel the space in front of you and imagine that the front of your body moves forward to meet that space. What happens to your breath? Now imagine the back of your body moving backward to meet the space in back of you. Watch what happens to your breath. Let the soles of your feet move down to meet the solid earth and at the same time, let the top of your head meet the space above you. What happens to your breath? From the core of your being, everything will soften and move outward. Can you feel the inner energy rising up like a fountain from under the ground, pouring up and flowing out the top of your head? The purpose of yoga is to create a balance in your body and your awareness.

3. Direct your attention to your feet. Simply stand, relax, feel your breathing, and have the intention to make contact with the floor. Inquire how the soles of your feet touch the floor. It is best if you are barefoot so that you can feel the texture of the surface of the floor. (To the person who wears shoes, the whole world is covered in shoe leather.)

Students often ask, "Should the weight be on the ball or the heel of the foot?" It should be balanced between the ball and the heel. Imagine that there are four tires on your foot, as if your foot were a small car.

Now puff up all four tires equally, so that the four corners of your foot make contact in a balanced way. Notice that you may have a habit of always standing with more weight on the inside, the outside, the front, or the back of the foot.

As your feet make balanced contact with the floor, the middle toes can relax and move forward. The balls of the big toes can find the floor. You can feel the first lift of energy coming up just behind the balls of the feet. The more you can root the base of your toes and heels the more safe you will feel. Send energy down into your legs and through the soles of your feet, being aware of how far your feeling can travel. Once again you are thinking of making contact with the floor; but now you imagine that you actually make contact with the ground underneath the floor.

If you slide your pelvis from left to right you will feel a pattern of pressure on the soles of your feet. Your feet will begin to widen. Take your time and allow your feet to grow comfortable. If you feel the pull of gravity and allow your legs to support you, you will begin to relax. This process is often accompanied by a prolonged exhalation and a sigh of relief as your shoulders relax and tension drops away.

4. Notice your shoulders. As our bodies release, they naturally lengthen, since a relaxed muscle is longer than a tight one. As the neck and shoulders and upper body relax, the head releases upward like a tortoise coming out of its shell. It helps if you allow your eyes to be as still as a very calm lake, so that the standing pose becomes one of repose.

To alleviate tension in the top of your shoulders, imagine that they are like a mailbox on a house, the kind that opens from the top. Imagine that you are opening the mailbox by moving the top edge of your shoulder blades away from your ribs. (The shoulder blades are, of course, positioned flat over the back ribs. This image of the shoulder blades moving away from the ribs is only an image. The bones do not actually move much at all. However, imagining that the top rim of the shoulder blade moves directly back away from the back ribs is an image that helps you to feel more space and softness in the region.) This gesture also helps to soften the tight muscles on the side of the neck. These muscles become chronically tight from the habit of holding the head forward and the habit of lifting the shoulders, which is a natural gesture in response to a threat. In the standing posture, you can undo the damage of poor posture habits. Your intention to allow the shoulders to soften is a powerful tool.

5. Bring awareness to your pelvis. You can examine the possibility of tightness in the lower back by moving the pelvis while standing. Your pelvic bowl is a large mass of fused bones at the base of the spine and torso that connects the legs to the body and supports the abdominal organs. It includes the sacrum, which is a flat bony plate at the base of the spine that is composed of five fused spinal vertebrae. This is your "sacred" bone. (The word *sacrum* is related to the word *sacred.*) The pelvis also includes the ilium and the ischium, the crest of bone on either side of the belly and the knobby bones that you sit on, respectively. Stiffness in the back and hips prevents the pelvis from moving freely. The pelvis often seems as solid as the rock of Gibraltar, a situation that can be caused in part by sexual fears and inhibitions. When the breath flows freely and fully into the lower abdomen for the first time, you may feel a bit uneasy. It can be scary to feel energy in the lower abdomen if you are in the habit of armoring it and holding it stiff and rigid.

Bend your knees slightly and move your pelvis to explore and test its range of motion. Imagine your pelvis is a silver basin filled with water and slowly tip it so that the water pours out the front. Then tip it so that you pour a bit of water out the back. Experiment until you discover a centered, balanced position for the pelvis that allows it to transfer the weight from the spine to the legs with a smooth suppleness.

Stand with your feet hip-width apart. Find the axis of your spine, the center of gravity of your body. Be aware that the front of the spine is actually near the center of your torso. When you are aware of this core, tension tends to drop away from the outer musculature, allowing a natural breathing pattern. Feel your heels in contact with the floor. Let gravity pull your heels down. Let the back of your pelvis drop. Relax your arms. Particularly think of lengthening the front of the arms on the thumb side to undo the residual tension that holds your arms slightly curled.

Using a long mirror, check to see if, from the side view, your ankle, knee, hip, shoulder, and ear are in a perpendicular line. Ours is a forward culture and our heads and upper chests tend to slouch forward. Bringing your head and shoulders back probably does not improve things much unless the rest of your spine adapts to the change without stress. Imagine that your spine is like the center pole of a circus tent. What would happen if all the ropes on one side were tighter than the ropes on the other side? The pole would suffer chronic strain. This is what we do to the spine by slouching and keeping the head in front of the shoulders.

6. Direct your attention to your head. Tip your head forward halfway and feel with your fingers how tense and tight the muscles down the back of your neck and shoulders have become. They have to be tense or your head would fall farther forward. We spend hours daily holding our heads like this and wonder why we have tension in the back of the neck. You can usually bring your head back by lifting the sternum or breastbone until the back of your neck softens and your head is balanced on the cervical spine. It is a bit like balancing a watermelon on a fishing pole.

7. Pay attention to the inner body. As you stand, imagine you are a seal standing under a fountain with the water falling down on your head. Lift your face and let the water fall inside you as your inner body lifts like a playful seal to play with the water.

In standing, you are relaxed and upright at the same time. This is a paradox, which is described in more detail in the sections on sitting meditation in chapters 6 and 7. You can practice the awareness of balance and ease that you learn in this posture any time you are standing still. It is a good place to begin, because if you master the principles of alignment, balance, and awareness in this one pose, you can employ them in the other postures.

REVIEW TIPS

- Stand up.
- Notice the pressure on the soles of your feet.
- Notice the sensations of gravity and bring your body into an alignment with it as you allow your muscles to relax.
- Continue making small adjustments as your body releases and changes.

SITTING

Siddhasana

There are several different ways to sit cross-legged or with the feet folded underneath the thighs. Since most Westerners sit in chairs instead of sitting on the floor, we have stiff knees, hamstrings, thighs, and hips. As a result, it is difficult for us to sit on the floor comfortably with an erect and aligned spine. If you wish to practice your sitting meditation in a chair, that is fine. But if you want to sit in one of the cross-legged postures on the floor or on a cushion, then you can benefit from yoga postures that help to give flexibility and suppleness to the body.

A very stiff body will not permit you to sit in a balanced and erect posture. The posture shown in the illustration is only one of many possible ways to sit. This is a simple cross-legged pose known as *siddhasana*. It is not a lotus or a half-lotus pose. Those poses are more difficult because they require more range of rotation in the hip joint. If you wish to practice any of the sitting cross-legged poses for meditation, you would be wise to put a bolster or firm cushion under your hips. This elevation of the hips makes sitting easier because it allows the knees to rest below the hip joints. If your knees are higher than your hips, it is much harder to keep the spine erect. If the spine slouches, you cannot breathe well. To raise the chest, the thighs have to descend. If you sit regularly, it is important to cultivate symmetry in your hips by alternating which ankle is on top. One suggestion is to put the right foot on top on Monday, Wednesday, and Friday and the left foot on top on Tuesday, Thursday, and Saturday.

Vajrasana

Virasana

On Sunday you can sit with your knees bent and your feet under your hips as in *vajrasana* (hero pose) or your feet just outside your hips as in *virasana* (thunderbolt pose). The illustrations show the poses without any supports. For most people it is not possible to be comfortable in these poses for a long time unless you support your hips on a firm cushion between the ankles or on a meditation bench, which lifts the hips off of your heels. The advantage of these poses is that they make it much easier to maintain an erect spine than the cross-legged poses.

Also, they are a counter pose for the hips. When you sit cross-legged your femurs or thighbones are rotated externally. If you sit in a cross-legged pose without also sitting in an internally rotated pose you might develop an imbalance in your hip joint.

In whatever fashion you have chosen to have your legs crossed or folded, there are many ways to explore the paradoxical demands of having the spine both erect and relaxed. You may even sit in a chair for this practice. However, if you practice sitting on the floor in various ways, you will develop more suppleness in your hip joints, knees, and ankles.

When you sit, see if you can focus on your intention to bring your body into accord with the image of an erect spine without actually using your voluntary muscles too much. Just your intention often allows the adjustment to occur with a quality of release and ease rather than a quality of self-criticism and overachieving concern. When you sit, see if you can internalize breathing deeply and easily for a moment; feel an opening at the base of the spine; and notice how the rest of the body responds to that opening. See if you can feel the top of your head and the base of your spine and the connection between the two, like the connection between the flower and the root.

An "erect" spine is not the same as a straight spine. The spine normally curves back in the lumbar (lower back) and cervical (neck) regions and forward in the thoracic (torso) and sacral (tailbone) regions. These curves give more springiness to the spine. Without them you would jar your head when you walked or ran, and your spine-bending movements would be less efficient. So, it is not necessary to "straighten" the spine.

However, sometimes one or another of the curves is relatively too deep or too shallow and the spine will need to be rebalanced. Never jerk or force your body into alignment. Schmoozing with your body is a method of working in which you relax and hang out with your body in the posture. You are having a dialogue with your body, giving it suggestions in a diplomatic way rather than ordering it around like a fitness fundamentalist. Then you listen to your body to get information. (You will find more information about the sitting meditation posture in chapter 12, Vipassanā.)

Sitting Exercise

1. In your sitting posture, without disturbing your body, think of the front of your body ascending toward the ceiling, without moving your head, so that the front of your body feels higher than the back part. As you hold this image in your mind, the front of the spinal column lifts and feels more active while the back of the spinal column feels like it is moving down through the tailbone to the floor. When you extend the spine in this way, be aware of what happens to the lower abdomen. These small meditative movements of postural adjustment should not impede the free flow of breath. On the contrary, they should enhance your breathing.

2. Pay attention to your spine. The spine is like a pile of blocks. Build them up by stacking one on top of the other in your mind's eye. Notice that as you inhale there is a bit more space between the vertebrae. See if you can sense a feeling of more space between the vertebrae even in exhalation.

Next, see if you can position your spine so that its natural relation to gravity produces a sense of balance and easy spinal lift. Do not use muscular force for this vertical lift of the spine. Try to sense that your spine is "active," but at the same time that you are not "trying" to hold it up. The great problem is the tendency to collapse the spine. You need to learn to keep it from collapsing without effort, and this paradoxical, almost magical, feat is accomplished by learning to think sensually.

3. Direct your attention to your head. Still sitting, keep the crown of your head facing the ceiling. Try some little head movements to discover the place where your head will be exactly in balance. For example, you might make some small circles with your head as you imagine you have a flashlight mounted upright on the crown of your head and you are drawing circles on the ceiling with the light. Then spiral in toward the center until your head feels balanced and there is a minimum of tension in your neck.

Consider the fact that your head is actually very heavy. Each movement of your torso requires the head to reposition itself to stay balanced. If you fail to keep it balanced, then you pay the price in tense neck and shoulder muscles.

4. Now focus on your arms. Lift the front of your armpits up without disturbing your arms. Let your arms and shoulders hang down passively. Then place your hands on your thighs, palms up or down, keeping your elbows hanging straight down from the shoulders. If your upper arms are held at an angle out in front of your torso while your hands are on your knees, it may place a strain on your back. Relax your thumbs. Be aware of your little fingers.

REVIEW TIPS

- If your knees and hips allow you to sit on the floor, practice sitting with your legs in various positions. If there is pain or stiffness, then sit on a cushion or in a chair.
- Notice the pressure underneath your hips as you sit on the chair or floor.
- Naturally climb the steps of your spine until you discover an alignment that allows your spine to be erect *and* relaxed.
- Continue sitting for thirty seconds to thirty minutes.

LYING

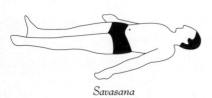

Savasana

Lying flat on your back is a pose called *savasana* in Sanskrit. In English it may be called the corpse pose or the sponge. Lying is one of the most important of yoga poses, and it will be the posture in which you will practice the body scan, which is described in chapter 30. You may practice the corpse pose at any time. Simply lie on your back on a pad or a blanket. Some people find that placing a rolled blanket or towel under their knees makes this pose more comfortable. Place your arms slightly away from your body on the floor. Turn your palms up, turn them down, then turn them up again and see what difference it makes in the way your shoulder blades fit against the floor. Usually you can feel your shoulder muscles soften if your palms face up.

Often when we lie down, we don't pay attention to the space our bodies occupy. The corpse pose provides a wonderful opportunity to direct your attention to your back in order to penetrate and touch your body with your mind's eye at a deeper level. If you can be very generous with yourself and open up your back like a fan, then you will spread out on the floor like a pancake.

See if you can feel how your ribs move away from the spine. Hold your breath and see if you can feel the skin of your back so much that as you begin to breathe, you can allow your breath to enter through your back. Gradually you will feel your breath rising as if from the floor through the torso to the front of your body. When you exhale, imagine you can feel your breath oozing out through the sides of your body as it widens. Don't disturb the front of your body. It is where we tend to breathe when we are in a state of panic. When your attention moves to the back of your body, your breath may become deeper and slower.

Since most kinds of meditation include the instruction to relax, it is important to gain some skill at relaxing voluntarily. Lying on your back is the best posture in which to practice relaxation. There are visualization practices to aid in relaxation in the following section called Lying Exercise and in chapter 38, Visualization.

Another famous relaxation technique is called autogenics. To practice this technique, say the following sentences to yourself as you lie on your back in a comfortable posture. "My right arm is growing heavier. My right hand is growing warm. My pulse is steady and regular. My breathing is slow and even. My solar plexus is growing warmer. My forehead is growing cooler." Take your time and really feel the effects of each suggestion as if your hand and belly actually grow warmer and your forehead grows cooler.

Relaxation includes the body and the mind. Usually you begin with the body and find a relaxed posture. If you are not comfortable, find some pillows or cushions to support your knees, lower back, or neck until you feel at ease. If any part of your body feels tight or painful or blocked, focus on that area as you breathe. Don't try to change it. Merely direct your awareness to that region. When we lie on our backs in *savasana* we often bring our tensions with us. You will relax more if you consciously practice the pose.

Lying Exercise

1. To acquire a balance between the cervical and lumbar curves of your spine, the curves in your neck and behind your waist respectively, rock your body gently by pointing and flexing your feet while pressing your heels into the floor. This movement will give you a sense awareness of the parts of your back that touch the floor and the parts that do not. When you become still, you may be better able to arrange your spine so that these two curves feel equal.

To study the relationship between the cervical and lumbar curves, first press down on one and then the other. Notice that when you press your lower back against the floor, your neck tends to arch higher off the floor. Seesaw back and forth between the two. Then let the rocking subside until your body is quiet and you are aware of your whole spine. As you grow more relaxed, the areas that make contact with the floor will grow wider and softer.

2. Lying in the corpse pose, ask yourself, "How can I do this pose with less effort?" Imagine that you are supported, not by the floor, but by the comforting warmth of a giant hand. How does this image enhance your feeling of safety and comfort?

3. Lying in the corpse pose, imagine that there is a small child lying within your body. Bring your attention to this image of the inner child. Remain in the *savasana* pose while you imagine the inner child turning to one side. Allow the child to roll over to the other side. Then let it roll and lie on its belly inside you while you still lie on your back. You might imagine having the child roll over onto its back and slowly stretch each arm out into the real arms of your body. Let your outer body fall away like a cobweb and your inner child's body, your new body, fill the space of the room. Feel the freedom of your inner child. If any part of the old body is still stuck, let it drop.

4. Imagine that your body is an ice cube melting on a hot sidewalk. Remain in the *savasana* pose as long as you like. It is fine to practice this pose in bed before you go to sleep. Even five minutes of deep relaxation on your back will restore your well-being. As you practice relaxing, you

will grow more skillful at relaxing quickly and deeply. The *savasana* pose will refresh you at any time and it is a great antidote to stress. It is like putting money in the bank, storing up reserves so that when you face stressful situations you are better able to respond efficiently.

REVIEW TIPS

- Find a quiet, safe place to practice.
- Lie on your back on a pad or a blanket.
- Place a pillow or rolled blanket under your knees, if necessary, to avoid pain.
- Place your arms on the floor slightly away from your body.
- Move your head and feet slightly until you feel comfortable.
- Remain quiet for one to fifteen minutes.

WARRIOR POSE

Virabhadrasana Two (Warrior Pose Two)

Many hatha yoga poses are named for and inspired by animals, plants, mountains, or mythological figures. This pose is named for a powerful hero in Hindu mythology named Virabhadra. For more information on Virabhadra, see The Shambhala Warrior in chapter 34, Nature.

Warrior Pose Exercise

The warrior pose is a lunge. Jump or step your feet apart to the distance that allows your right knee to be bent at a 90 degree angle with your right foot turned forward. Your right thigh is horizontal. Your left leg is straight and the toes of your left foot point left at a 60 degree angle from your right foot. A line drawn straight back from your right foot should intersect the arch of your left foot. Center your erect torso above this line and face front, that is, the direction you were facing before you took the lunge. Extend your right arm forward and your left arm backward from the shoulder horizontally. Look out over your right arm. Bring your coccyx (tailbone) down in order to prevent your lumbar spine from arching and your shoulders from rising. Soften your jaw and eyes, breathe easily, and hold for thirty seconds.

Then bring your feet together and release all tension. Repeat the pose on the other side. In all standing poses keep your feet balanced, that is, do not allow the outer or inner edge of the foot to lift off the floor. In the *virabhadrasana* pose, the bent knee tends to move forward, so keep it back over the outside of the heel. This powerful pose does tend to cause some compression in the lower back, so keep extending the tailbone down and lifting the back ribs up out of the pelvis. In the face of this effort, see if you can avoid the tendency to become rigid and stiff. Remember that true strength is peaceful.

REVIEW TIPS

- In all standing poses keep your feet balanced.
- Keep extending your tailbone down and lifting your back ribs up out of your pelvis to relieve possible compression in your lower back.

RESOURCES

Feuerstein, Georg. *Encyclopedic Dictionary of Yoga.* New York: Paragon House, 1990.

Feuerstein, Georg, and Jeanine Miller Feuerstein. *Yoga and Beyond.* New York: Schocken, 1972.

Iyengar, B. K. S. *Light on Yoga.* New York: Schocken, 1960.

Miller, Barbara Stoler, transl. *Yoga: Discipline of Freedom. The Yoga Sutras Attributed to Patanjali.* New York: Bantam Books, 1998.

Ornstein, Robert. *The Right Mind: Making Sense of the Hemispheres.* New York: Harcourt Brace & Co., 1997.

Chapter 7 • Yoga Breathing

Your hand opens and closes and opens and closes.
If it were always a fist or always stretched open, you would be paralyzed.
Your deepest presence is in every small contracting and expanding,
the two as beautifully balanced and coordinated as bird wings.

— Rumi

Pranayama is a Sanskrit word that means the "control of the breath." It is the fourth limb of the eight limbs of *ashtanga* yoga. In the *Yoga Sutra*, Patanjali asserted that disturbances of the mind cause irregular breathing, whereas regulating the breath leads to tranquility, which prepares the mind for meditation. Many meditative traditions around the planet have included breathing practices. Even folk wisdom advises us to take a deep breath to help survive all kinds of stress and trauma. It is something that we can almost always do, and that changes our physiology both electro-chemically and neurologically. Under duress, fear, or anger the breath becomes short and tight. It may be spastic and shallow. Taking a deep breath is the antidote.

Our very language reflects the connection between breath and spirit. Think of the word *inspire.* It means both "to breathe in" and "to stimulate, encourage, or arouse." The word *spirit* means both "breath" and "courage." And, of course, the word *expire* means both "to breathe out" and "to die." There are similar double meanings in many languages for both root words *spirit* and *breath.* In Sanskrit the word for spirit is *prana;* in Chinese, *chi;* in Japanese, *ki;* in Hebrew, *kath;* and so on. The first breath you take when you are born is an inspiration and your last breath at the moment of death is an expiration.

CONTEMPORARY USES

Today, modern Western medicine recognizes spirotherapy, which is the use of breathing exercises to improve health. There are some studies on the multiple effects of correct voluntary respiration. When you try to breathe slowly and deeply, you probably experience a few hitches where the movement of air is not smooth. These resistances may be the result of injuries or habits that have scarred your torso, leaving it stiff in some places.

If you are emotionally distraught and near tears, for example, you probably cannot take a smooth breath. This illustrates the powerful way in which emotions can affect the breath. Consider how you breathe when you are laughing. Laughing is great! It is jogging for the diaphragm. Consider the breath control required of a singer, a chanting monk, an actor, or a musician playing a wind instrument. How about the difference in breath quality between an asthma attack (long, gasping breaths) and a moment of sexual passion (short, panting breaths)?

Conscious breathing simply means that you are directing your awareness to your breath while you breathe. One breathing practice is to notice your breathing without trying to do anything to change it. It is almost impossible because we have lost our capability to breathe naturally. We could breathe naturally when we were babies. In fact, one of the best ways to entice your own breathing into a natural rhythm is to imagine the breath of a sleeping baby, and then try to synchronize with the image. It takes a lot of training and practice to simply be aware of your breath because you tend to want to fix it and make it better. You may need years of yoga stretching practice before your ribs and diaphragm can move without resistance, and years of practice focusing your attention so that you can simply watch your breath without interfering with it. You will ultimately learn to become the audience for your breath instead of the director, as well as how to dwell in witness consciousness.

The reason chronic shallow breathing deprives us of energy is that it reduces the working capacity of our respiratory system to about one-third of its potential, diminishes the exchange of gases, and deprives us of the natural healthful circulation of oxygen into our body. After general anesthesia, surgical patients are often given a device that encourages deep breathing to help flush the poison out of their systems. This is an example of spirotherapy.

The lungs are one of the organs of the excretory system. They remove waste products like carbon dioxide. The alveoli in your lungs have an enormous surface area. These small air sacs, if spread out flat, would cover a tennis court. It is across this huge surface that gases, moisture, and waste products are transported by diffusion and osmosis.

Breathing deeply helps to prevent disease. It makes use of the entire body. Natural breathing is a powerful form of self-healing for the body and even for the mind. We often find that freeing ourselves from restrictive breathing also frees us from the many narrow, unconscious attitudes we have about ourselves and the world. These attitudes often cause a hard, rigid body, so your first step is to "stop the hardening of the attitudes."

But what is normal breathing? There are many different kinds of normal breath because the breath responds to the circumstances and the needs of the body. If you are sprinting up a hill, your breathing grows deeper and faster. That is normal. So it is difficult to describe a normal breathing pattern. At rest, each one of us has an individual breathing pattern. If the movement of our breath were carefully recorded it would be as individual as a fingerprint.

The physiological mechanism of normal human breathing has a double set of nervous system controls. The speed and depth of breathing is regulated by the voluntary nervous system and the involuntary nervous system. Usually your breath is under the control of the autonomic or involuntary nervous system with sympathetic nerve messages serving to speed up the breath and parasympathetic nerve messages slowing it down to adapt to the needs of your body for more or less oxygen. But you can decide to hold your breath or to breathe in many different ways voluntarily. That is what I mean by a double set of controls.

So, since our breathing is regulated by both the conscious and unconscious parts of the brain, it serves as a kind of gateway from one to the other. This gateway works both ways. When you are agitated your breathing is fast and shallow. When you are in a meditative state your breathing acquires four characteristics: it becomes slow, deep, smooth, and abdominal. If you wish to acquire a meditative state, you can help the process along by making your breathing slow, deep, smooth, and abdominal. That is the physiology behind the adage, "Take a deep breath." Abdominal breathing is belly breathing. It means that the abdomen expands upon inhalation so that the wave of the breath moves through the whole torso, all the abdominal organs receive a massage, and the lower lobes of the lungs are filled.

How to Begin

Before you begin to practice much *pranayama*, practice some yoga postures or *asanas* to develop a good awareness of your body. The movements of *pranayama* breathing are infinitely subtle and refined. It is easier to detect them if you have a comfortable body that is quiet and still. The yoga postures serve to accomplish this. Then you need to pay attention to your breathing.

The *pranayama* practices cultivate what they require. They should be performed in a gentle manner and never forced. The breath is powerful; you can kill yourself, for example, by holding your breath under ten meters of water and then quickly rising to the surface. The expanding air ruptures the alveoli, and this allows air bubbles to enter the blood stream. The rupture of the alveoli is different from compression sickness. In scuba diving and martial arts, one is trained to avoid holding the breath because breath holding combined with force may damage your nervous system or worse.

Observe the Breath While Lying

To learn to observe your breath without interfering with it, lie in a comfortable posture on your back with your knees bent up or draped over a pillow. Lying on a mat or carpet on the floor is better than a soft bed.

Place one hand on your chest and the other hand on your belly. With your fingers lightly sensing your body, you should now be able to detect the movement of each breath. Be very gentle with yourself. Invite your breath to move through your body like a wave. Do not force anything. Just observe, and see if you can detect the very beginning of each inhalation. Does your belly move first or does your chest move first? Is there more movement in your belly or in your chest?

Wait for the onset of inhalation. Let it be a surprise. Do not hurry it or retard it. The inhalation is a contraction of the diaphragm whereas the exhalation is a relaxation. The onset of inhalation is a particularly useful point in the breath cycle at which to observe the details of your body. Does your body seem to move freely in response to the wave of the breath or do you sense that it has some places that are frozen or stuck?

Now place your hands on the region of your diaphragm, or lowest ribs. See if you can sense a spreading and opening in this region during inhalations. The diaphragm is where inhalation begins. The wave of movement travels through the soft organs of the body and causes some movement in the hard muscles and bones. Even the arms and legs respond to the movement of the breath.

Now let your arms rest on the floor beside your body, palms up, a few inches away from your hips. Can you sense any little tugging or rising and falling movement in your upper arms with each breath? Where, exactly, does your body move in response to your breath? Which portions of your back are pressing into the floor and which areas seem to move with your breathing? Is your right shoulder blade pressing into the floor in the same way as your left shoulder blade? Which ribs on your right side are making contact with the floor? Are there any ribs on your right side that do not make contact with the floor? Is it the same on your left side? By asking questions such as these you tend to promote a breathing pattern that approaches the meditative state. In the meditative state, the breath is calm, smooth, slow, and deep. If your mind wanders, gently bring it back to the task of watching your breath movement.

PRACTICE IN A SITTING POSTURE

Find a comfortable sitting posture. See chapter 6, Yoga Asanas, for more information on the practice of acquiring an erect posture with good alignment and relaxation. The spine and ribs are designed to function most efficiently when the torso is upright. If you are slumping or crooked, the breath wave will be impeded by the strains and stiffness. Notice the difference between lying and sitting. The relationship to gravity has changed, so it is useful now to observe any differences.

Notice the flow of air through the tip of your nostrils. Feel the coolness of the air as it enters and the warm moistness as it leaves. Feel the air flow and observe whether it is smooth. Can you sense the flow of air across the membranes of your nose and throat? Imagine that the air flows across these moist mucous membranes so smoothly that it makes absolutely no turbulence. How quietly can the river of air flow?

In the sitting posture it is quite wonderful to allow your breath to help keep you erect. Do this by watching for two things. First, observe the inhalations as they fill your upper chest with air and allow this filling with air to help lift your upper chest. Second, observe the exhalations and as you come to the end of each exhalation, squeeze the abdominal muscles just slightly to allow a bit of extra air to go out. This same squeezing of the abdominal muscles that helps push the last bit of air out also serves to stabilize the lower spine and keep it erect. So each wave of the breath in the sitting posture helps to support your spine.

The breath also helps to prevent rigidity. Allow the movement of your breath to massage the stiff places that tend to arise in your torso while sitting. As you attempt to remain erect and aligned in your sitting posture, your back, sides, and shoulders may become rigid or even cramped. Use the movement of your breathing to introduce resiliency and a slight motion to the rigid areas.

You can almost always find some place in your shoulder or neck or back where you are holding unnecessary tension. Looking for it is like a treasure hunt. But the treasure is not just in finding the hard muscles, the treasure is the moment of Aha! when you succeed in transforming hard, immobile places into living, breathing flesh that can tirelessly reside in the sitting posture.

The movement of your breath massages your whole body. Your body cannot live without it for more than a few minutes. Many of us live in bodies that have a limited capacity for breathing as a result of the inhibition or blocking of movement, resistance to movement, or tension. Capillaries actually become blocked and the blood flow constricted as a result of hard, tight, rigid muscles. If you can learn to watch your breath and remain relaxed, you will enhance the flow of blood and the oxygenation of your muscles and other tissues.

REVIEW TIPS

- Choose a comfortable posture, either sitting or lying.
- Close your eyes and observe your normal breathing rate.
- Without any unnecessary effort, slow your breathing rate until it
  is twice as slow as normal.

- Continue to relax as you monitor your posture.
- Get closer to your breath by noticing each moment of the inhalations, the exhalations, and the pauses between.

RESOURCES

Aranya, Swami Hariharananda Aranya. *Yoga Philosophy of Patanjali.* Albany, N.Y.: State University of New York Press, 1987.

Farhi, Donna. *The Breathing Book: Good Health and Vitality through Essential Breath Work.* New York: Owl Books, Henry Holt, 1996.

Hendricks, Gay. *Conscious Breathing: Breathwork for Health, Stress Release, and Personal Mastery.* New York: Bantam Books, 1995.

Iyengar, B. K. S. *Light on Pranayama.* New York: Crossroad, 1981.

Lewis, Dennis. *The Tao of Natural Breathing: For Health, Well-Being, and Inner Growth.* San Francisco: Mountain Wind Publications, 1997.

Miller, Barbara Stoller. *Yoga: The Discipline of Freedom. The Yoga Sutras Attributed to Patanjali.* New York: Bantam Books, 1998.

Mishra, Rammurti S. *The Textbook of Yoga Psychology. The Definitive Translation and Interpretation of Patanjali's Yoga Sutras.* New York: Julian Press, 1987.

Rama, Swami, Rudolph Ballentine, and Alan Hymes. *Science of Breath: A Practical Guide.* Honesdale, Pa.: The Himalayan Institute, 1979.

Chapter 8 • Yoga Meditation

The yogi in whom the turnings of thought have ceased recognizes that thought, thus purified, is really colorless. But like a flawless crystal, it reflects, without distortion, the color of any object presented to it.
— Barbara Stoller Miller

The complete program of practices in the eight limbs of yoga begins with moral and ethical concerns, moves on through the body and breath, and, with the last four limbs, describes meditation. The first of the four meditative steps is called *pratyahara*.

The Sanskrit symbol for AUM

PRATYAHARA

This step involves a withdrawal of attention from the senses. You choose to pay attention to the inner world and to ignore messages from the physical body. This withdrawal occurs involuntarily during sleep and when we are engrossed in thought, but in meditation it is voluntary. You can direct your attention to a mantra, a visualization, or an image of some sort. Or, you can direct your attention to the thoughts and sensations that arise, and practice the art of allowing them to pass away so that you can return to stillness. In *pratyahara* meditation, in your seeing there should be only seeing; in your hearing nothing but hearing; in your smelling, tasting, touching nothing but smelling, tasting, touching; and in your thinking, nothing but thinking.

75

DHARANA

In *pratyahara* meditation, your attention is not so distracted and it is more consistently focused on the inner state. When you focus your attention on one thing, you achieve the beginning of meditation. The human mind has the capacity to direct its attention like a laser beam of awareness toward one object. The object can either be external, such as music you may be playing, or internal, such as thought itself. The possibility of the mind examining thought itself is very important in the process of meditation. It is the basic mechanism of the second of the four meditative limbs called *dharana*, or concentration.

The word *concentrate* means "to direct one's thoughts or attention." It is the opposite of diluting or scattering thoughts. If your mind is jumping uncontrollably from one thought to another, it is not concentrated. If your mind is obsessively repeating and dwelling on some unpleasant or pleasant image, it is not concentrated. Concentration requires both intention and awareness.

In *dharana* one is holding the mind still. But the mind is movement. The mind is like the wind. The wind is created by air movement; when this movement stops, the air is still here, but the wind has disappeared. The goal of yoga is the gradual ceasing of the movements of thought. If you are watching a movie, concentrating on the plot for an hour and a half, is that yoga meditation? No, this is not what yoga means by concentration. The difference is that you concentrate on the movie because it is interesting. In yoga concentration, you choose an object and dwell on it even if it does not spontaneously enchant you. You are training the mind.

By letting go of your customary stance of judging and probing with your intellect, you open up to an astonishing realm of other modes of knowing and being. It is a challenging luxury to explore this exalted state of consciousness every day. It is hard for most of us to do nothing, simply to be in a state of watching and waiting. You are attuning yourself to subtle insights and energies that you may never be able to describe in words. But knowing them is impossible until and unless you spend time in this state of observing.

You enter a witness consciousness where the observing mind quietly watches the chosen object of meditation. If your mind jumps around, it does not mean that you have failed, because every time you begin again you derive some benefit from the practice. You are taming the mind. After a period of regular practice you will be able to focus your attention on your chosen object, at first for ten or twenty seconds, and then for minutes. Once you have trained your attention so that it can remain still for a long period, then you have reached the next stage of meditation in yoga called *dhyana*.

DHYANA

In *dhyana*, or contemplation, the concentration is even more complete. The last three stages of yoga meditation can be compared to falling in love. The stage of *dharana* can be compared to studying love as a Western biomedical scientist might probe into it, analytically and intellectually. *Dhyana* can be compared to falling in love. You are absorbed by the object of your affection and think of this person all the time. The meditator thinks of the mantra or object of meditation all the time. Likewise, the stage of *samadhi*, the final limb of the yogic path can be compared to the rapturous condition of love in which you do not need any other person in order to simply *be* love. The absorption is complete.

When mental concentration becomes permanent during meditation, this does not mean that you are asleep. You watch the show, including your free associations and responses to the object of meditation. This is not brainstorming or discursive thinking. This is more like the absorption of the mystic. According to Carl Jung, *dhyana* allows the unconscious to take on form through the sinking into and deepening of contemplation. The light of consciousness now illuminates the unconscious rather than the external world.

SAMADHI

Samadhi is the final limb of the yogic path where subject and object merge into one experience. The goal of most meditative practices is to achieve a state of deep mental absorption. This concentration calms the mind by diverting its attention from aversion and craving. Counting to ten slowly is a rudimentary form of *samadhi*. But the calm state achieved in this way only works at the conscious level.

True *samadhi* is a state that cannot be defined because it has no content. Its function is to unhook the consciousness from the ego. Jung felt that the various states of *samadhi* were all different forms of unconsciousness. Yoga teachers disagree with this. After experiencing the state of *samadhi*, the yogi returns to ordinary consciousness and dons the ego as one would an old jacket. According to Roman Dina, in his book *The Mystery of Meditation, Part 1*, "In *samadhi*, only the object awareness remains, as if the consciousness of individuality disappears. Actually, the individuality of the practitioner does not disappear, but the practitioner's consciousness telepathically identifies with the object of meditation."

Words are inadequate to describe *samadhi*. It is said to be the highest state of consciousness, associated with the direct mystic experience of reality. The senses and the mind are at rest. The mind loses its identity and is absorbed into a higher state precluding any awareness of duality, although a form of unitary awareness of the conventional world is retained. *Samadhi* can include bodily awareness or it can go to a level in which you lose awareness of your body and the material world.

How to Begin

The point of departure for yoga meditation is to concentrate on something. This can be a physical object or a thought.

Patanjali's *Sutra 1–39* advises the meditator to contemplate whatever object he or she chooses, according to Barbara Stoller Miller, author of *Yoga: Discipline of Freedom*. Your skill in concentrating will be improved by practice. Choose an object that suits your general goals. Preferred meditation objects are those that evoke feelings of equanimity and harmony. More information about the mantra as an object of meditation is presented in chapter 9, Mantras.

Meditation Exercise

1. Sit in a comfortable posture in a safe place, free from distractions, with your spine and neck upright. Close your eyes and relax deeply. The posture of meditation is described more fully in the section on asanas in chapter 6, Yoga Asanas.

2. Regulate your breath so that it becomes long, slow, deep, and abdominal. Allow your breath to be unmanipulated and natural.

3. Turn your attention inward. Withdraw your attention from any sense awareness of your body and the environment.

4. Concentrate your mind on the object of your choice, for example, the syllable *aum*. Your mind will wander and stray. This is normal. You will become lost in thought or in a daydream, or you may get lost in your plans for the future, memories, or other diversions. This is not meditation. These fantasies are obstacles. Whether they are pleasant, unpleasant, or neutral, when you "wake up," simply bring your attention back to your meditation object. Gently begin again.

This is the essence of sitting meditation. You begin again a thousand times. The way in which you direct your attention to your object of meditation is not at all like solving a problem with your rational intellect. It is not "thinking" about it. It is not wallowing. You approach the object with your awareness, with a "beginner's mind," as if you knew nothing. You make contact in new ways each time you sit and practice. Nothing is expected. If you have an agenda of hopes and expectations, you will be impeded. Enter a state of "no mind." This is not sleep. You are aware that you have "no mind." In deep sleep you are not aware. The process of quieting the thoughts in your mind is like cleaning out your house. When the furniture is gone, you have more space.

REVIEW TIPS

- Choose a quiet, safe place to meditate.
- Sit in a comfortable posture.
- Gently allow your breathing to become long, slow, deep, and abdonimal.

RESOURCES

Dinu, Roman. "The Mystery of Meditation, Part I." www.spiritweb.org/Spirit/Yoga/mystery-meditation.html.

Feuerstein, Georg. *Encyclopedic Dictionary of Yoga.* New York: Paragon House, 1990.

Feuerstein, Georg. *The Shambhala Guide to Yoga.* Boston, Mass.: Shambhala, 1996.

Jung, Carl. *Psychology and the East.* Bollingen Series XX. Princeton, N.J.: Princeton University Press, 1978.

Miller, Barbara Stoller. *Yoga: Discipline of Freedom. The Yoga Sutras Attributed to Patanjali.* New York: Bantam Books, 1998.

Chapter 9 • Mantra

"When I use a word," Humpty-Dumpty said in a rather scornful tone,
"it means just what I choose it to mean — neither more nor less."

— Lewis Carroll

Etymologically the word *mantra* is made up of the Sanskrit words for the phrase "instrument *(tra)* of reflection" *(man)*. In other linguistic traditions it means "a thought" *(manana)* "that saves" *(tra)*. Part of the rituals of Hinduism, mantras may resemble the prayers or hymns of Christianity, but they are fundamentally different in nature. In the Hindu tradition there are many different words for ritual speech. The word *mantra* means a word or phrase that has power. "The source of that power is the truth and order that stands at the very center of the Vedic universe," says Ellison Banks Findly in his essay *"Mantra kauisasta:* Speech as Performative in the Rgveda." *Mantra* is a general name for formulas, verses, or words that are believed to have magical, religious, or spiritual significance. Their purpose is to produce a change in the mental state of the person who uses them. They arose in the Vedic period of India, but became more clearly defined in the Upanishadic era, and have changed and evolved since then. In the Vedic rituals, mantras were used in many ways; sometimes they were shouted and chanted by groups, and sometimes repeated silently. They were created or discovered by the Vedic poet-sages, and in one Hindu tradition they were believed to have been a gift from the god, Shiva.

Mantra, like poetry, expresses the awareness of spiritual reality. Unlike poetry, a mantra is used in a ritual context, and, unlike poetry a mantra is a word of power. One recites the mantra with an intention. The mantra is a catalyst that enables the sacred potential of the ritual to become a reality. Mantras have different uses: propitiation where one wishes to appease a Deity; acquisition where one is asking for something; and summoning help from some supernatural force.

Mantras do not *express* a thought, they *generate* a thought or even a concrete manifestation of that thought. This distinction reflects the fact that in India, language is considered to have an effect on things. The usual functions of language are to inform or communicate, but the mantras have the purpose of accomplishing an action, generally a ritual or psychological or mystical action. This action is the purpose and meaning of the mantra. Ritual language does not communicate information, but serves to "create and allow participation in a known and repeatable situation." The mantra is not mechanically repeated. It must be accompanied by the proper thought, for the goal of the ritual is realized when the consciousness of the worshipper blends with the image or symbol represented by the mantra.

In ancient India, diseases were thought to be sent by supernatural beings. Mantras were used in elaborate rituals by the shamanic healers to exorcise the demons who caused diseases. These procedures certainly addressed the psychosomatic elements of illness, and were exclusively used for psychological disorders. For the physical elements of illness, the healers used practical methods such as surgery, herbs, and therapy. When the healer prepared medicines, he would use mantras. By the beginning of the Christian era, the magico-religious element of medicine had given way to the more empirically and rationally based Ayurvedic system, according to Kenneth G. Zysk, author of "Mantra in Ayurveda: A Study of the Use of Magico-Religious Speech in Ancient Indian Medicine." But even today in many, if not all, countries, patients sometimes turn to spiritual healing practices, inspired by the accounts of supernatural healings found in many traditions.

Most mantras are in the ancient Sanskrit language. One of the more widely known mantras is *aum* or *Om. Om* appears thus in Sanskrit.

It is a primal sound that is pronounced ah-oo-mm. It is one of the letters of the Sanskrit alphabet, all of which may be regarded as mantras. Mantras are words that satisfy longings to be free from fear. They may be wishful thinking or they may really work, if only from the placebo effect.

Although the mantra is extensively used and occupies an important place in the spiritual exercises of Hinduism and Buddhism, it is also known in the West. An example is the Prayer of Jesus, used within the Eastern Orthodox Church. See chapter 20, Contemplative Prayer, for more information about the Christian uses. It has also been suggested that many spiritually minded Catholics, particularly in religious orders, make use of the rosary as a form of mantra, a means of keeping the mind in a state of recollection. An example of Christian prayer is, "Lord Jesus have mercy upon us. Hail Mary, mother of grace, blessed is thy name and the fruit of thy womb." In Islam, a related technique is that of the Sufi's repetition of God's name, or a holy word or formula, either audibly or inaudibly, to achieve a state of recollection. In the Sufi tradition this is called *dhikr.*

CONTEMPORARY USES

Many mantras have no meaning in ordinary language. This suggests that they are abracadabra words. They do affect the feeling tone of the persons hearing them or making them. Many mantras have a numinous effect that is as ineffable as a religious experience. They are not the same as prayers or spells, which is difficult for the Westerner to understand since most of our examples of religion come from Christian monotheism or the animistic or magical practices of tribal peoples.

Mantras are many-sided instruments and can be understood in many ways. Some of them elicit a mystical state of consciousness. Mystical perception is a special kind of awareness that is marked by greater clarity than ordinary sense perception. Many mantras are relaxing, soothing, and serve to lessen suffering. These consciousness-raising and healing mantras are used today by Westerners. These mantras are very meaningful to the person who uses them to dispel ignorance and realize release from suffering. This lofty intention to be released from suffering is a big goal to claim for the power of words.

In "Consclusion: Mantras — What Are They" author André Padoux believes that it is not entirely legitimate to transfer mantras from their Indian source into our Western culture because we cannot really adopt all the Indian cultural context in which they are grounded. If we are to use them, it must be within a philosophical framework of our own traditional notions concerning the powers of speech, which differ from Indian notions.

However, mantras may still prove useful for improving mental concentration or mystical life. Harvard University professor and physician
Herbert Benson recognizes that meditation on religious words is the most
healing of all mantra techniques.

According to Dr. Benson, the *physical benefits* of reciting mantras as a
meditative practice include the following: (1) a lower pulse rate, (2) lower
blood pressure, (3) a sense of relaxation known as the relaxation response,
and (4) a slower breath rate. The *mental benefits* of mantra meditation
include: (1) more control over one's life by gaining control over the mind
and senses, (2) more awareness of one's true identity as a spiritual being
instead of one's identification with the body, job, race, religion, etc.,
(3) more awareness of and synchronization with the oversoul, universal
energy, supreme truth, or whatever term one would like to use, (4) more
inner peacefulness, which leads to stress relief, (5) the unfolding of one's
full potential, the enlivening of the inner intelligence of the body, and the
development of higher states of consciousness, and (6) more orderliness,
dynamism, and creativity within the meditator, which results in greater
effectiveness and success in daily life.

How to Begin

The first three requirements of a meditative practice remain the same
in most forms or styles of meditation. First, you need a quiet place; second, you need a comfortable and stable posture; and, third, you need an
open and receptive mind.

The fourth requirement of a meditative practice is a meditative device
of some sort, which could well be a mantra. If you do not have a mantra
provided by a teacher or a short prayer from your personal spiritual tradition, you could not do better than to consult Vietnamese Buddhist monk
Thich Nhat Hanh's wonderfully poetic and creative book on meditation
entitled *The Long Road Turns to Joy* to find a suitable meditation device. For
example, each time you inhale repeat the phrase "Breathing in, I calm my
body." Each time you exhale repeat the phrase "Breathing out, I smile."
The next inbreath say, "Dwelling in the present moment." Breathing out
say, "I know this is a wonderful moment."

REVIEW TIPS

- Be sure that you are in a safe, quiet place.
- Sit and practice at the same time every day, even if it is only for five minutes.
- Do not expect anything or try to do anything
- Remember the "passive attitude" that enhances letting go.
- If you forget your mantra and begin daydreaming, be gentle with yourself and gently return to your practice.
- Notice each experience that arises with a detached awareness.

RESOURCES

Alper, Harvey P. *Mantra*. Albany, N.Y.: State University of New York Press, 1989.

Ashley-Farrand, Thomas. "A Selection from Mantra: The Original Power of the Spoken Word." www.sanskritmantra.com/what.htm.

Ashley-Farrand, Thomas. *Healing Mantras*. New York: Ballantine, 1999.

Findly, Ellison Banks. *"Mantra kavisasta:* Speech As Performative in the Rgveda" In *Mantra*. Albany, N.Y.: State University of New York Press, 1989.

Hanh, Thich Nhat. *The Long Road Turns to Joy: A Guide to Walking Meditation*. Berkeley, Calif.: Parallax Press, 1996.

Hanh, Thich Nhat. *Being Peace*. Berkeley, Calif.: Parallax Press, 1996.

Oberhammer, Gerhard. "The Use of Mantra in Yogic Meditation: The Testimony of the Pasupata." In *Mantra*. Albany, N.Y.: State University of New York Press, 1989.

Padoux, André. "Conclusion: Mantras — What Are They?" In *Mantra*. Albany, N.Y.: State University of New York Press, 1989.

Zysk, Kenneth G. "Mantra in Ayurveda: A Study of the Use of Magico-Religious Speech in Ancient Indian Medicine." In *Mantra*. Albany, N.Y.: State University of New York Press, 1989.

Web site for mantra help: www.geocities.com/Athens/Parthenon/7534/mantras.html

part 3
buddhism

Introduction • Buddhism

Whatever has the nature of arising
also has the nature of cessation.

— Buddha

Buddhism evolved from the meditation of Siddhārta Gautama, an historical figure who experienced a transformation and became the Buddha — a fully enlightened being — in the sixth to fifth century B.C.E. The Buddha is regarded as an earthly man and teacher, not as a transcendent being. Meditation is central to all Buddhist practice. The Buddha enumerated approximately forty different techniques of meditation. The word *buddha* also refers to the enlightened nature of mind and experience. So there is a buddha mind within us all. It is not something we have to create. It is already there.

Buddha expounded the four noble truths, which make up the core of his teaching. These are (1) the truth of suffering; (2) the truth of the origin of suffering; (3) the truth of the cessation of suffering; and (4) the truth of the path that leads to the cessation of suffering.

There are various schools and branches of Buddhism. They teach a practice called *vipassanā*, which is described in chapter 10. Buddhism spread to Tibet, Burma, and Thailand, to China (as Ch'an), to Korea, and to Japan, where Buddhism evolved into Zen.

Buddhism encourages individuals to think for themselves. This story illustrates how the teaching works.

The Buddha once visited a small town called Kesaputta in the kingdom of Kosala. The inhabitants of this town were known by the common name Kalama. When they heard that the Buddha was in their town, the Kalamas paid him a visit, and told him:

"Sir, there are some recluses and brahmanas who visit Kesaputta. They explain and illumine only their own doctrines, and despise, condemn, and spurn others' doctrines. Then come other recluses and brahmanas, and they, too, in their turn, explain and illumine only their own doctrines, and despise and condemn and spurn others' doctrines. But, for us, Sir, we have always doubt and perplexity as to who among these venerable recluses and brahmanas spoke the truth and who spoke falsehood."

Then the Buddha gave them this advice, unique in the history of religions:

"Yes, Kalamas, it is proper that you have doubt, that you have perplexity, for a doubt has arisen in a matter which is doubtful. Now, look you Kalamas, do not be led by reports, or tradition, or hearsay. Be not led by the authority of religious texts, nor by mere logic or inference, nor by considering appearances, nor by the delight in speculative opinions, nor by seeming possibilities, nor by the idea; 'this is our teacher.' But, O Kalamas, when you know for yourselves that certain things are unwholesome (*akusala*), and wrong, and bad, then give them up . . . And when you know for yourselves that certain things are wholesome (*kusala*) and good, then accept them and follow them."

The Buddha went even further. He told the bhikkhus that a disciple should examine even the Tathagata (Buddha) himself, so that he (the disciple) might be fully convinced of the true value of the teacher whom he followed.

— Walpola Rahula
What the Buddha Taught

RESOURCES

Rahula, Walpola. *What the Buddha Taught.* New York: Grove Atlantic Monthly Press, 1986.

BUDDHISM WEB SITES

For more information, consult these Buddhist web sites.
www.geocities.com/Athens/Parthenon/7534/ (Tibetan Buddhism)
www.parallax.org/ (Thich Nhat Hanh)
www.ncf.carleton.ca/dharma/introduction/buddhism.html
hawaiian.net/~dsparks/
www.dhamma.org/ (*Vipassanā* as taught by Goenka)
www.buddhanet.net/
www.naropa.edu/degreesmfa.html

Chapter 10 • Mindfulness

Practicing mindfulness in Buddhism means to perform consciously all activities, including everyday, automatic activities such as breathing, walking, etc., and to assume the attitude of "pure observation," through which clear knowledge, that is, clearly conscious thinking and acting, is attained.
— *The Shambhala Dictionary of Buddhism and Zen*

Mindfulness, as a meditative path, evolved from the Buddhist practice of *vipassanā*. Mindfulness is not a technique, it is a state of awareness. By evoking mindfulness the models you hold about yourself and the world become clear, your emotions are released, and you become fully aware of what is happening. The state of mindfulness is the result of a deliberate choice to be vulnerable and sensitive. You drop your defenses and choose to take what comes. Since some of the stuff that comes up may be negative, you need compassion and nonviolence in order to practice mindfulness with safety.

Most of the time our clear or quiet mind is cluttered with noisy chatter. Awareness lowers the noise. Mindfulness lowers the noise. In a state of mindfulness you pay attention to the present moment and as you do, the other things fall away. The focus is on the present experience as it is in other consciousness disciplines. When the mind has become silent, when you have lowered the noise, then the signal that is the beauty and reality of spirit will simply emerge. That signal is always present, but as the stars in the daytime are hidden by light, the signal of quiet spirit is often hidden by the noise we make. The signal is the realization that there is more to life than we think.

Contemporary Uses

Mindfulness meditation is a skill and involves the training of our attention. It has great therapeutic value in preventing depression. Mindfulness is not a dogma or another burden to add to our long list of things we ought to do. Mindfulness happens naturally when we are awake to the present moment and are able to drop our projections, obsessions, complexes, concepts, and habits of mind. It allows us to reexamine our assumptions.

When we stop the "hardening of our attitudes," we get unstuck and start enjoying a natural abundance of vitality that gives us endless energy. In these moments of quantum shift and leaps of consciousness, we can sometimes get free of old dysfunctional habits and get a glimpse of reality and of who we are. Mostly we see that we are not who we thought we were. Instead of recoiling with timidity and uncertainty at this realization, we discover how to love it as a new kind of freedom.

That is why one of the best meditations is a practice described by Ram Dass. The practice is simply to ask yourself the question, "Who am I?" then note the answer and respond with, "Not this." Kriyananda describes the same practice but uses the word *"neti"* instead of "Not this." If you repeat this process you will get a long list of the labels you use to identify your personality, your persona, your presumed position in society, and what you hold as descriptions of yourself. The process is interminable until you get to the level of "Who is asking the question?" or "Who is minding the store?" The moments when you get to this question and then ask, "Hello! Is anybody home?" may be the only times that you are truly awake, alive, and aware.

These moments of mindfulness expand our consciousness. They usually occur spontaneously, by accident, but there are things we can do to make ourselves more "accident prone." Moments of mindfulness tend to cut through our list of illusory labels and bring us face-to-face with the entity who is minding the store. This turns out to be just another concept, of course. We practice mindfulness not with the aim of experiencing any particular kind of sensation, but in order to free our mind from all conditioning. When we open and soften, and become quiet enough to listen to the inner landscape, it is possible to be more insightful. It is often very freeing and exhilarating. We see that the ephemeral nature of all phenomena means no clinging, even to the concept of no clinging.

Attachments are ubiquitous, they smell of dependency, they make us cling. We cling to our old habits, labels, and passions to say nothing of obsessions, addictions, and compulsions. We cling to security as Linus clings to his blanket in Charles Schultz' Peanuts cartoons. We see others and ourselves clinging to dysfunctional relationships or habits or jobs and wonder how to use the practice of detachment to break free from the habits that do not serve us.

Cultivating detachment can appear to be coldhearted and unloving if it is not balanced by compassion. Can we cultivate compassion that is free from attachment? If we make an axis on which we plot the range of human conditions from attachment to detachment, can we learn to love each unselfconscious passionate movement inferred in the dance along the axis? The rhythms of our excursions from one pole to the other give us endless opportunities to improvise and cultivate our skill at spontaneous right action.

As soon as you try to practice focusing your mind on your breath or any other meditation object, it becomes very clear that the mind is out of control. The mind keeps jumping from one thing to another like a spoiled child who reaches for one toy, becomes bored, and then reaches for another. This ingrained habit of restlessness and dullness changes when you try to fix your attention on your breath and then calmly bring it back again every time it wanders. Simply begin again and again, smiling gently, without tension.

This is how you develop an awareness of reality. This is the right effort. Awareness means watchfulness. By practicing awareness of your breath, you notice the here and now. You are observing the autonomic functioning of the breathing cycle, an activity that continues unconsciously whether you pay attention or not. This practice begins to develop an awareness of a subtler reality. If your mind is totally focused on your breath, it is free from the hindrances of desire or aversion.

The task that meditators undertake is to understand their own transient nature. The first stage is simply to learn the technique, how it is done, and why. The second stage is to put it into practice. Finally, with persistence, one grows more skillful at sustaining one's attention and it becomes possible to pierce one's inner reality. Outer, ordinary, everyday reality and consciousness remain the same, but not quite the same because there is an extra dimension, the inner reality. You penetrate the apparent reality of mental processes and physical forms. According to William Hart, author of *Vipassanā Meditation As Taught by S. N. Goenka*, you discover that "as matter is nothing but subtle wavelets of subatomic particles, so strong emotion is merely the consolidated form of momentary likings and dislikings, momentary reactions to sensation. Once strong emotion dissolves into its subtler form, it no longer has any power to overwhelm."

How to Begin

Although you can practice mindfulness anywhere or anytime while you are engaged in ordinary pursuits, it is useful to practice mindfulness while you are simply sitting quietly and comfortably. Then, with fewer distractions and stimuli, you have the opportunity to direct more of your attention to the perceptions of your senses. The Buddha considered thinking to be one of the senses, like smelling and touching. In mindfulness practice, observe whatever comes to your attention.

First, pay attention to your body, get comfortable, close your eyes and watch for whatever sensations of touch, pressure, tightness, or temperature may be present. Second, pay attention to your breath. If you direct your attention to the movement of your breath, you will always have something to observe that is changing since the breath is always moving. Some people prefer to direct their attention to the belly, while others feel that the sensations of the air moving in and out the nostrils is a smaller area and therefore allows a more concentrated focal point for their attention. Third, direct your attention to the sounds around you. Notice that whatever you hear comes into your ears and awareness without any effort on your part, you do not have to reach out or try. Your eyes are closed, so sight is not relevant. Finally, direct your attention to the thoughts that arise. Some of them may have rather strong emotional content, but view them as passing sensations and let them go. Keep on letting go. At the very end, you may enjoy a feeling of release and calm when you let go of all your goals, including the goal of letting go.

REVIEW TIPS

- Practice at the same time every day.
- Choose a safe, quiet place to practice.
- Sit comfortably in an erect and stable posture with your eyes closed.
- Pay attention to your body and any sensations that arise.
- Pay attention to your breath.
- Pay attention to the sounds you hear.
- Direct your attention to the contents of your mind, and notice any thoughts that may arise.
- When your mind wanders, gently return to the practice with a sense of forgiveness and compassion toward yourself. It does not serve to berate yourself for failing to maintain one-pointed concentration on the moment-to-moment arising of experiences. Hardly anyone can do this. We learn from our failures. If we did not have knots there would be nothing to untie.

RESOURCES

Grof, Christina, and Stanislav Grof. *Spiritual Emergency.* New York: Putnam, 1989.

Hart, William. *Vipassanā Meditation As Taught by S. N. Goenka.* New York: Harper, 1987.

Salzberg, Sharon, and Joseph Goldstein. *Insight Meditation. Correspondence Course Workbook.* Boulder, Colo.: Sounds True, 1996.

Fischer-Schreiber, Ingrid, Franz-Karl Ehrhard, and Michael S. Diener. *The Shambhala Dictionary of Buddhism and Zen.* Boston, Mass.: Shambhala, 1991.

Spiritual Emergence Network, Institute of Transpersonal Psychology, 250 Oak Grove Ave., Menlo Park, CA 94025; (415) 327-2776

Chapter 11 • Lovingkindness

Where love rules, there is no will to power;
and where power predominates there love is lacking.
The one is the shadow of the other.

— Carl Jung

E quanimity, lovingkindness, and sympathetic joy are the essential facets of compassion. For centuries the teachers of the major Buddhist traditions have preached the value of loving others. The Buddha taught that to have a direct experience of the wondrous reality that is beyond concepts, we need to be free from the idea of the individual self, so that when we are generous we do not attach any strings. Buddhists call lovingkindness meditation *metta. Metta* embraces all beings and differs from conventional ideas about love, which often connote possessiveness. It is more like the spiritual love of the Christian saints known as *agape.* In the Hebrew tradition, lovingkindness is called *chesed.*

CONTEMPORARY USES

Lovingkindness is a special kind of love. It is one of the essential aspects of compassion. It does not mean that you ignore hurtful actions, but it does help you see the good in others. Cultivating lovingkindness is a remedy for fear. Whereas some meditation teachers would advocate imagining that you are filling yourself with peace and light and ridding yourself of pollution and disease, the teachings of *metta* in the Buddhist tradition describe practices that do just the opposite. If you are advanced in your practice, you can breathe in the difficulties and pains of the world and imagine breathing out pure lovingkindness. Instead of just trying to heal yourself, you are trying to heal others.

You begin with learning to love yourself. This is not narcissistic or selfish because your intention is to develop the wisdom and strength to love others. Even though we may not achieve perfection, we keep trying because the practice of lovingkindness brings benefits to the practitioner. Using the lovingkindness meditation with the intention of cultivating good will strengthens your will power. It brings peaceful sleep. It makes other people more friendly toward you. It brings serenity. It tends to make you less judgmental toward yourself and others. It is an antidote to fear.

When you see suffering in the world, on television or in the street, see if you can open your heart to it. Don't be afraid of the feeling. Be vulnerable: use that quick, bright uprush of compassion, focus on it and deepen it. You will see how blind you have been to suffering. Compassion is nobler than pity. Pity has its roots in fear, arrogance, and condescension. Lovingkindness is not sentimentality, which distorts reality. Lovingkindness is not attachment or codependency. In *vipassanā* practice many schools and teachers save the *metta* for the last five minutes of the session. However, one can take retreats where the *metta* practice is the main theme, instead of only a minor element, of the practice.

How to Begin

First, you have to awaken lovingkindness within yourself toward yourself. This is not self-indulgent because it is the work you do for yourself that gives you the strength to do good work for others. When you feel that you do not have lovingkindness to give, try this method for discovering the love that is within you. Go back in your mind and remember a time when someone loved you in a way that really helped you and felt wonderful. Was there someone who was kind to you in your life? Remember them and let that memory fill you with gratitude. If nobody ever gave you unconditional love, then simply imagine such a being and pretend that you have received such love. This will allow your love to flow naturally toward the person who was kind to you. Now, let this lovingkindness extend to some other person. It is easier to focus your attention if you direct the lovingkindness toward a specific person, particularly a loved one.

A second powerful way to evoke compassion is to think of other people as exactly the same as you. We are all made of the same star dust and breathe the same air and drink the same water.

A third practice of lovingkindness is this: divide yourself into two parts, *A* and *B*. *A* is the aspect of you that is whole, capable of unconditional love, and wise. *B* is the aspect of you that is suffering and confused. Now, as you breathe in, imagine that *A* opens his or her heart completely, and warmly accepts and assimilates all of *B*s suffering. Let *B* allow all of the pain and suffering to flow out of his or her heart. As you breathe out, *A* sends abundant healing love, comfort, and happiness to *B*.

Do your acts of lovingkindness bind you to the one you are intending to benefit, or do they distance you? Often people give financially in order not to have to give of themselves. Whether called *chesed, metta,* or *agape,* lovingkindness builds an attachment between giver and receiver in which both benefit. The result is a union that bears fruit. Throughout the day, examine your habits of giving and lovingkindness. Are they intended to draw giver and receiver closer, or allow the giver to remain distant? The classic example of parental lovingkindness that is in severity is forbidding a child to touch the fire or play with a knife out of concern for the child's welfare.

Throughout the day, examine your habits of self-restraint and judgment. Is your intent lovingkindness, or are your habits a projection of your own shortcomings? Look for aspects of your behavior, thought, speech, or deed that reflect a loving self-restraint. Does your love or giving tend to overwhelm those persons you intend to benefit? Healthy lovingkindness must be tempered by a recognition of the capacity of the recipient. A master may wish to give over everything he knows to his student, but doing so would only overwhelm and confuse the student. Similarly, parental lovingkindness without discipline can lead to a spoiled child, or one suffocated with love.

TRADITIONAL *METTA* PRACTICE

In *Insight Meditation* by Sharon Salzburg and Joseph Goldstein, the Buddhist practice of *metta* is described as beginning with the repetition of four phrases:

May I be free from danger.
May I have mental happiness.

May I have physical happiness.
May I have ease of well-being.

We begin by extending these wishes to ourselves. Then we move on to the rest of the six categories of beings to whom we extend lovingkindness. Repeat the same four phrases and direct them to someone in each of the six categories. The six categories are:

1. Ourselves
2. A benefactor
3. A good friend
4. A neutral person
5. An enemy or person with whom we experience difficulties
6. All beings without exception

THE PRACTICE OF *TONGLEN*

The *tonglen* practice of giving and receiving is to take on the suffering and pain of others, and give them your happiness, well-being, and peace of mind. This is an advanced practice, not to be undertaken unless you have strong compassion and confidence. You should establish a regular sitting practice of meditation and feel quite centered before you begin *tonglen*. It is best to start practicing on yourself in order to heal yourself. Begin by sitting and allowing your mind to settle. Sit with your mind and feel its mood. Breathing in, mentally absorb any negative or harmful thoughts of any sort and, as you breathe out, mentally give out calm, clarity, and joy. The purpose of this practice is to purify your own mind.

When you become more advanced, you learn to take on with compassion all the various mental and physical sufferings of all beings and give them, through love, all your happiness, well-being, peace of mind, healing, and fulfillment. You may worry that practicing *tonglen* will harm you because you are taking in suffering. The only thing it can harm is your ego. If you have the strength to take on the suffering of others and transform it, you will be greatly benefited yourself.

Lovingkindness and Guilt

Lovingkindness can be used to change guilt into remorse. This is an important healing step because remorse contains more compassion and lovingkindness than guilt, and includes a positive determination to make amends for whatever wrong was done. To do this, as you breathe in, accept total responsibility for your actions in that situation and wholeheartedly ask for forgiveness. Direct the *metta* instructions toward yourself. Now, as you breathe out, send out forgiveness, healing, reconciliation, and lovingkindness. You breathe in the blame, and breathe out the undoing of harm. This exercise may give you the courage to actually talk to the person you have wronged and ask for forgiveness from the depths of your heart.

Review Tips

- Begin with healing and comforting yourself so that you are feeling strong enough to expand your compassion toward others.
- When you direct lovingkindness toward others, it is important to realize that all human beings have the same flesh and blood, and the same desire for happiness.
- When someone is suffering and you find yourself at a loss to know how to help, imagine what you would feel if you were suffering the same pain. This is the meaning of the word *compassion.* It means the deep awareness of the suffering of another coupled with the wish to relieve it.
- When you realize that other beings have the same components of life that you do, you begin to appreciate the fact that we are connected. This awareness of the interconnectedness of all life is conveyed by the term *interbeing.* When you see that you are interconnected to the spotted owl, then you feel that harming the owl will be harming yourself. This is the perspective of the compassionate and enlightened heart.
- Direct your thoughts toward yourself.
- Ask that you be free from danger.
- Ask that you be free from suffering.

RESOURCES

Hanh, Thich Nhat. *Diamond That Cuts Through Illusion: Commentaries on the Prajñaparamita Diamond Sutra.* Berkeley, Calif.: Parallax Press, 1992.

Salzburg, Sharon, and Joseph Goldstein. *Insight Meditation. Correspondence Course Workbook.* Boulder, Colo.: Sounds True, 1996.

Salzburg, Sharon, and Jon Kabatt-Zinn. *Lovingkindness.* Boston, Mass.: Shambhala, 1996.

Sogyal Rinpoche. *The Tibetan Book of Living and Dying.* San Francisco: HarperSanFrancisco, 1992.

Chapter 12 • *Vipassanā*

The Master sees things as they are,
without trying to control them.
She lets them go their own way,
and resides at the center of the circle.

— Lao-tze, *Tao Te Ching*

V*ipassanā* is a technique of meditation presented by the Buddha in the *Satipatthana Sutta*, in the "Discourse on the Establishing of Awareness." The Hinayana school of Buddhism, which is preserved today as the Theravada school, is centered primarily in Southeast Asia, especially in Sri Lanka, Myanmar, and Thailand, and uses *vipassanā* as its representative practice. It is a practical method for developing self-knowledge through self-observation. The word *vipassanā* is the same in Sanskrit and Pali, which is the language used in Buddhist sacred texts. It means insight, clear seeing, and intuitive knowing. *Vipassanā* is mindfulness of what is, or bare attention. Mindfulness is the microscope of the mystic. *Vipassanā* is also called insight meditation, and is meant to lead you to examine the nature of things for yourself.

CONTEMPORARY USES

Today there are Buddhist centers around the world where lay persons can go for instruction in meditation for short periods or long retreats. Persons of other faiths are usually welcome in Buddhist retreats. If you want to learn *vipassanā* meditation without going to a retreat center for personal instruction, there are books, tapes, web sites, and interactive e-mail correspondence courses available. Weekend retreats or three-day retreats might be a good way to begin if you do not live close enough to a teacher to go to regular weekly meditation classes. Ten-day retreats provide an opportunity for deeper exploration into the practice. *Vipassanā*, like Zen, alternates periods of sitting meditation and walking meditation. This rhythm of practice prevents the body from becoming too stiff during long sittings.

Most *vipassanā* retreats are bare-bones awareness practices that do not require you to adhere to any tenets other than the conviction that this practice will be of benefit. Unlike Zen, which proposes an instant and irreversible enlightenment, other schools of Buddhism suggest that there is a gradual improvement in the skill of the practitioner with occasional breakthrough moments and occasional setbacks. You experience your own inner space and inner truth. The experienced teachers can help you with any difficulties you may have. They have worked with so many students that they can provide reassurance, such as letting you know that your particular problem is quite common, or they may be able to give specific remedies for your particular hindrance. The names and addresses of a few of *vipassanā* teachers are listed at the end of this chapter.

Vipassanā practice leads you to examine the nature of things for yourself. The first step is to develop steadiness of mind. It is a formal meditation practice. Here you develop the skill of concentrating your mind, which is the basis for all kinds of meditation and most other endeavors. After you have developed steadiness of mind, then your unbroken attention can discover increasingly subtle perceptions and sensations.

Eventually you glimpse the ephemeral nature of being. It can be quite a jolt to discover that there is nothing to cling to, nothing to defend. This transformation into clear seeing involves body knowledge. You begin with an intention to sit and observe the moment-to-moment rising and falling of phenomena. This intentionality is the psychic equivalent to gravity. It helps you to get started. But eventually you will let go of the intention because it empowers the plane of ego consciousness. When you discover the larger dimensions of awareness, you see that your initial attitudes were limiting or one-sided. This more all-encompassing perspective may astonish you as you acknowledge and assimilate elements of your psyche that you may have been resisting or denying.

How to Begin

Sitting Meditation for Beginners

1. Sit comfortably and pay attention to the sensations that arise in your body. The important thing is to be aware of the sensations, not the cause of the sensations, and to perceive whatever sensations come into awareness without allowing your attention to be drawn into any one particular sensation. At first there will be some places in your body where the sensations are unclear. As you grow more skillful you will be able to experience sensations in more parts of your body. Whether the sensations are pleasant or unpleasant is irrelevant in meditation. The task is simply to observe objectively. By examining a sensation with dispassionate detachment you learn that it is not necessary to expand your sensation into an emotion of liking or disliking. The cause of suffering is this habit of reacting to thoughts or sensations with likes and dislikes. When you stop making yourself suffer you achieve equanimity.

2. Spend five to twenty minutes in your sitting posture, breathe smoothly and naturally, and observe the thoughts that arise. You do not need to make any effort to stop the thoughts from arising. This does not help anyhow. But you do make an effort to avoid getting lost in the thoughts. You are observing the thoughts as a witness. You are not the director of your thoughts, you are the audience. If you follow a train of thought, you have forgotten the practice. That is fine. When you remember the practice, gently bring yourself back to watching the thoughts with a sense of delight and appreciation for the gift of this practice. Berating yourself for forgetting the practice serves no purpose.

3. After practicing being mindful of your thoughts, notice your intention to quit, notice how it feels to move your body, and notice the aftertaste. Do you experience a sense of clarity and equanimity after your meditation? Could you possibly manage to bring this sense of clear mind into your day's activities?

As a beginner, it is probably best to practice Buddhist meditation without mixing it with other paths. This is not to say that you may never practice any other path. But to experience the benefits of this traditional practice you should give it a chance for at least a month. Buddhist practice has a complex and variegated lineage with many aspects to it. You can certainly shop around for other ways to meditate, but you should not window-shop forever. Sooner or later you will want to settle into a formal meditative practice that suits you. And one of the various Buddhist paths may well be the meditation technique for you.

THE POSTURE OF MEDITATION

What all of the various techniques of sitting meditation have in common is the sitting posture itself. Since different states of mind are dependent on and produced by different body postures, one may conclude that the most useful thing to do as a first step is to achieve the posture of meditation. A meditation teacher will usually start with two instructions for sitting: keep the spine erect and relax. You may assume any sitting posture that is comfortable to you, sitting in a chair is fine if you cannot sit crosslegged due to stiffness or injury. The spine should be balanced. It is also very useful to practice some of the other postures of hatha yoga to gain a relaxed balance in the body. See chapter 6, Yoga Asanas, for more information on other postures.

Will Johnson, author of *The Posture of Meditation*, says the sitting posture for meditation is supposed to be comfortable and natural. You are not trying to be anything other than what you are. But the two orders — (1) keep the spine erect and (2) to relax — lead one into a paradox. If you hold the spine straight it often becomes rigid and stiff. If you relax the spine it often slouches and collapses. The posture of meditation requires that you solve this paradox. It is a bit like solving a koan from the Zen school. This same posture will occur in other sitting traditions such as the Christian contemplative school or Sufi meditation.

The body carries a great load of residual tension and pain. Unfortunately, the effort to create alignment often serves to increase the tension. Living in such a body, the mind feels compressed, compacted, and bound up. If we can bring our bodies into a state of internal alignment and balance, then our minds begin to soften and expand as well. The feeling of ease is the best guide in your search for alignment. This path of settling into the awareness of your own body is called embodiment.

Posture Exercise

1. Begin by sitting in a comfortable posture: it may be on a bench, on cushions, or in a chair. If you are in a chair, do not lean against the back, but bring your hips forward toward the front edge of the seat. Your spine should be free to move a bit.

2. Now examine your body for the feelings of tension that this posture may cause. See if you can allow the tension to subside. If you cannot, you will need to experiment with different sizes of cushions, bolsters, or chairs to find a supportive setup for your body. If you add more cushions under your hips, you will be able to allow your knees to move down toward the floor. This is especially important if you are sitting cross-legged because your knees should be lower than your hips in order to allow your spine to be aligned.

3. Now move your torso and head very slowly, very gently, very slightly in different directions, front, back, side to side, and in a circle. Notice the sensations of tension that arise when you lose the verticality of your axis. Discover the sensation of no tension when you bring your axis into the center. These small movements will continue spontaneously throughout a sitting session. They change endlessly because your body changes, and the position that provided alignment ten minutes ago may not be exactly the location or position that is optimum now. Only when you are aligned is relaxation possible.

REVIEW TIPS

- Find a quiet, safe place to sit.
- Sit in a comfortable posture, relaxed and with an erect spine.
- Examine your body for feelings of tension.
- Allow the thoughts to arise, and then allow them to subside.

RESOURCES

Fischer-Schreiber, Ingrid, Franz-Karl Erhard, and Michael S. Diener. *The Shambhala Dictionary of Buddhism and Zen.* Boston, Mass.: Shambhala, 1991.

Friedman, Lenore, and Susan Moon. *Being Bodies: Buddhist Women on the Paradox of Embodiment.* Boston, Mass.: Shambhala, 1997.

Fuerstein, Georg. *The Shambhala Dictionary of Buddhism and Zen.* Boston, Mass.: Shambhala, 1991.

Goldstein, Joseph. *The Experience of Insight: A Simple and Direct Guide to Buddhist Meditation.* Boston, Mass.: Shambhala, 1987.

Goldstein, Joseph, and Jack Kornfield. *Seeking the Heart of Wisdom.* Boston, Mass.: Shambhala, 1987.

Hanh, Thich Nhat. *Being Peace.* Berkeley, Calif.: Parallax Press, 1982.

Hart, William. *The Art of Living:* Vipassanā *Meditation as Taught by S. N. Goenka.* New York: HarperCollins, 1987.

Johnson, Will. *The Posture of Meditation.* Boston, Mass.: Shambhala, 1996.

Kabat-Zinn, Jon. *Full Catastrophe Living.* New York: Delta, 1991.

Kabat-Zinn, Jon. *Wherever You Go There You Are.* New York: Hyperion, 1994.

Reps, Paul, comp. *Zen Flesh, Zen Bones: A Collection of Zen and Pre-Zen Writings.* New York: Anchor Books, 1955.

Young, Shinzen. *Meditation: Escaping into Life. Dialogue with Michael Toms.* Los Angeles: Vipassanā Support Institute, 1998.

Vipassanā Centers

- Insight and Spirit Rock Meditation Centers: Joseph Goldstein, Jack Kornfield, and Sharon Salzburg studied in Asia, Thailand, and Myanmar in the seventies, and then returned to America where they have been teaching this form of meditation to thousands of students. They established two centers. The Insight Meditation Center is located at 1230 Pleasant St., Barre, MA 01005. The Spirit Rock Meditation Center is at P.O. Box 909, Woodacre, CA 94973.

- The *Vipassanā* Meditation Center, based on a teacher named Goenka, is at P.O. Box 24, Shelburne Falls, MA 01370.

- Many *Vipassanā* retreats in America and Canada are cited in the journal *Inquiring Mind*, P.O. Box 9999, North Berkeley Station, Berkeley, CA 94709.

- Jon Kabat-Zinn has created a mindfulness meditation program in the Stress Reduction Center of the University of Massachusetts Medical School at Amherst, Massachusetts where he takes the pain-ridden patients whom the other doctors have given up on and gives them instruction in meditation based on the *Vipassanā* training. He has removed all the Sanskrit words and cleared the practice of any particular spiritual tradition.

Although he studied the techniques of *Vipassanā* meditation, he has translated the practice into Western biomedical terms. Stress management programs modeled after Kabat-Zinn's center have been developed in other hospitals. Kabat-Zinn was featured on the Bill Moyers public television program *Healing and the Mind.*

• There are correspondence courses such as the one from Dharma Foundation. Email course@dharma.org for more information.

BUDDHISM WEB SITES

Buddhism web site: www.ualberta.ca/~slis/guides/religion/buddhism.htm
Tibetan Buddhist web site: www.geocities.com/Athens/Parthenon/7534/

Chapter 13 • Za-Zen

To know what Zen is, and especially what it is not,
there is no alternative but to practice it,
to experiment with it in the concrete so as to discover
the meaning which underlies the words.

— Alan Watts

To describe Zen in words is by definition impossible, because Zen is experience — unique and individual, embodied yet timeless. And one of the primary experiences of Zen is the practice called *za-zen*.

We say "primary experience," rather than meditation, for, to the Zen believer, to sit *za-zen* is not to practice a sitting meditation, but to experience sitting. Just that. For *za-zen* must be purposeless and without intention. It is, arguably, not a form of meditation at all, though most people who practice it find benefits similar to those experienced by others in meditation. But if one sits *za-zen* in order to lower blood pressure, one is not really sitting *za-zen*. If, in sitting, one's blood pressure diminishes, that is simply an observable fact. The purpose of sitting must be simply sitting.

Is Zen therefore without any purpose at all? Not quite. There is a goal in Zen, which is to receive illumination, called *satori*. But to strive for that goal is to miss the point, for it is in the elimination of striving that the goal can be reached.

Paradoxical? Why, yes! Zen is full of teasing paradox. That is both the delight and, to some, the frustration of Zen.

One of those paradoxes revolves around *za-zen*, the sitting meditation. For, if one follows the logic of Zen thoroughly, it should not matter whether one is walking or eating, riding a tricycle or knitting. Illumination

113

should arrive at any instant, no matter what your activity. Yet satori favors the prepared mind, apparently, for the sitting meditation is virtually synonymous with Zen.

We will encounter Zen in several different ways in this book, for in addition to *za-zen*, Zen offers a walking meditation, meditation with word puzzles (koans), and work meditation *(samu)*, which are covered in chapter 14, Zen in Action; haiku (chapter 29) and brush painting also derive from the Zen tradition. All of these practices have in common the elimination of striving — the focus on being here, now, just acting, not planning and strategizing and worrying. Chopping wood and hauling water — as the Zen saying goes — that is the goal of Zen practice.

This tradition is part of the great stream of Buddhism that began in India in the sixth century B.C.E. Arriving in China several centuries later, Buddhism encountered and absorbed some of the insights of that land's indigenous philosophy, Taoism; it was there called *ch'an* Buddhism, the word being a translation of the Sanskrit word for meditation, *dhyana*, which later became Japanized into Zen. Then, traveling down the finger-shaped peninsula of Korea to Japan, Zen collided with Shinto, the way of the *kami* or nature deities, and further transformed itself. So, what we know as Zen embodies at least three different Asian religious systems. Yet Zen is not any of them, despite its heritage; it has grown well beyond its roots.

What distinguishes Zen from other types of Buddhism is the belief that enlightenment arrives suddenly. From its beginning, Zen masters questioned how the enlightenment that Buddhism sought could arrive in any other fashion than like a flash of light. The slow, steady accumulation of wisdom could not, they argued, lead to nirvana — for nirvana is the opposite of striving (or, perhaps, the essence of nonstriving), so how could one reach it through steady steps as though toward a goal? No, Zen says. Satori is attained suddenly, when the world is seen exactly as it is, with no illusions cast by our striving thoughts.

When satori is reached, one realizes an unbreakable and constant connection to the universe — that, in the language of Zen, one is always of the Buddha-mind. When illumination has been attained, one lives completely in the present, utterly spontaneous and natural. There is neither past nor future, simply an eternal present. The world is not divided into self and other, self and outside-the-self, self and nonself. There is a unity of the observer, the observed, and the act of observation itself. That is satori.

To assist students in reaching this illuminated state, Zen masters used what is called "direct pointing," nonverbal ways of showing rather than telling the way to satori. Zen stories, some of them marvelously whimsical and surreal, depict Zen masters answering questions about illumination with strange actions and apparently unrelated comments. The truth that could be told, they claimed, was not the truth. What they would — or, perhaps, could — teach was the sitting meditation, which is the foundation of Zen practice.

CONTEMPORARY USES

Zen is variously described as a religion, a philosophy, even an existentialist way of life. Because it is based in experience rather than theory, it does not necessarily entail giving up other religious ways; there are Jewish Zen practitioners, Quaker and Catholic ones. There are, however, many masters who demand adherence to such Buddhist doctrines as a cycle of reincarnations that continue until nirvana (nothingness) is reached. This is by no means the case with all Zen masters or practitioners, however.

Similarly, there are several sects within Zen Buddhism, most prominently the Rinzai and Soto schools; one distinction between them is the avoidance, by the latter, of the word puzzle called the koan. All sects employ meditation, predominantly the sitting meditation, as a means toward enlightenment. In some of these sects, it is vitally important that one's satori be vouched for by a master, called a *roshi,* whose illumination was similarly vouched for by a master. Such masters encourage students to move beyond the illusory limits of the mind into direct experience. While it is not necessary, in theory, to study with such a master in order to receive illumination, study in a *zendo* (Zen school or monastery) is certainly useful in becoming skillful in this practice. (Some anarchic Americans, pointing out that the earliest masters received satori without such training, resist becoming part of organized Zen.)

It is possible to study Zen privately, through inspirational texts, attempting to gain enlightenment that way. More commonly, individuals seeking instruction in Zen practice attend classes or retreats at a *zendo,* where a master who has received satori leads the meditation, gives instruction, and examines students to determine their degree of success in attaining enlightenment. It should be noted that some Zen masters call such untraditional means of study "degraded Zen" or otherwise dismiss it; others, however, accept such practices.

Although it is far from Zen philosophy to ponder the physiological effects of sitting *za-zen*, it is clear that the deep relaxation that Zen encourages has healthful effects similar to those found in other breathing meditations. However, it must be said that to concern oneself with such matters would not, in any school, be considered to be practicing Zen. The by-product of health should not be sought after, for the only goal of Zen is to be totally and spontaneously in the present. A famous Zen story tells of Yen-t'ou, a Zen master who, set upon by sword-wielding bandits, screamed so hideously that he was heard for miles around. Was this a failure of Zen practice, to scream so loudly in fright? No, for his illumination was so strong that he was able to completely and spontaneously act in the most human of ways: to scream in fear for his life. That his scream did not deter the bandits was not, again, a failure of illumination, for he died in satori, utterly at peace.

How to Begin

For most beginning Zen students, the surest way to learn to sit *za-zen* will be to locate a *zendo* and to attend classes, meditation, and/or retreats conducted by *roshi* there. Many major cities have such centers. For those in areas without a *zendo*, weeklong or even longer retreats at some of the centers listed in the resource list are a way to get started.

Typically, a Zen retreat or class will consist of joining other students in sitting meditation for a set period, often for several hours; at many monasteries, students get up and walk (see chapter 14, Zen in Action) at irregular intervals, either under the command of the master or when the body calls for movement. At some monasteries, an attendant with a *keisaku* (warning stick) gives a sharp nudge to anyone who seems to be drifting or dozing. A complete training in Zen will usually also include some instruction in the philosophy, as well as individual meetings with the *roshi*, who will evaluate the student's progress toward satori and, when appropriate, confirm that illumination has been achieved.

You should be aware that you may find that daily routines and practices vary somewhat according to the monastery and the *roshi* who manages it. It is well to think through your personal goals and your temperament before interviewing at a *zendo* or attending a retreat. If you sleep poorly away from home or find sharing space with strangers trying, for instance, enrolling at a retreat center with only a dormlike facility will make your practice more challenging. Similarly, do not expect necessarily to like the Zen master; his or her role is not to be charming, but to assist you toward illumination. However, serious distrust of the master can make it extremely hard to learn the practice; follow your best instincts in making the choice of this or any other spiritual instructor.

If you would like to attempt this practice without instruction by a *roshi,* begin by selecting a place in your home where you will practice *za-zen.* Generally, one sits *za-zen* on the floor, in an upright posture with legs crossed akimbo. Placing a pillow called a *zafu* under the buttocks makes for greater comfort in most cases. It is also possible to sit on a couch or chair, with the back supported. In *za-zen,* posture is extremely important. You are expected to sit with back straight, head balanced, and hands resting comfortably in your lap; the left hand cradles the right, thumbs touching. Your eyes are half-closed, gazing but not looking at the space in front of you. Although you may wish to alter this posture slightly if you sit in a chair, be careful to hold your body erect and don't slouch.

Many people find it helpful to use a timer for sitting meditation. In a *zendo,* regular gongs mark the passage of the hours, while you sit in meditation until told to stop. At home, it is often difficult to let go of the consciousness of time passing. So, a small silent timer (one that does not tick), such as those sold in housewares stores, can be useful in assisting meditation. (Even a loudly ticking timer can serve, although the beginning meditator will often find this almost hopelessly distracting.)

Few beginners can sit for an hour or more, but rarely can one attain a composed state in less than ten minutes. Try, when you begin your practice, to extend the length of meditation slightly until you find a span that is comfortable for you; begin at ten minutes and increase your time by two minutes each day. Most practitioners suggest that meditating every day is important. Engaging in longer meditations at regular — say, weekly — intervals can assist the beginner in settling into shorter daily meditations more readily.

At the beginning of the meditation, bow slightly, hands folded as if in prayer, and elbows raised; this hand position, called *gassho,* is traditional to Zen meditation, and over time serves as a cue to the body-mind that meditation is about to begin. Then sit, breathing deeply and freely and regularly. Clear your mind of all thought, and seek to remain simply within the moment. Experience noises and lights and fragrances and odors without remarking upon them. When the timer goes off, bow again to close the meditation.

Beginners usually find sitting *za-zen* extraordinarily difficult. It is as though, once the body is silent, the mind becomes furiously loud. Thoughts race across the mind like Ping-Pong balls or ricocheting bullets. This is the "monkey mind" of which Zen speaks: the mind that worries, doubts, frets about the past, makes lists, all the time chattering like a monkey.

A common piece of advice given to meditators who encounter this hyperactive monkey is to picture the mind as a sky full of clouds. Each thought, then, becomes a cloud drifting past. However, Zen does not normally rely upon such visualizations. Rather, the meditator is encouraged to simply accept the chattering mind and to listen behind it for another more powerful kind of thought, what Zen calls "wild mind." It is to this other mind that one seeks to attend in *za-zen.* There may be thoughts there in the wild mind, but they will be thoughts of startling originality and freedom. There may be visions, there may be inspirations; however, it is not the point of the meditation to solicit or capture them, but simply to experience them. What is important is not to cling to the thoughts, ideas, and opinions that pass through the mind during meditation, but simply to observe them and let them go.

Similarly, beginning meditators are often counseled to concentrate on their breath — to count breaths from one to ten, then to start over again. This has the effect of keeping the monkey mind busy at a mundane task, which makes it less annoyingly verbal than usual. However, such counting should be done with the realization that concentration is not the goal of *za-zen.* Or perhaps it could be said that its goal is concentration on all parts of experience at once — the cat's slight purr from across the room, the shaft of sunlight against the mottled rug, the damp smell from the potted plant — and the body's gentle breathing, in and out. These are all part of one great unity.

Such a multiple focus is especially difficult in early meditation, when the senses act just as does the mind. No matter how carefully you have selected a quiet room for meditation, suddenly every whisper from the heating system seems gratingly loud, every movement of the cat seems to scream with energy, the room's colors grow shrill. Because so much of one's life is passed in not noticing, settling down to be aware — simply aware — is often a bit overwhelming. Like the chattering monkey mind, the senses become overwrought and exaggerated with anxiety. This feeling of sensory overload diminishes as practice is continued.

No matter how much one practices, however, there will be times when the monkey mind and monkey sense seem as vivid and uncontrollable as in early meditation. The more advanced student will simply be less distraught at encountering these familiar experiences, remembering always that the purpose of sitting meditation is not to control the mind, but to sit. Just that: to sit. It is both the simplest and the most profound of understandings.

REVIEW TIPS

- Determine if you wish to study with a master, or attempt sitting *za-zen* alone.
- If you decide to study with a master, research the possibilities, conduct interviews, make a selection, and attend classes and/or retreats.
- If you decide to attempt *za-zen* on your own, select a place for meditation to occur.
- Locate or purchase a timer, preferably one that does not tick loudly.
- Sit on the floor or in a chair, with your back straight, and your arms resting in your lap.
- Before beginning, set the timer for between ten minutes and one hour.
- Bow slightly to begin.
- Sit. Count your breaths (one to ten, then begin again) if necessary.
- Bow slightly at end of meditation.

RESOURCES

Abe, Masuo. *Zen and Western Thought.* Honolulu: University of Hawaii Press, 1986.

Bonnefoy, Yves. *Asian Mythologies.* Translated under the direction of Wendy Doniger. Chicago.: University of Chicago Press, 1993.

Briggs, William. *Anthology of Zen.* Westminster, Calif.: Grove Publishing, 1961.

Dogen. *Dogen's Manuals of Zen Meditation.* Translated by Carl Bielefeldt. Berkeley, Calif.: University of California Press, 1988.

Harding, D. E. *On Having No Head: Zen and the Rediscovery of the Obvious.* New York: Viking Penguin, 1986.

Johnston, William. *Christian Zen.* New York: Fordham University Press, 1977.

Kapleau, Philip. *Three Pillars of Zen: Teaching, Practice, and Enlightenment.* New York: Doubleday, 1989.

Merton, Thomas. *Zen and the Birds of Appetite.* New York: New Directions, 1968.

Omori, Sogen, trans. *An Introduction to Zen Training: A Translation of Sanzen Nuyman.* New York: Kegan Paul International, 1996.

Scott, David. *The Elements of Zen.* Boston, Mass.: Element, 1992.

Suzuki, Shunryu. *Zen Mind, Beginner's Mind.* New York: Weatherhill, Inc., 1980.

Tworkov, Helen. *Zen in America.* New York: Kodansha International, 1994.

Watts, Alan. *Talking Zen.* New York: Weatherhill, Inc., 1994.

Watts, Alan. *The Way of Zen.* New York: Vintage Books, 1989.

ZEN CENTERS

San Francisco Zen Center, San Francisco, Calif. (415) 863-3136

Green Gulch Farm Zen Center, Sausalito, San Francisco, Calif., (415) 383-3134

Tassajara Zen Mountain Center, Carmel Valley, Calif., (415) 431-3771

Providence Zen Center, Providence, R.I., (401) 658-1464

Zen Mountain Monastery, Mount Tremper, N.Y., (914) 688-2228

Cloud Mountain Retreat Center, Castle Rock, Wash., (360) 274-4859

Chapter 14 • Zen in Action

Calm, activity — each has its use.
— Shaku Soen, Zen master

Although it is common to speak of "Zen meditation" as the seated meditation called *za-zen*, in fact Zen Buddhism encompasses much more than that practice. The enlightened person, one who has achieved satori, is able to meditate continually, whether washing dishes or walking, whether shooting an arrow or reading a book. Action without striving, action with complete concentration — that is the essence of Zen in daily life. Perhaps the most famous example of the grace and focus of this style of meditation is the Japanese tea ceremony. The simple ritual of making and serving tea, when infused with great attention and deliberateness, becomes as deeply spiritual as a solemn High Mass.

The great Buddhist teacher Bodhidharma, often credited as the founder of Zen, was an Indian monk who taught sitting meditation at the Shaolin Temple in China. There, he found that monks nodded off during the *za-zen* sessions — and so he invented movement meditation, which formed the basis for what we know today as the martial arts. So, meditation in action was part of Zen tradition from its earliest days.

"Chop wood, carry water," a famous Zen phrase, tells of the difference between the enlightened and the unenlightened state. Before enlightenment, it is said, we chop wood, carry water. After enlightenment, we chop wood, carry water. There is, in other words, no real difference, to the observer, in the actions of an enlightened master and a complete fool. What is different is that the Zen master chops wood and carries water simply, without thinking about whether the wood should have been carried yesterday or the water carried tomorrow, without fretting about why someone else isn't carrying the water and chopping the wood, without daydreaming or worrying. Zen in action is action, simply, for its own sake, focused upon completely and utterly.

But this nonresisting mind is not passive: it is intensely focused. Satori or "seeing" is attained by attending with complete, laserlike attention to what one is doing. This permits, in a paradoxical way, enlightenment to flood in. The story is told of how Hui-k'o, the sixth Zen patriarch, attained enlightenment. Sitting in the marketplace, selling firewood, he heard someone reciting the famous "Diamond Sutra," a Buddhist prayer. At that moment, he became enlightened: not by the words of the sutra, not by his own actions, but by his attention and openness to what he was doing and the world in which he was doing it.

There are several Zen traditions that can assist the student in attaining satori. One of these, the koan, is difficult if not impossible to practice without studying with a master. The most famous koan to non-Zen folk is probably the riddle, "What is the sound of one hand clapping?" Another one that is widely known is the demand, "Show me the face you had before you were born." These koans are given to Zen students by their *roshi*, or teacher, to snarl up the intellectual part of the mind with the impossibility of the puzzle. The "answers" to these riddles, which are transcribed in the collections called the *Hekiganroku* and the *Mumonkan*, are not linear responses; a laugh, a shout, a dance may be the answer as much as an apparently irrational change of subject. The point of meditation with the koan is to reach a point where everything is new — what is called in Zen "beginner's mind" — and to respond to the world from that position.

Zen stories, used for teaching purposes, have the same nonlinear quality of koans. A monk came to the famous teacher Choa-chou and asked to be enlightened. "Have you eaten?" the teacher asked. "Yes," the monk replied. "Then go wash your dishes," Choa-chou said. At that moment, the monk achieved enlightenment.

This tale makes little, if any, sense to the logical mind. But it is consistent with Zen teaching that meaning is found in action, rather than in thought. This Zen-in-action is called *samu*, or work practice. This is the special heritage of Japan, to which Zen migrated after it had become established in China. There, a style of meditation emerged that emphasized the melding of the meditative stance with daily life: the "chop wood, carry water" school of meditation. Sitting meditation still formed the basis of Zen training in this tradition, but meditation now included everything in life. Even war could be meditative, as training of samurai warriors in medieval Japan stressed.

CONTEMPORARY USES

As mentioned in chapter 13, Zen became part of American life through the migration of Japanese masters after World War II. Such renowned schools as the Tassajara Zen Center and the San Francisco Zen Center have trained thousands of Americans in both sitting meditation and work practice.

Zen's influence on American culture has been, perhaps, never greater than in the 1950s, when the Beat poets embraced its precepts (often translated in ways that would have surprised earlier practitioners). Since then, Zen has exerted a strong influence among American artists, as evidenced by the classic on-the-road novel, Robert Pirsig's *Zen and the Art of Motorcycle Maintenance.* Among contemporary practitioners, the most notable is Natalie Goldberg, whose Zen-influenced books on writing have drawn huge audiences to this tradition. This contemporary American phenomenon echoes that of Japan, where Zen gave rise to the poetic form called the *haiku* (see chapter 29).

Zen work practice today overlaps to some extent with concepts of other body-centered meditations, even those that do not arise from Buddhist origins. The idea of focusing on action, rather than on the mind, is found in a kind of dance called authentic movement, in which motions are permitted to arise naturally from the body's own wisdom; another form of dance, contact improvisation, similarly demands utter attention to the moment in a way that combines action and meditation.

HOW TO BEGIN

A simple way to experience Zen work practice is a meditation called *Kinhin,* often called in English "Zen walking" — although, technically, the meditation should really just be called "walking," for it is simply walking in its purest state, unencumbered by the distractions of doing anything but walking. This practice often alternates with sitting *za-zen* in monasteries or *zendos*, but can be performed at home as well.

You need not have instruction in this practice before beginning; it is perfectly safe and relaxing even for the complete novice. The only caution that needs to be given is that it's useful to walk on a level surface. While it is possible to do Zen walking up a steep hillside or over a rocky path, it's easier to start on a simple, flat floor.

To perform this meditation, just walk.

It's that simple. And that difficult.

Stand still and center yourself within your body. When all striving has vanished, slowly lift your right foot. (Striving feels like an urgent itch; wait until you don't feel any need to move on, before moving on with the next motion.) Feel your heel leave the ground; feel the ball of your foot stretch upward; feel your toes slowly, one at a time, pull off the floor.

Move as slowly as you possibly can without losing balance. Hold each position for as long as you can, only moving when all striving has subsided. Hold your foot just above the floor before letting your knee loosen and your leg stretch forward. Hold this position — hold, in fact, each of the many positions that the foot and leg go through as the step unfolds.

Slowly put your foot down on the floor. Feel your weight shift from one hip to the other as you begin to move your attention to the other leg, which is, very slowly, going to be moving up from the floor in the same slow way as the first foot: heel up, then ball, then finally toes, holding each position as you go; stretching your leg forward, placing your foot, letting your weight shift, moving forward.

In the most traditional form of *kinhin* or walking meditation, the hands are held in a position called *shashu:* making a fist with the left hand, enclosing the thumb, place that hand to the heart and cover with the right hand. Now raise the elbows so that the arms are parallel to the floor. Walking with arms in this position is typical of *kinhin* as performed in *zendos* or monasteries, where the pace is often relatively speedy. In such training, it is also important to breathe in rhythm to the steps: one half-step for each full breath.

It can take as long as twenty minutes to walk across a room this way. Even those who often snooze off during seated *za-zen* can find this kind of movement meditation profoundly peaceful and relaxing. Beginners often express surprise at the enormous attention demanded by moving slowly in this way. And often, they are surprised at how calm they feel after this brief and simple exercise.

If you find Zen walking to be a suitable meditation for you, you may wish to expand into other forms of *samu*. The essence of Zen work practice is to do whatever you are doing. Washing dishes can become a meditation if, in place of rehashing the difficulties of the day or rehearsing the next day's meeting, you wash the dishes. Pay attention to every plate; notice the way the food catches on it in a specific pattern; the way it gleams slickly when covered with soap; the way the water strikes it and bounces off from the faucet, spraying other dishes; the way it rests, solidly, in the dish drain.

Or try *samu* when you are standing in line at a grocery store (this is, to some minds, a very advanced form of meditation). Instead of raging at the slowness of the clerk, simply stand. Move forward, one foot at a time, when you can. Otherwise, simply stand. Take in the roar of the crowd, the harsh lights overhead, the slight odor of human anxiety. Do nothing that you do not have to do; don't push your cart forward and back, don't tap your fingers, don't pick up magazines and shuffle through them. Just stand, wait, and move forward.

As the above suggestion demonstrates, the practice of *samu* may alter your life. You may find that some situations are so stressful that to maintain a meditative calm amid them is well-nigh impossible. You may choose to simplify your life, eliminating din-filled public rooms and choosing instead to gather peaches in a quiet orchard. It is no accident that we find a tradition of meditative monks living in simple ways. Do not underestimate the power of opening your senses to the world around you. The more you practice *samu*, the more you feel the quiet centeredness it can bring, the less you may choose to be away from that still point of calm.

REVIEW TIPS

- Try Zen walking as a first step into *samu*. It is the easiest and yet one of the most effective forms of work practice.

- If you decide to continue, you may wish to seek out a *roshi* or Zen teacher. The most complete Zen training traditionally comes through being shown, rather than told, the way.
- Any action can be imbued with meditative intention. You need not change your life to meditate. Be aware, however, that many who adopt this style of meditation decide to simplify their lives, the better to more fully enjoy the calm that comes from practicing *samu.*

RESOURCES

Abe, Masuo. *Zen and Western Thought.* Honolulu: University of Hawaii Press, 1986.

Beck, Charlotte Joko. *Nothing Special: Living Zen.* San Francisco: HarperSanFrancisco, 1994.

Dogen. *Dogen's Manuals of Zen Meditation.* Translated by Carl Bielefeldt. Berkeley, Calif.: University of California Press, 1988.

Enomiya-Lassalle, Hugo M. *The Art of Zen Meditation.* San Francisco: Thorsons, 1987.

Joshu. *Recorded Sayings of Zen Master Joshu.* Translated and introduced by James Green. Boston, Mass.: Shambhala, 1998.

Kapleau, Philip. *Three Pillars of Zen: Teaching, Practice, and Enlightenment.* New York: Harper & Row, 1966.

Kasulis, J. P. *Zen Action, Zen Person.* Honolulu: University of Hawaii Press, 1981.

Kaye, Les. *Zen at Work.* New York: Crown Publishers, 1997.

Scott, David. *The Elements of Zen.* Boston, Mass.: Element, Inc., 1992.

Simpkins, Alexander, and Annellen Simpkins. *Meditation: From Thought to Action.* Rootstown, Ohio: Tuttle, 1998.

Suzuki, Shunryu. *Zen Mind, Beginner's Mind.* New York: Weatherhill, Inc., 1980.

ZEN WEB SITES

The Electronic Bodhidharma, web site of the Research Institute for Zen Buddhism, Kyoto, Japan: www.iijnet.or.jp/iriz/irizhtml/irizhome.htm; Mailing address: Hanazono University, Nakakyo-ku, Nishinokyo, Tsubonouchi-cho 8-1 Kyoto, 604 Japan.

Web links to Buddhist sites: Dharma Rain Zen Center: http//www.teleport.com/~ryanjb/STILLPOINT/SP.html

Zen@Sunsit supplies randomly selected koans: www.sunsite.unc.edu/zen

Chapter 15 • Tantrism

Tantra shows that within every moment of our lives — within every feeling and thought and activity — are contained deep and powerful truths which, if examined in a clear light, can lead to true personal freedom.

— Marc Allen

In Sanskrit, the word *tantra,* means "expansion" or "weaving." We invoke the Tantric spirit by expanding our ways of giving or receiving sexual energy. Tantric Buddhism developed in India in the region of Old Bengal in the fifth through thirteenth centuries C.E. during a time of tremendous chaos, invasions, wars, and epidemics. Tantric Buddhism, which is a continuation of Hinayana and Mahayana Buddhism, arose outside the Buddhist monasteries as a protest movement by people who felt that desire, passion, and ecstasy should be included among spiritual practices.

The Tantrics made the brave and daring assertion that enlightenment can be found in all activities including those that were forbidden; so it has always been controversial. The criticism that Tantrism is degenerate is countered by the assertion of its adherents that greed, ignorance, and aggression are the degenerate pitfalls of Buddhism, not ecstasy. In the Tantric view, prudishness can be a form of aggression. There is a possibility of decadence in Tantric practices if the goal of compassion is forgotten, and hedonistic adventurism takes precedence. To counter this, the Tantric teacher insists on a sense of responsibility.

Sufism resembles Tantrism, and was probably influenced by it, since both traditions share the image of the lover and the beloved as characters in the sacred play of the divine. Taoism includes Tantric elements. There was a parallel development in Hinduism that emerged from communities devoted to the feminine goddess, Shakti. In the *Yoga Sutras* of Patanjali, there is no mention of a feminine divinity; she appeared with the Tantric texts.

There are very old chthonic elements in Tantrism, which emphasizes the awakening of the *kundalini* or divine energy, symbolized by the rising of a sleeping serpent at the base of the spine. An East Indian would never say "I thought it" of an inner revelation. To them the revelation comes from the gods.

Tantrism celebrates and honors the body in all its human functions, including sexual intercourse. Sexual union is practiced as part of the initiation process and as an ongoing ritual for the purposes of bringing about religious transformation and providing a bridge between humanity and divinity. Exponents of the tradition say embodiment is not a "soul" in a "body," but rather a multilayered mind-body continuum of corporealness, affectivity, cognition, and spirituality whose layers are subtly interwoven and mutually interactive. The Tantric goal is to maintain a clear realization of emptiness in the midst of passion. Tantrism offers many exotic rituals and methods such as feasts, poetry, dance, song, and the use of meat and alcohol, and many practices for partners.

The enlightened mind is a natural state of being fully present in the moment with no thoughts to interfere with the clarity of the next moment of awareness. Tantrists and other pan-Buddhists meditate on Avalokitesvara, who is the "Lord who regards the cry of the world." In China, the goddess of mercy, Kuan-yin, is a similar figure because she gives compassion. The gurus in Tantrism can be male or female. Today, the Tantric Buddhist or Hindu of India enjoys the continuity of a very ancient, aboriginally influenced tradition.

In the Tantric view, there is a clarity to any sense experience or emotion when it first arises, but then the clarity is obscured by judgments. There is no need to prevent thoughts from arising, one simply appreciates the true nature of mind in the experience of the moment. The language of Tantric texts contains veiled allusions and metaphors. This ambiguity provides a superficial meaning for the ordinary person, and many layers of hidden meanings for the initiate. This twilight language is used to alter the consciousness of the disciple and to produce more compassion and wisdom.

For example, the texts often refer to the union of a lotus and a *vajra*, or diamond scepter. Clearly, these are metaphors. They can be interpreted as referring to psychic processes such the uniting of wisdom and compassion, or bliss and emptiness. Simultaneously they can mean bringing together the female and male organs in physical union. The multiple meanings are all intended.

CONTEMPORARY USES

Tantric practices use materials from everyday life and the practices include a wide diversity of material. In this era of AIDS, we can study Tantrism to learn ways of sexual intimacy that involve all the senses. Tantra provides a new definition for lovemaking, which may be sexual or may involve reverence for another's body in a nonsexual way. Tantrism asserts that the energy becomes concentrated in the spine during sex; but the point of Tantric practice is not just to have better sex. The goal is to consciously transform sexuality into a religious experience.

Another goal of Tantrism is to experience orgasms that are not exclusively genital. Sex gives us a feeling of oneness, but there are other ways to gain this feeling. The point is to bring awareness into everything you do, including sex.

Tantrics use the image of *kundalini* awakening, but this is not just an Eastern notion. Carl Jung argues that the *kundalini* awakening of the East is the same as the psychic objectivity of Western psychology. On the path of Tantra, one indulges — but with awareness. Tantric Buddhist love creates a subtle ecstasy that results in a more permanent mental enhancement than the temporary satisfaction of ordinary sensuality.

In the tradition of Tantrism, the disciple must have a guru for a personal initiation. The disciple must also practice many kinds of meditative disciplines and rituals in order to be qualified and become adept enough for the initiation of physical union. In the West today, there are many books, teachers, and web sites that call themselves Tantrist but omit these prerequisites and go right to the instructions for practice.

These instructions do emphasize that the practice has a spiritual goal rather than a goal of simple hedonism. The pleasure is not an end in itself. The goal is a meditative bliss. For example, the idea of mindfulness is one guideline. If one is mindful during the pursuit of the bliss of sexual union then one will not be doing anything to harm oneself or another. This connotes a sense of responsibility and it precludes unbridled promiscuity as part of the practice.

According to Miranda Shaw, author of *Passionate Enlightenment: Women in Tantric Buddhism,* another characteristic of Tantric spirituality is that the practitioner "must relinquish attachment to the pleasure and meditate that everything, including their bliss, is devoid of intrinsic reality. In the midst of intense desire, it is necessary to renounce desire by seeing it as dualistic grasping for something that ultimately does not exist. At this point it may be helpful to imagine oneself as a thirsty person pursuing a mirage in the sky. Ordinary bliss can never bring ultimate realization, just as a mirage cannot quench thirst. Analyzing that the object of the bliss is no more real than a mirage in the sky may help to dissolve attachment into the expanse of skylike awareness."

The goal of Tantric yoga or Tantric Buddhism is the same as the goal of other traditions and branches: it is awareness. The difference is that Tantrists use every aspect of everyday life for the development of this awareness, including sex. Passionate desire arouses a great fire of energy that can be used to fuel the aspirant toward greater spiritual understanding. This is not a dull path.

How to Begin

Tantric practice includes much body awareness and many ways to appreciate the divinity within one's own body and the body of one's partner. One of the most universal metaphors for the divine or spiritual element of a human body is energy. So to begin, you need to develop your skill at sensing and manipulating your "energy body" or "kinesthetic body." Before you can be sensitive enough to sense such a subtle thing as your energy body, you need to relax. This can be done by sitting in a comfortable posture. Let all your expectations, assumptions, and resistances melt away and become very aware of your sensory experience in the present.

Then imagine that your real, physical body has a three-dimensional copy. Call it the energy body or the kinesthetic body or the subtle body. It is not your aura. It is simply an imagined duplicate of your real, physical body. As you remain quiet with your physical body, imagine that your energy body expands to fill the room and then contracts down to a single point. This is an energy exercise. The purpose of this kind of exercise is to gain skill at sensing your energy body and then using it in ways that enhance or support the movements of your physical body.

A second exercise for the energy body is this: slowly lift both your physical arms and your kinesthetic arms and lower them again. Then lift and lower your physical arms but leave your kinesthetic arms quiet. Then lift and lower your kinesthetic arms and leave your physical arms quiet. Then lift both your kinesthetic arms and physical arms simultaneously and notice the difference in quality. The refined and subtle perceptions that you begin to notice may reveal that your energy body and your physical body are not always doing the same thing. In lovemaking, for example, if the energy body is not totally involved and supportive of the act of intercourse then the partners may feel that there is something missing in the experience.

With a partner, sit facing each other and remain still and quiet for some minutes as you gaze into the left eye of the other person. Imagine that you are gazing, not into the eye or brain of the person opposite you, but all the way through them to infinity. This soft gaze enlarges your perception from its usual narrow focus. Take several minutes for each of the following experiences. Notice the sounds, notice the smells, notice any peripheral visual impressions, and notice the way your body feels. Allow your breathing to settle down. If thoughts arise, allow them to do so but do not get lost in thought. Wait and continue to notice the moment to moment experience of your own body and the sight of your partner's body. You will probably begin to experience your own body and its relationship to the other person in new ways that may be astonishing, fresh, direct, even scary. Stop if you feel panic coming on. Know that you are practicing the art of direct sensory experience with a quiet mind. This in itself is a spiritual experience.

Review Tips

- Sit quietly and become aware of your real, physical body.
- Then imagine an energy body within your physical body that is identical in size and shape.
- Experiment with your energy body. First expand it to fill the room and then contract it down to a point.

- If you have a partner, sit facing each other quietly while you perceive the sounds and other sense impressions around you.
- Gaze into your partner's left eye with no intention of doing anything else.

RESOURCES

Anand, Margo. *The Art of Sexual Ecstasy: The Path of Sacred Sex.* Los Angeles: J. P. Tarcher, 1991.

Cleary, Thomas. *The Ecstasy of Enlightenment: Teachings of Natural Tantra.* York Beach, Maine: Samual Weiser, Inc., 1998.

Johnson, Will. *The Posture of Meditation.* Boston, Mass.: Shambhala, 1996.

Muir, Charles, and Caroline Muir. *Tantra: The Art of Conscious Loving.* San Francisco: Mercury House, 1989.

Osho. *The Book of Secrets: The Science of Meditation.* New York: St. Martin's Griffin, 1974.

Peterson, Brenda. *Nature and Other Mothers: Personal Stories of Women and the Body of Earth.* Columbine, N.Y.: Fawcett, 1992.

Shaw, Miranda. *Passionate Enlightenment: Women in Tantric Buddhism.* Princeton, N.J.: Princeton University Press, 1994.

TANTRA WEB SITES

www.luckymojo.com/tktantradefinition.html
www.luckymojo.com/sacredlandindex.html (sacred landscape)

part 4
taoism

Introduction • Taoism

The Tao is hidden and nameless.
Yet Tao alone supports all things and brings them to fulfillment.

— Lao-tze

One of the world's most ancient religions, Taoism (or Daoism), can as readily be described as a spiritual philosophy. "The Way" is the simple meaning of the word *tao*, and that way is to balance the apparently opposite energies of this world, referred to as *yin* and *yang*. This philosophical Taoism, which does not emphasize the gods and rituals and magical practices that are part of popular Taoism, is what is best known outside China. But philosophical Taoism does not exhaust the rich resources of this tradition, which has provided imagery for many centuries of Chinese art and served as the bedrock of such meditative traditions as Qigong and T'ai Chi.

Taoism has its roots in the most ancient religions of China, those practiced long before Confucianism and Buddhism were adopted. The earliest historical records, dating back to as long as twenty-five hundred years ago, indicate that early China was home to tribal peoples whose shamanic religion resembled that of their Asian neighbors. As government and culture became centralized under ruling dynasties, these tribal religions were absorbed, together with some of their ancient spiritual techniques.

Among many of these peoples, the shaman was a woman; the Taoist emphasis on balancing yin (feminine) and yang (masculine) elements is a distant echo of the spiritual prestige of early Chinese women. Recent scholarship affirms that Taoism grew from these shamanic roots, although it developed well beyond them. The meditative disciplines of Taoism, then, have deep connections with shamanic disciplines, which are covered in Part I: Shamanism.

Traditionally, the founder of Taoism is the philosopher Lao-tze. He seems to have been a true historical figure, a librarian who, retiring from the pressures of court life, wrote the spiritual masterpiece *Tao Te Ching,* or the *Book of the First Principles,* which codified the spiritual insights of the aboriginal Chinese religion. Legend embellished the facts known about the philosopher, transmogrifying him into a demon-fighting elemental force who never died but disappeared instead, riding a green ox toward the west.

This semi-mythical founding figure provided the basic sacred text. But it was the next great master of the tradition who provided Taoism's elaborate and complex myth. Chang Tao-ling lived in the second century C.E., almost eight hundred years after Lao-tze. Not much is known of his actual life, but his legend claims that he fought demons with his magical powers, subduing them through the use of talismans. He also found a way to make a drug that guaranteed immortality. Drinking it with his wife and two friends, he ascended into heaven, from where he continues to observe his distant followers today. Chang Tao-ling was called *T'ien-shih,* "Heavenly Master." After his ascension, Chang Tao-ling's son took that title, which was thereafter passed along the family line, right down to the twentieth century.

Other important sages of the Taoist tradition were Chung-li Ch'uan, who attained immortality through a process of inner transformation that resembled Western alchemy. Sometime during the Sung Dynasty (960–1368 C.E.), the now-divine Chung-li Ch'uan taught these arts to a mortal named Lu Tung-pin, who codified them so that others, too, could attain immortality. From this period onward, Taoism became so intertwined with other Chinese occult arts that it is difficult to distinguish them.

Like Chang Tao-ling and Lao-tze himself, most Chinese divinities are deified mortals, people who have attained great spiritual power during their life on earth and are transmuted into gods. In the Taoist celestial sphere, gods and goddesses come and go like government employees; there's always someone charged with each important task, but the divinity may be different in different eras. The other world looks, in fact, a great deal like this world, with the August Personage of Jade (Yu-Ti) supervising a complex bureaucracy of the spirit.

PHILOSOPHICAL CONCEPTS OF TAOISM

The idea of cosmic unity is very important in Taoism. This unity, according to Lao-tze, extends from the time before time, from the moment of the very origin of the universe. Something then existed called the Tao, which preceded even "the one" that was born of it; the one divided into two, which gave birth to three, and so on to the "ten thousand beings." Later Taoist philosophers offered a slightly different version of this primordial myth: the Tao, they said, divided itself into yin and yang; unity became duality, then multiplicity.

Much of ancient Taoist writing concerns itself with articulating what the Tao is. Yet this very project is self-defeating, for the Tao eludes capture in words. "The Tao which can be spoken is not the true Tao," the *Tao Te Ching* tells us. Meditation on this primordial unity is part of the way that is Tao.

So, all life on earth exists as a play of the forces of yin and yang. Health and happiness come from these forces being in balance; unhappiness and disease, from their imbalance. Much of Chinese medicine and health philosophy, as well as such arts as *feng shui* (geomancy) and brush painting, are based upon this search for balance. If we cannot return to that primordial unity that was the undivided Tao, we can seek to keep the elements in balance as they were immediately after the Tao separated itself.

Both philosophical and mystical Taoism seek to move beyond oppositional thinking. So, it is wrong to think of yin and yang in a dualistic framework, with yin being "bad" because it is connected with shadow and darkness, while yang is "good" because it is connected with light. Rather, Taoism sees both as necessary in this universe — both as expressions, ultimately, of the great unity from which they emerged. Understanding this, and moving beyond the apparent opposites of this world, is the goal of the Taoist practitioner. The familiar yin-yang symbol — a circle divided into light and dark portions by an S-shaped line, each side bearing a dot of the other color within it — represents this insight.

It is the great power and exquisite wisdom of this tradition that demands we recognize that dualistic thinking is an artifact of consciousness, that it is not found in nature. Without darkness, there would be no light; without rest, no activity. All aspects of nature are in harmony; we cannot choose birth over death, youth over age, day over night. All Taoist practices seek to break the hypnotic spell of dualistic thinking and to allow us to reconnect with the simple, natural state of unity that is the Tao.

The dance of life within this world, seeking to maintain a perfect balance between yin and yang, is called *chi,* or life force. *Chi* exists everywhere, not only in animate objects but in rivers and mountains, in rocks and air. Even human structures have a flow of *chi* within them, which can be stimulated or thwarted just as flowing water might be. *Chi* wishes to move, unimpeded, according to Chinese philosophy. And it will do so, provided we do not set up blocks to its free movement.

From ancient times, Taoism has placed great emphasis on longevity; many of its spiritual techniques are connected with a search for long and healthy life — or even, if at all possible, to avoid death entirely. Some esoteric sexual techniques were practiced by early masters, and are still practiced by some Taoists, as ways of maintaining energy rather than dissipating it. Even Lao-tze himself is said to have known techniques for extending his life through sexual control (see chapter 15, Tantrism, for other approaches to this subject).

Taoist meditation techniques, from the start, have had physical components, for if the ultimate goal is to become immortal, it is necessary to bring the body to a high spiritual state. There was less distinction in ancient China between what was called "physical" and what was "spiritual." The ideal was to practice a spiritual and physical asceticism that ultimately transforms the body into a luminous being of light. Though it traveled far from its ancient shamanic roots, this vision of the transformed body is, finally, almost identical to that sought by arctic shamans who wished to mount to the upper world in ecstatic trance.

TRADITIONS OF TAOISM

Given its great antiquity, it is not surprising to find that Taoism has many varied traditions. Over many centuries, believers remolded Taoism to reflect the historical and social realities of their times. In the West, the most familiar version for most of this century has been philosophical Taoism, based in the great texts such as the *Tao Te Ching.* In recent years, however, such arts as *feng shui,* derived from magical Taoism, have been introduced and popularized in Europe and America. The Chinese divination system called the *I Ching,* as well as talismanic magic and exorcism, are clearly derived from the shamanic background of Taoism.

Alchemical Taoism, which teaches that the body can be transformed through consciousness of the energy or chi of the universe, is the basis of Qigong and other forms of meditation. In this mystic system, the universe is seen as not only derived from the primordial Tao, but able to return to that stage through specific practices. We each have, alchemical Taoism teaches, an "energy body" that can be reunited with the Tao. Esoteric traditions of sexual energy exchange, which resemble East Indian Tantrism, are part of this tradition.

From these varying strands of Taoism emerge the Nine Healing Arts, ways of attuning the physical body and its environment to the inner *chi* or life force that undergirds and sustains the universe. These are meditation, nutrition, movement, herbal medicine, acupuncture, *feng shui,* sexual practices, divination, and body work. These practices are based in the concept of *wu wei,* which means that the least possible action should be taken to achieve the desired results. Based in the observation of nature, especially of the flow of water, this way of acting is believed to bring us directly in touch with the Tao. Whether we are cutting wood or creating art, moving *with* the energy rather than *against* it is the Taoist way. As the *Tao Te Ching* puts it, "Go against the stream not by thrashing about, but by standing still and letting the water do the work. To the outside, wisdom seems to lie in taking no action, but, in fact, wisdom lies in foreseeing the need for action long before others can see it."

Chapter 16 • T'ai Chi

Tao is the way but it is not the ordinary way.

— Lao-tze

The martial art of Shao-Lin arrived in China from India as early as the fifth century C.E. where it was cultivated in the Taoist monasteries. It was changed into the great system of T'ai Chi (pronounced tai jee) in a continuous development over the last thousand years. T'ai Chi is a form of moving meditation. Along with the postures of hatha yoga, the movements of the Taoist healing arts were influenced by the behavior of animals. Many of the movements have animal names. The Taoists learned from nature, and the very name *tao* means the "path" or "way" that is the natural way. Originally T'ai Chi was practiced for two reasons, both for the rejuvenation of the monks who needed exercise and for self-defense. The postures and the transitions between the postures are performed in such a way as to stretch and contract every one of the 710 muscles of the body.

Due to the great antiquity of the form and the huge population of China it is no wonder that there are many different variations or styles of T'ai Chi along with hundreds of forms of the other martial arts. T'ai Chi combines wisdom from Buddhism, Confucianism, and Taoism. In recent years, a form of T'ai Chi has been practiced by great masses of Chinese people for mind and body conditioning, although Taoism is illegal under the Communist regime along with all other religions.

CONTEMPORARY USES

Today, one can find a T'ai Chi teacher in most American cities. The whole set of movements, or exercises, takes about ten to fifteen minutes to perform. There are many different types of T'ai Chi from short forms of 37 movements to long forms of 108 movements. The movements are slow, continuous, light, gentle, and balanced. The purpose of the practice includes the development of strength, flexibility, and balance. The symbol for the balance between the energies of yin and yang is a circle divided into white and black portions by an S-shaped line with each side bearing a dot of the other color within it.

In this symbol the small, white dot inside the black portion and the small, black dot inside the white portion represent a harmonious relationship between opposites. There is not only a balance between the two, but there is a bit of the opposite within the center of each half. This harmony between opposites is one of the goals of T'ai Chi.

Another goal is the development of *chi*, which means "life force." Taoism is not a dualistic sort of philosophy, nor do the black and white colors of the yin-yang symbol represent the opposites of good and evil. Good is considered to be a balance or harmony between the black and the white. *Chi*, or *ki*, in Japanese, is the same as *prana* in Sanskrit. It means energy or spirit. After practicing the T'ai Chi form you feel recharged and restored. Your blood circulation is stimulated, and your nervous system and muscular system are in balance. It concentrates your mind and calms your emotions.

T'ai Chi has a relationship with another, even more ancient, healing art called Qigong, which also controls the flow of energy, *chi*, within the body through breathing and mental intention. Most Qigong exercises are stationary, whereas in T'ai Chi you also develop balance when you perform movements that require you to lift one foot and balance on the other leg while moving the lifted leg slowly to take a step. This develops a greater capacity for both strength and calmness in the mind and body. Both Qigong and T'ai Chi promote healing and rejuvenation with the same qualities of smoothness, slowness, and groundedness.

Research on T'ai Chi shows that this practice reduces anxiety after stressful situations, increases flexibility and strength in elderly persons, and reduces the instance of accidental falls among its elderly practitioners. T'ai Chi trains more than your muscles and nerves. By turning your attention to the inhalation and exhalation of the breath, it develops "intrinsic energy" or *chi*. Two unique features of T'ai Chi as a form of exercise are its beauty and slowness. As in yoga and other meditative practices, T'ai Chi adheres to the notion that the process is the goal. In other words, the path is the destination.

HOW TO BEGIN

Although you will eventually need to study the movements of the form with a teacher or a video tape, you can begin by practicing a very simple, repetitive form of T'ai Chi called T'ai Chi Chih. It was created specifically to serve the needs of people who do not have time to take a class. It is so simple and safe that you can begin right now.

To prepare yourself for the movements of T'ai Chi Chih, stand in a relaxed posture. Be sure your shoulders, elbows, and wrists are relaxed and your head is balanced in its position at the top of the spine so that there is minimal tension in the muscles of your neck. Let your weight sink into the ground and your attention drop to your belly, about two inches below your navel. This is the *tantien* or *hara*, which is the center of gravity of your physical body. Watch the movement of your belly as you breathe in and out and continue relaxing the rest of your body. Sense that you are sinking deep into the ground.

Maintaining relaxation during the practice of T'ai Chi Chih requires continual monitoring of your attention and concentration. You don't want to be as limp as a dishrag, but you don't want to be holding unnecessary tension either. So you monitor your posture endlessly to maintain that wonderful amount of tension that is just right, enough to remain vertical and to move and to walk with no extra effort. This type of relaxation is used in the walking meditations of Buddhism and the labyrinth walking meditation.

T'AI CHI CHIH

There are two simple forms of T'ai Chi Chih that you can learn from reading this book. The forms are Round the Platter and The Bass Drum.

Round the Platter

From the standing position, raise your two wrists slowly and gently in front of you, while allowing your elbows to bend and your hands to hang loose. The image for this move is of a begging dog. Now, bend your knees a bit and place one foot a comfortable distance in front of the other while keeping both knees slightly bent.

To practice Round the Platter, you simply rock your weight forward onto the front foot and backward onto the back foot nine times. Your feet never leave the floor. It is as if they are glued to the floor. While you move slowly and smoothly forward, you circle your hands left and forward. While you move slowly and smoothly backward, you circle your hands right and backward, so that your hands trace the rim of the "platter" at just below shoulder level. When you come back the ninth time you bring your front foot back to join your back foot. You complete the nine rounds by lowering your two forearms and hands like a chiffon scarf drifting down through the air. Then practice nine rounds with the other foot forward.

Breathe slowly out as you go forward and slowly in as you come backward. Keep your torso erect throughout the entire form. Students often lean forward as their weight goes forward or lean back as their weight comes backward. By keeping your spine in alignment during the movements, you practice the great art of maintaining equanimity even when you are moving. You also keep your head at the same level. This will require a bit of effort and suppleness in your legs and hips. The practice can be quite a good exercise. As you grow stronger and more flexible you can spread your feet farther apart. A very low form of Round the Platter in which the feet are wide apart is quite strenuous. This practice can be as challenging as you wish.

The less strenuous or high form is suitable for anyone who can stand on their feet, even the elderly or infirm. In fact, it is particularly beneficial for those who have suffered a disability of some sort and need to improve their strength, suppleness, and balance in a safe manner.

The Bass Drum

The foot position and body movement are exactly the same as in Round the Platter, but in The Bass Drum the palms of your hands face each other and the circular path of the hands follows the rims of a large imaginary bass drum held in front of your body. Your hands are about 12 to 15 inches apart. As in many forms of T'ai Chi and Qigong, the palms of the hands are sensitive to the energy that connects them to each other and to the universe. Sometimes this form is practiced while holding a light bamboo stick between the two palms at the center of the life line. The life line is the prominent line that runs across the palm of the hand nearest to the base of the fingers. Using the stick helps direct your attention to your palms.

As with the Round the Platter form, The Bass Drum can be practiced at any standing height level by widening or narrowing the distance between your feet. You choose a level that is just deep enough to be challenging to your body and mind, enough to keep you alert and mindful, but not so deep as to be a struggle or an effort. If you push yourself too hard you will lose your relaxed balance.

The two exercises are poetic, releasing, natural forms that can be practiced any time, anywhere. If you do not feel like using the arm movements in a public place, such as at an airline terminal or in line at the post office, you can still practice the forward-backward movement of the torso in order to protect yourself from stress while you are standing and waiting. These forms serve as a standing meditation.

Imagine yourself visiting a marvelous natural wonder, perhaps the top of a volcano, a cliff overlooking the sea, or a splendid pristine waterfall. Just standing still is fine, but the walking or forward-backward movements of T'ai Chi can serve to direct your attention to your connection with the external world. That is their purpose. They alter your chemistry in a way that can make you more skillful in many areas, including the arena of perceiving the whole ambience of an inspiring natural site. They almost serve as a prayer celebrating the fact that you are in such a place.

REVIEW TIPS

- The purpose of T'ai Chi practice includes the development of strength, flexibility, and balance.
- As in yoga, T'ai Chi adheres to the notion that the process is the goal.
- Study the movements with a teacher or video tape.
- T'ai Chi Chih is a very simple, repetitive form of T'ai Chi.

Resources

Chia, Mantak. *Awaken Healing Energy through the Tao.* New York: Aurora Press, 1983.

Feng, Gia-Fu, and Jerome Kirk. *Tai Chi: A Way of Centering and I Ching.* New York: Macmillan, 1970.

Huang, Wen-Shan. *Fundamentals of Tai Chi Ch'uan.* Hong Kong: South Sky Book Company, 1973.

Jin, P. "Efficacy of Tai Chi, Brisk Walking, Meditation, and Reading in Reducing Mental and Emotional Stress." *J. Psychosm. Res.* vol. 36, no. 4 (May 1992): 361–370.

Lan, C., J. S. Lai, S. Y. Chen, and M. K. Wong. "12-Month Tai Chi Training in the Elderly: Its Effect on Health Fitness." *Medical Science Sports Exercise* vol. 30, no. 3 (March 1998): 345–351.

Lewis, Dennis. *The Tao of Natural Breathing.* San Francisco: Mountain Wind Publications, 1997.

Chapter 17 • Qigong

*The Way is constantly inactive and yet
there is nothing that remains undone.*

— Lao-tze

"The scholar learns something every day, but the Taoist unlearns something every day," said Chinese philosopher and Taoism founder Lao-tze. One of the most effective ways to "unlearn" — which in Taoist terms means to put oneself gracefully into the flow of universal life force — is the discipline called Qigong (also spelled *Chi-Kung* and *Chi Gong*). Sometimes called "Taoist yoga," Qigong was also influenced by Buddhism, which became a significant part of Chinese culture in the seventh century C.E. Despite this influence, Qigong derives most of its primary concepts and techniques from Taoism, which in turn is based in ancient shamanic traditions.

The word Qigong is translated in many ways. The first syllable refers to the *chi* or life force that flows, like an invisible river, through the entire universe. The word *chi* is used in China to describe electricity *(diann chi)* as well as heat *(reh chi)*; human vitality is called *ren chi*. The second syllable, found also in the Chinese martial art kung fu, means "work" or "effort" — not simply modest effort but work that involves training, discipline, and dedication. So, Qigong can be understood to mean "working with the life force" or simply "energy work." A generic term, Qigong is used to describe many "forms" or series of meditations, including that known as T'ai Chi Ch'uan.

This *chi* or energy is described as a unified, inseparable, eternal, and omnipresent force that permeates the universe. In nature, the two aspects of this force — the yin and the yang — exist in harmony, each with its own contribution to the sustaining of life and existence. We humans, however, get out of balance. Our yin energy grows too strong, and we become passive and cold. Or our yang energy overbalances the yin, and we become angry and too passionate. Through Qigong, the practitioner encourages the natural *chi* flow, removing blocks and restoring balance.

Qigong, one of Taoism's Nine Healing Arts, relies upon the same basic physical map as acupuncture, acupressure, and shiatsu. According to this understanding, a series of lines — called meridians — runs through the human body carrying the universal force of *chi* in much the same way as a streambed directs the flow of water. The intersections of such lines are particularly powerful points for healing; it is into such points that acupuncture needles are inserted or acupressure applied. In Qigong, such points and meridians are also important, for the various exercises are designed to "activate" or restore the flow of *chi* to them.

CONTEMPORARY USES

Although T'ai Chi has been taught in the West for many years, only recently has Qigong begun to be as widely known. T'ai Chi entered Western consciousness at approximately the same time that other Asian martial arts became popular, during the mid-twentieth century. American servicemen who had been stationed in Korea and Japan brought back interest in karate, jiujitsu, and other martial arts. T'ai Chi, which has a more martial aspect than most other forms of Qigong, was the earliest of the Qigong forms to become widely known outside China. Though introduced as a martial art, in the United States T'ai Chi quickly became a healing discipline for older citizens, who, like their peers in China, found that T'ai Chi helped them remain flexible and healthy even into advanced age.

Increased public interest in complementary healing techniques in the 1980s and 1990s has opened the door for other forms of Qigong. Most of the currently available books on Qigong have been published since 1990; classes in Qigong are also much more widely available. Most emphasize the yogalike exercises that are part of Qigong. Another aspect, the art described as "sending the *chi*," in which a practitioner assists a client in improving the balance of *chi* with hands-on healing (or sometimes even hands-off, for this can be done at a distance), is still better known in China than outside it.

In China, Qigong is used at "medicineless hospitals" that rely upon Qigong to treat disease, especially chronic illnesses. Patients perform Qigong exercises for many hours each day. They also receive healings from Qigong specialists who "send the *chi.*" Dramatic videotapes of tumors visibly shrinking while Qigong doctors hold their hands over the patient, offer a compelling witness to the efficacy of the cure. Whether a placebo effect, in which the body's own healing systems create a cure, is at work or not has not been studied. But there is no doubt that there are many documented cases in which Qigong eased, or even helped put into remission, life-threatening illnesses such as diabetes and cancer.

Outside China, Qigong is more typically encountered as a kind of physical exercise. Using one or more of the sequences of movement meditations that are part of the Qigong heritage (Soaring Crane Qigong, Intelligence Qigong, and other traditions), a teacher will lead students to focus on an inner vision of *chi* circulating freely through the body. Visualization and meditation are as important as physical movement. In fact, some teachers emphasize that inner intention is more important than movement — that a vivid visualization of a movement is more powerful than the same movement done unconsciously. Qigong continually stresses the idea that mind, body, and spirit are an indivisible unity. There can be no such thing as Qigong done merely for fitness, for true fitness can only be attained — so Qigong masters say — by attuning oneself to the universal force, which requires inner as well as outer effort. The outer or physical aspect of Qigong is called *Wai Dan,* while the inner work is called *Nei Dan* — and both are necessary to attain the balance sought by Taoist philosophy.

How to Begin

While the best way to learn Qigong is to attend classes with someone who has trained in this discipline, it is possible to experience some of the benefits through solo study and practice. With one of increasing number of videotapes and audiotapes that lead the viewer or listener through specific Qigong forms, one can now practice this healing art even if there are no trained teachers in the community. There is no question, however, that the combined energy of a group of students enhances the meditative effects of the exercises. There is, similarly, no question that the energy and skill of a master teacher are an incomparable advantage to those for whom such teaching is available.

However, not everyone has access to such teachers, especially outside the major urban centers of the United States. Those interested in pursuing Qigong need not pack up the household goods and pets, for if the *chi* is everywhere, it is as fully in Pocatello or Homer as in San Francisco or Chicago. Tuning in to the eternal, ever-flowing life force is possible in any location or community.

The few simple exercises given below will give you the flavor of Qigong. To truly experience the healing effects of Qigong, however, you will need to learn a complete form and practice it regularly — daily, if possible. A complete form may take between twenty and thirty minutes and will activate all the major energy points of the body. Regular practitioners report increased vigor and vitality, as well as a calmer, more serene attitude toward life's challenges.

Begin with a series of seated exercises. Two, which seem almost childishly simple to perform, are reported nonetheless to be very powerful in increasing the flow of *chi*. First, pound your feet on the floor like a spoiled child. Hit them on the floor hard enough to feel a slight tingle in the soles of your feet. Keep this up for at least five minutes. This will open the *chi* points on the base of the feet.

Then, shake your hands from the wrists, fast, as though you were shaking water off your palms. Continue this for five minutes. You can also shake your hands downward, with palms faced upwards, for an additional few moments. These actions will activate the *chi* points at the wrist and in the palms.

Then, stand upright. Imagine yourself as a tree, rooted in earth, reaching toward the sky. Breathe normally, but with each exhaled breath imagine yourself expanding outward into the farthest reaches of the universe. With each inhaled breath, imagine yourself drawing in the energy of the entire universe. Expand into the universe, then contract and pull the universe back within you. Do not let thoughts and worries intrude; if they appear, simply concentrate on your breath and on the vision of expansion and contraction. Expand and contract for approximately five minutes.

The next few motions are the beginning of the *Chi-lel* or "Intelligence" form of Qigong. They represent only a few of the movements that, in the full form, will draw energy along all the major meridians of the body.

Standing upright with palms relaxed by your sides, slowly turn your palms so that they face backward. Then elevate your fingers until your palms form a right angle to the floor. Hold this position for a moment, then make three slow circles forward and backward, while continuing to keep your wrists bent sharply. As you do so, imagine gathering *chi* from the earth and pulling it into your body.

Now relax your hands again and let your palms drop to your sides. Slowly raise your arms, palms facing each other, until they are at navel level. Cup your palms slightly towards your navel and imagine *chi* flowing from hands to torso.

Turn your palms to face the floor and point them forward. Gradually draw them in a circle around your body until they reach the back. Imagine a point opposite the navel; send energy from your middle finger to that point, called the *mingmen.*

Then simultaneously draw the hands at an angle up to the armpits, pausing to direct *chi* with the middle fingers to the *dabao* points, which are located on the chest approximately one-third of the distance from the shoulders to the waist, and the same distance from breastbone to underarm. Pour *chi* into the *dabao* points, then extend your arms directly forward from them as though you are reaching toward the horizon.

In the full *Chi-lel* form, you would direct *chi* to every part of the body, stretching and bending to do so. During this, or any other, Qigong form, visualization and meditation are as important as the physical movements themselves. Imagining the *chi* pouring through the body, as one does in the preliminary standing meditation, is said to have dramatic healing effects even without the attendant movements.

REVIEW TIPS

- If you suffer from extreme anxiety or another mental imbalance, some specialists advise against Qigong. The flow of energy that it creates can seem overpowering to some individuals. If there is any history of mental imbalance, it is best to study Qigong only with a well-trained teacher.

- While it is possible to do Qigong in any kind of attire, including business wear, clothing that does not constrict will be more comfortable, especially for beginners.
- If possible, locate a teacher who can lead you through an entire form. Be aware, however, that the recent increased interest in Qigong means that there are some teachers who charge exorbitant rates for their services. While there are esoteric aspects to Qigong that an expert teacher may include in his or her training, the beginner is unlikely to pursue them, and need not pay for the opportunity.
- Similarly, prospective students should be aware that there is a kind of sexual Qigong that some masters practice. If you are uncomfortable with such traditions, do not study with those who profess it, or simply decline that aspect of the teaching.
- If you are unable to locate a teacher at your level or in your area, videotapes and audiotapes can be used. For most students, however, it is difficult to maintain the discipline of regular practice when their support is limited to tape player or television. Occasional weekend or vacation workshops can supplement solo work and sustain the solo practitioner.

RESOURCES

Chan, Luke. *101 Miracles of Natural Healing.* Cincinnati, Ohio: Benefactor Press, 1996.

Cleary, Thomas. *The Essential Tao.* San Francisco: HarperSanFrancisco, 1993.

Cohen, Ken. *The Practice of Qigong: Meditation and Healing.* Audiotape. Boulder, Colo.: Sounds True, 1997.

Cohen, Ken. *Qigong.* Tapeworm Video, 1998. Videotape.

Cohen, Ken. *The Way of Qigong: The Art and Science of Chinese Energy Healing.* New York: Ballantine, 1997.

Dreher, Diane. *The Tao of Womanhood: Ten Lessons for Power and Peace.* New York: Morrow, 1998.

Kuei, Steven. *Beginning Qigong: Chinese Secrets for Health and Longevity.* Boston, Mass.: Tuttle, 1993.

Lao-tze. *Tao Te Ching.* New York: Vintage Books, 1989.

LeGuin, Ursula. *Lao Tzu: Tao Te Ching: A Book About the Way and the Power of the Way.* Boston, Mass.: Shambhala Publications, 1997.

Lu, Ke Yun. *The Essence of Qigong: A Handbook of Qigong Theory and Practice.* Translated by Lucy Liao. Abode of the Eternal Tao, 1998.

Ming-Dao, Deng. *Scholar Warrior: An Introduction to the Tao in Everyday Life.* San Francisco: HarperSanFrancisco, 1990.

Sommer, Deborah, ed. *Chinese Religion: An Anthology of Sources.* New York: Oxford University Press, 1995.

Towler, Solala. *A Gathering of Cranes: Bringing the Tao to the West.* Abode of the Eternal Tao, 1996.

Tse, Michael. *Qigong for Health and Vitality.* New York: St. Martin's Press, 1996.

Watts, Alan. *Tao: The Watercourse Way.* New York: Random House, 1977.

Wong, Eva. *The Shambhala Guide to Taoism.* Boston, Mass.: Shambhala, 1997.

Yang, Jwing-Ming. *Eight Simple Qigong Exercises for Health: The Eight Pieces of Brocade.* Rosindale, Mass.: Ymaa Publications, 1997.

TAO WEBSITES

Tao of Healing: www.geocities.com/HotSprings/2426/

Taoism by Alan Watts: www.alanwatts.com/taoism.html

Taoism General Page: www.interinc.com/Allfaiths/Taoism/

part 5
islam

Introduction • Islam

Meditation is to the soul as breath is to the body.
— Richard Cambridge

Although it is common today to speak of meditation as a nondeistic Buddhist discipline, in fact some form of meditation is found in every major spiritual tradition. Those who define meditation as clearing the mind of all thought in order to encounter the void that is existence speak from a Buddhist perspective. We have, in this book, defined meditation more broadly: as a way of calming the mind, changing its focus from pesky externals to a more timeless perspective, releasing creative flow, and promoting a sense of well-being and communion with the cosmos. This can be done either in the context of a traditional religion or in the absence of such a context; it can be done with or without belief in a supreme divinity. In this, we speak from a postmodern, multicultural, relativistic perspective that is not necessarily the perspective of the traditions we chart. Practitioners of many traditions in this book expect that followers of their form of meditation will honor the totality of the beliefs and insights of their religion, not merely take what is comfortable or seems useful within it.

This is certainly the case with Islam, the youngest among the world's great monotheistic religions, founded in the seventh century C.E. by the Arabic prophet Mohammed. The word *islam* itself conveys the importance of "submission" or "surrender," understood to be surrender to the divine will, the will of Allah (which means "god" in Arabic). More than 700 million people today follow the path of Islam — almost 20 percent of the world's total population.

Like most religions, Islam grew from polytheistic roots; like most religions, too, it has taken on slightly different flavors in the various cultures where it thrives. However, it remains centered in the land where it was born, in desert Arabia; the primary shrine of Islam remains Mecca, the town that was the central site of the Quraysh tribe, of which Mohammed was a member. There, a pre-Islamic shrine, the Ka'aba, was chosen by Mohammed and sanctified to become the preeminent sacred site. It remains so, and it is to that site that Muslims travel on the pilgrimage (see chapter 33, Pilgrimage) called the *haij,* which is one of the major meditative forms of Islamic worship.

Many important parts of Muslim tradition are based in the life of the prophet Mohammed. Born in 570 (or as late as 580) C.E. in Mecca, Mohammed's father was already dead when the child was born; his mother died shortly afterward, and so he was raised as an orphan by a kinsman, Abu Talib. His life was one of genteel hardship until his marriage to a considerably older and very wealthy woman, Khadijah. She was one of his earliest supporters when he began to receive visionary messages. Not all his clan, the Bani Hashim, was pleased with the revolutionary monotheism that Mohammed preached, but until the deaths of his wife and his uncle, he was supported and sustained.

Thereafter, however, the new head of the Bani Hashim as well as the powerful Quraysh made life for the prophet difficult, and he migrated to Yathrib, which became known as Medina, the city of the prophet; this move, which took place in 621 C.E. during the traditional pilgrimage time, was known as the *Hegira* or exile. There he assisted the villagers in making peace with other nearby tribes, in a document called the *ummah* or Constitution of Medina. Even this work, however, did not eliminate unrest among non-Muslims, and the prophet's life was sometimes in danger from them. Several battles, including a massacre that effectively eliminated all Jewish residents of the city, were necessary before the prophet's power was consolidated in Medina.

Even during the prophet's life, warfare was common as a means of extending the domain of Islam. An unrelenting war on Mecca, which even included a raid deemed sacrilegious during the sacred month of Rajab, resulted finally in the establishment of Islam in the city that had previously spurned the prophet. Despite the history of continual internecine warfare among Bedouin tribes, Mohammed succeeded in uniting the entire Arabic peninsula under his control before his sudden death in 632 C.E.

The religion, which was still very new at the time of its founder's death, grew exponentially in the decades that followed. Several contenders to the position of Islamic leader emerged, but finally Abu Bakr was named caliph — successor to the prophet. Under his leadership, renegade Bedouin tribes, who had left the faith upon the prophet's death, were brought back into the fold through warfare. Then, under the flag of Islam, a series of aggressive campaigns into neighboring lands began. Syria, Palestine, Turkey, Iraq, and other lands were brought into the faith by famous Arab generals. Slowly, even more territory, including such distant places as Azerbaijan, were added to the Islamic fold. Later, even Spain became Islamic, though the Battle of Tours in 732 C.E. ended Muslim expansion into Europe; Spain, too, was later lost to Islam, in the fifteenth century, as was Sicily, but all other lands conquered in those early days remain firmly Islamic.

With the murder of the third caliph, Uthman, contention over succession arose. The elected caliph was Ali ibn Abi Talib, son-in-law of Mohammed, but a Syrian contender, Muawiyad, eventually held sway. From that time dates the major division in Islam between the Shiah (Shiite) sect, which accepts the caliphate of Ali as the beginning of the true lineage from Mohammed, and the Sunni, the most widespread of the sects and the one most based in conservative custom or *sunnah*, which accepts the first three caliphs as legitimate. The Sufi, the most mystical of the Islamic sects, arose several centuries later, and is the source of the meditative traditions in this chapter. Finally, Baha'i, a religion that stems from Islam but has moved away from it, was born in Iran in this century; followers of that religion have suffered martyrdom in their home country, but the religion has appealed to many worldwide for its mystical pacifism.

THE IMPORTANCE OF THE KORAN

Like other traditions based in sacred scripture, Islam finds its greatest truths recorded in a single work, the Koran (also spelled Qur'an), a collection of revelations given to Mohammed by an angelic messenger. In 114 chapters, these "recitations" (which is the meaning of the word *koran*) were said to have been dictated to Mohammed, but are thought to be the exact words of Allah. These words were being read, according to tradition, from a source called The Mother of the Book, a heavenly work written by God that was also the source of the Bible and other written scriptures — hence the similarity among them.

While prophecy itself is a mystic art, there is no prophetic tradition in Islam. Mohammed is said to be the "Seal of the Prophets," the last prophet in a line of perhaps a quarter million prophets who preceded him. As Allah's truth had to be said in each language individually, earlier prophets such as Moses and Jesus are acknowledged within Islam. However, such direct guidance from the divine stopped with Mohammed. And the language of the Koran is considered the final language of revelation; the book cannot, in mystical tradition, be truly translated, so devout Muslims learn Arabic in order to read the sacred book with its perfected words.

Given that revelation was still in progress at the point of Mohammed's untimely death, the Koran could not have been assembled by him. Rather, it was the work of Zay ibn Thabit, the prophet's secretary, who gathered all the documents of revelation after Mohammed's death. Paper was not used by the Arabs at the time, so various revelations turned up written on leaves, bone, leather, and stone. Others had been memorized by the prophet's followers. All these were brought into a single work that was then given to Hafsah, daughter of the caliph Umar, to transcribe. From this document all copies of the Koran descend.

Several other books are also recognized as important, although not of the prestige and spiritual value of the Koran. These are called the Six Sound Books, and include the words of great Islamic poets and scholars. These books include sayings attributed to the prophet and anecdotes from his life. Much of the text of these books has to do with custom, or *sunnah*, which has formed a backbone of Islamic practice since the beginning. Some contemporary Muslims have questioned the authority of these books, claiming that only the Koran itself should be consulted as the word of Allah.

Because the divine cannot be pictured in human form in Islam, there is no tradition of sacred art that corresponds, for instance, to the European medieval paintings of the resurrection of Jesus Christ. The same religious impulse in Islam found its way into calligraphy. Using phrases, or even single words, from the Koran, sacred artists attempted to capture the inner significance in magnificent and often quite elaborate patterns. This calligraphy is a form of meditation unique to Islam.

Another Islamic meditative form, similar to Buddhist chanting (see chapter 9, Mantra), is the recitation of words or lines from the Koran from memory. Even when Arabic is not the language of the worshiper, the words must be spoken in the original language. The continual recitation of significant words creates a somewhat hypnotic effect similar to other forms of meditation.

THE FIVE PILLARS OF ISLAM

There are five religious practices of Islam, called the Five Pillars, each of which is similar to meditative practices of other traditions. The first is basic to the others: confession of faith, the *shahadah,* in which the Muslim believer attests that "There is no God but the One God, Allah, and his prophet is Mohammed." The recitation of this phrase is often used as a meditation by Muslims. The second, the ritual prayer, or *salat,* is said five times daily, following a purification and accompanied by a series of prescribed gestures (reminiscent of the yogic sun salutation). The third pillar is *zakat,* the paying of alms, while the fourth is *sawm,* the daily fast observed during the month of Ramadan, an ascetic technique whose spiritual efficacy has been widely noted. Finally, the pilgrimage or *haij* to Mecca is the fifth pillar (see chapter 33, Pilgrimage).

THE SUFI MOVEMENT

There is no question that the great prophet Mohammed himself was a mystic; yet because he was said to be the Seal of the Prophets or the final prophet, there was no mystical movement in Islam for almost four centuries after the founder's death. Yet mysticism is a natural human trait, as the great philosopher William James so effectively argued. Mystics seek a sense of timeless union with the cosmos — and mystics are born into Islam, just as into other religions.

Despite the strictures against prophecy, a movement emerged in Islam that has sustained itself to the present, producing some of the most famous and emotionally moving literary works of the entire Muslim culture. This is the Sufi movement, named from the Arabic word *suf*, meaning "wool," for the original practitioners wore white wool robes.

Islamic Sufism aims at direct, face-to-face union with Allah, resulting in a loss of that sense of the isolated self that afflicts us daily. This is attained only through contact with a saint *(walis)*, who in turn received inspiration from another saint in a chain *(silsilah)* going back to Mohammed himself. These saints might pass unnoticed among ordinary people, but they are invariably found to have special powers and a kind of personal holiness called *barakah*. Even after death, this *barakah* continues, so that pilgrimage to the burial places of Sufi saints is seen as a means of attaining peace and even physical health.

But the primary way of attaining holiness, to the Sufi, is through *fana* — turning away from the world, turning toward god. One way this "turning" is literally experienced is through whirling, which is discussed in chapter 19, Sufi Dancing. Other practices, such as asceticism and self-mortification, are also used to attain *fana*, that ecstatic union with god in which all ordinary desires and concerns melt away. It is expressed in the great Sufi poetry as a kind of drunkenness, an intoxication with god. After this union comes another stage, called *baqa* — living in god. Not as ecstatically joyous as *fana*, the state of *baqa* is the holiest state that humans can attain.

There are several orders of Sufi, each of them claiming descent from a specific saint. Usually these brethren live communally, but some wander as penniless ascetics; these are called dervishes. Part of the regular worship of each Sufi brotherhood was a specific form of worship called a *dhikr* — many of which were forms of practice that produced a light trance or meditative state. These included repetition or chanting of names or qualities of god, or sometimes physical prayer like the whirling dance of the Mevlevi order.

Chapter 18 • Sufi Breathing

The drop loses its limitations when it falls into the boundless ocean.
— Shah Ghasemn Feibakhsh

Founded in the middle ages (tenth to eleventh century C.E.) in Arabia by mystically-inclined poets and philosophers, Sufism embraces the idea that it is possible to be directly in touch with divinity, called Allah in that faith. Intoxicated by this deep and immediate connection, Sufis experience ecstasy or "extinction" *(fana)*, described as a kind of drunkenness in which all barriers to union with god are dissolved. Practices such as whirling and fasting are commonly used to attain *fana*.

Non-Muslims typically become familiar with Sufism through its great poets, for there have been few spiritual traditions that have been so magnificently expressed in poetry as this one. The great Persian Sufi poet and mathematician Omar Khayyám became popular in mid-Victorian England, eight hundred years after his death, when his *Rubáiyát* was translated by Edward Fitzgerald. A rubáiyát is a series of verses in the interlocking rhymed form called *rubai;* Robert Frost's poem "Stopping by the Woods on a Snowy Evening" is the best-known non-Muslim example. Khayyám's simple yet sensuous verses were lauded by the British public, who alas did not generally understand that the "Thou" of the poems was Allah, not some medieval sweetheart. Even better known today is Jalaluddin Rumi, the thirteen century mystic who founded the Sufi order called the Mevlevi. His ecstatic verses, especially in the translations of Andrew Harvey and Coleman Barks, are among the bestselling poetry in the world.

Sufi wisdom does not stop with ecstasy. Once the union with god is attained comes the challenge of living in that union, to live in *baqa,* a special kind of holiness. This holiness is not a matter of simply following rules or praying at the proper times and in the proper ways. It more resembles Zen Buddhism in assuming that the utterly holy person may seem childish or unassuming — even eccentric — to others. A tale is told of Rumi that he was preaching one day in the open air. Some dogs came up, sat on their haunches in the crowd around the poet, and listened, wagging their tails and panting sloppily. With great enthusiasm, Rumi proclaimed them enlightened, for their attentive posture and joyous response to his message. Only a great spiritual leader, or an utter fool, could have made that proclamation.

The place of women in Islam has been a source of much controversy. Many people contend that women are excluded from real participation in a religion in which only men can visit the most sacred place and hold positions of religious power. Others, however, contend that the Islamic picture of god is not gendered, which allows women as well as men to fully participate in the spirituality of Islam. The strong role that women, including Mohammed's wife, Khadija, and his daughter, Fatima, played in the early faith is also offered as testimony. Women have occasionally become renowned Sufi teachers as well as writers, especially poets; one of the earliest Sufi woman mystics was the poet Rabi'a al-Adawiyya, who established the tradition of speaking of god as "the Beloved." Famous among Sufi women were "the weeping ones," also known as "the sighing ones," women who wept continually from the force of divinity that they experienced.

In most Sufi orders, provision is made for women, sometimes in integrated, sometimes segregated, groups. Irina Tweedy, an Englishwoman who studied with the India Sufi order called the Naqshabandi, established that order both in England and, recently, in the United States. The Chishti order, brought to the United States by Hazrat Inayat Khan, is best known for its work with children's spirituality. The order founded by Rumi, the Mevlevi, is also one that emphasizes women's spiritual agency; one of that order's great female saints was recently exhumed, and her body was discovered uncorrupted and smelling of roses.

It is important to note that Sufi teaching is not conveyed through writing and study, but rather directly through contact with an individual

teacher. These teachers are affirmed by the various orders, who legit-
imize their conveyance of Sufi wisdom through the mechanism known as
nisbath, or linking of student and teacher. Rituals, prayers, even meditative practices may be learned from books, but real learning comes only
through direct teaching.

CONTEMPORARY USES

As mentioned in the section above, the meditative and spiritual practices of Islam are part of a complex and deeply tradition-bound religious
culture. While some other forms of meditation can be readily extracted
from their original settings, the case of Sufi practice is somewhat more
complicated. Some Sufi teachers welcome those of other faiths — or who
practice no faith — who wish to learn such techniques as Sufi breathing,
but others object to the dislocation of any practice from its Islamic context.

Among the Sufi practices that have become somewhat disconnected
from their original setting is a form of breathing meditation. This is used
in a non-Muslim context among some performing artists who seek to make
a connection to a spiritual essence in their work. Such breath practice is similar to that found in other traditions such as Zen Buddhism and yoga. What
distinguishes the Sufi practice are the prescribed visualizations that accompany the breaths, as well as the variations of mouth and nose breathing.

Breathing meditations are especially practiced by the Naqshabandi
order, which emphasizes *hosh dar dam* or conscious breathing. Referred to
as "safeguarding your breath from heedlessness," this meditation strives
for a continual awareness of the divine presence. Some Sufi breathing meditations use the name of god, Allah, or some of the ninety-nine names and
attributes of Allah as words for vocalized breath meditation. Another
requires the continual repetition of the words *La ilaha Illallah,* ("there is no
god but Allah") thousands of times daily; this repetition can be murmured
but is more often recited in the mind while simultaneously concentrating
on the breath.

HOW TO BEGIN

While the Sufi breath tradition is as complex as any other spiritual tradition, it is possible to share part of it through use of the Five Purification

Breaths. These breaths are traditionally performed daily, usually at dawn — while standing outdoors, if possible, or facing a window if not. If you are immobilized, it is possible to perform these breaths from a seated or prone position. Try to keep your spine straight, whatever posture you use.

While called the Five Breaths, there are in fact twenty: four sets of five breaths each. Each set has a name, an associated color, and a prescribed way of breathing. The entire sequence is centered upon the idea of purifying the soul by renouncing anything that gets in the way of daily, continual connection with the divine.

For each set of breaths, breathe slowly and deeply. Attempt to make each breath approximately the same length as the others. While breathing, visualize its designated color, element, and form of purification. Each series is five breaths, each breath including both inhalation and exhalation.

The first series is the earth breath. Breathe in through your nose, then out again through your nose, envisioning the color yellow. In this breath, you imagine taking in energy from the earth that travels up your spine and into your crown, and then flows up and out to be reconnected with the earth, which replenishes the energy. This is the breath that asks the earth to filter all our impurities.

The second series is the water breath. Breathe in through your nose, then exhale through your mouth. As you breathe, stand on your toes, letting your hands hang down by your sides as though they are wet and dripping. Visualize the color green washing through you, washing out all impurities from your soul. Feel yourself become completely liquid.

The third series is the fire breath. Breathe in through your mouth and out through your nose. Imagine fiery red energy coming into your heart and envigorating you. Imagine fire flooding through you, consuming any impurities that keep you from union with the divine.

The final series is the air breath. Breathe in through your mouth, and exhale again through your mouth. Imagine light blue energy blowing through you, driving out any remaining impurities. Imagine yourself expanding through the universe as a wind pours through all the spaces between the atoms of your body. As you do so, expand into space, and let all your being be replenished by the great purity of space.

Upon completion, recite the following Islamic prayer:

Beloved Lord,
almighty God,
through the rays of the sun,
through waves of the air,
through the all-pervading Life in space,
purify and revivify me,
and, I pray,
heal my body, heart, and soul,
amen.

REVIEW TIPS

- Determine if you feel that you can ethically engage in Islamic practices. If you feel at all hesitant about your ability to use these practices respectfully, seek another form of meditation.
- Use the breath work regularly, if possible. Setting a specific time and place for this practice makes its impact greater.
- As you practice, focus on the purification that is its intent. You may wish to tape-record the instruction above until you become familiar with the connection of color, image and mouth/nose alternation.

RESOURCES

Ali, Ahmed, contemporary trans. *Al-Qur'an.* Princeton, N.J.: Princeton University Press, 1984.

Bair, Puran. *Living from the Heart: Heart Rhythm Meditation.* Pittsburgh, Pa.: Three Rivers Press, 1998.

Bayat, Mojdeh, and Mohammed Ali Jamnia. *Tales from the Land of the Sufis.* Boston, Mass.: Shambhala, 1994.

Chishti, Hakim Moinuddin. *The Book of Sufi Healing.* Rochester, Vt.: Inner Traditions, 1991.

Chittick, William C. *The Sufi Path of Knowledge.* Old Westbury, N.Y.: State University of New York Press, 1998.

Cleary, Thomas, trans. *The Essential Koran: The Heart of Islam.* Memphis, Tenn.: Castle

Books, 1993.

Cornell, Rkia Elaroui. *Early Sufi Women.* Durham, N.C.: Duke University, 1998.

Esposito, John. *Islam: The Straight Path.* New York: Oxford University Press, 1998.

Fadiman, James, and Robert Frazer, eds. *Essential Sufism.* San Francisco: Harper-SanFrancisco, 1997.

Godlas, Alan. "Sufism, Sufis, and Sufi Orders: Sufism's Many Paths." www.arches.uga.edu/~godlas/Sufism.html

Harvey, Andrew. *Love's Fire: Recreations of Rumi.* Los Angeles: Meeramma Publications, 1988.

Helminski, Camille Adams. "Women and Sufism." *Gnosis* (winter 1994).

Helminski, Kabir Edmund. *Living Presence: A Sufi Way to Mindfulness and the Essential Self.* New York: J. P. Tarcher, 1992.

Nicholson, R. A. *Rumi, Poet and Mystic.* New York: George Allen and Unwin, 1952.

Schimmel, Annemarie. *I Am Wind, You Are Fire: The Life and Work of Rumi.* Boston, Mass.: Shambhala, 1992.

Shah, Idries. *The Way of the Sufi.* New York: Arkana, 1991.

Smith, Margaret. *Rabi'a the Mystic and Her Fellow Saints in Islam.* New York: Rainbow Press, 1977.

Star, Jonathan, and Shahram Shiva. *A Garden Beyond Paradise: The Mystical Poetry of Rumi.* New York: Bantam Books, 1992.

Tweedie, Irina. *Daughter of Fire: A Diary of a Spiritual Training with a Sufi Master.* Inverness, Calif.: Golden Sufi Center, 1995.

Upton, Charles. *Doorkeeper of the Heart: Versions of Rabi'a's Poetry.* Brattleboro, Vt.: Threshold Books, 1988.

Wilcox, Lynne. *Sayings of the Sufi Sages.* Riverside, Calif.: M. T. O. Shahmaghsoudi, 1997.

Sufi Order International Secretariat, P.O. Box 30065, Seattle, WA 98103

Chapter 19 • Sufi Dancing

How long will you move backward? Come forward; do not stray in unbelief; come dancing to Divine Knowledge.

— Rumi

Dancing — twirling, really — is the *dhikr*, or meditative form, of the Mevlevi, an order of Sufi Muslims from Turkey, founded by the mystic Jalaluddin Rumi. Better known today simply as Rumi, he was one of the greatest poets Islam has produced, author of thousands of poems and the spiritual treatise called the *Mathnawi*. He was also a great religious leader whose influence is still felt throughout Islam. His meditative style of dance inspired wandering ascetics sometimes called "whirling dervishes," for they twirled and twirled until they attained a sense of unity with the divine.

Rumi was born in 1207 C.E. in what is today Afghanistan. Mongol invasion threatened the area, and Rumi's parents moved to Turkey, where the poet was raised. His father was a renowned religious teacher who died when Rumi was in his early twenties. For more than a decade thereafter, Rumi traveled, studying with various spiritual masters. He had already become what one teacher called "a lion of knowledge" when he met the wandering sage Shamsuddin of Tabriz, who so inspired him that all his previous knowledge seemed slight in comparison. Afire with divine love, Rumi began composing the poetry that has been, for untold numbers, their first introduction to Sufism. Although Shams disappeared from Rumi's life soon afterward, the poet-mystic's course was set. He continued to compose poetry with great fire and passion until his death in 1273.

The use of dance as a technique for consciousness alteration is as old as human history; it appears and reappears as a religious ritual in varying settings and cultures. Such outbreaks of dance as worship are not necessarily connected to each other. The American Shaker movement, for instance, had many similarities to Rumi's Mevlevi. In that religious society, daily life was fiercely ascetic; the spare style of Shaker furniture is still known today. But joined with this intense self-denial was an ecstatic style of movement in which men and women — separately, for sexuality was forbidden, which ultimately led to the religion's disappearance — twitched and twirled, shaking from direct contact with divinity. Yet this ecstatic-dance religion was in no way connected with Islam.

Traditional Sufi dancing continues in Turkey, where the distinctive traditional garments — puffy pantaloons, short white jackets, stiff hats — of the Mevlevi are also still worn. To the sound of the reed pipe and the kettledrum, the dancers whirl with their right palms turned upward and their right hands raised, while their left hands are turned down toward the earth. Keeping the left foot solidly on the ground, the dancer uses the right foot to propel the body around. Women as well as men dance in the Mevlevi, although usually separately. The date of Rumi's death, December 17, is the order's major festival, which is celebrated with dancing.

CONTEMPORARY USES

In the 1960s, a new variety of Sufi-inspired dancing was developed in the United States. Founder Samuel L. Lewis joined the ideas of the American dancer and spiritual leader Ruth St. Denis with the Sufi teachings of Hazrat Inayat Khan and developed some fifty dances, calling upon many different spiritual traditions to do so. Now practiced worldwide, the Dances of Universal Peace is a nondenominational meditative practice that combines simple chants with simple movements.

Dances of Universal Peace brings together mystical traditions from around the world, to be practiced in a spirit of inclusiveness and openness of spirit. In addition to regular dance meetings, often at churches and other religious centers, Dances of Universal Peace adherents host conferences and encampments that bring together their danced meditation with other spiritual traditions.

Typically, one or several leaders teaches a song and the movements that go with it; there are some five hundred songs and dances in the repertoire. One does not need to be an excellent dancer to be able to join in the dances. Most rely on walking rather than bounding, and most are performed slowly. The songs, too, are easy to learn; usually only a few lines in length, they are sung repeatedly in a chantlike manner. In keeping with the nondenominational focus of the dances — which aims to show the universal truth beneath differences of religion — the chants will include prayers from Buddhism, Christianity, Judaism, Native American religions, women's spirituality, and Islam. The combination of repetitive motions with repetitive singing evokes a calm, somewhat trancelike state in most practitioners.

How to Begin

For most non-Islamic individuals interested in Sufi-style dancing, participation in a session of Dances of Universal Peace is often the best introduction to this tradition. The international office of Dances of Universal Peace will provide callers with information on a local contact, who will in turn provide information on when and where dances are held. In addition, there are newsletters that list conferences and workshops that offer Dances of Universal Peace as part of their program.

Generally, Dances of Universal Peace requires a group of four or more; many of the dances are danced in pairs, which makes it difficult for individuals to practice alone. In addition, most participants report that they find the occasion more spiritually moving, and their own meditation more profound and focused, when there are others dancing with them. Instruction is offered before each dance, so even beginners can join without hesitation. It is important to note that Dances of Universal Peace is not a performance occasion; expect to participate, not watch, if you attend.

Those who wish to experience Sufi dancing in its original form should consider how best to respect the religion from which it comes. Unlike yoga, for instance, which is taught by non-Hindus and does not require adherence to Hindu beliefs, Sufi practice is tied with a specific vision of the divine, and the role of humanity in relationship to the divine. Those who wish to believe in a polytheistic divinity, or who reject asceticism as a spiritual discipline, would probably be viewed by true Sufi believers as interlopers in their religious ways. For those who readily accept the Islam — the surrender — to a monotheistic divine being, which is at the heart of their beliefs, Sufi prayer through movement can be an extremely moving and important spiritual practice.

During a dance evening at a Sufi center, the dancers will chant and sing, often using the name of Allah as the basis of the chant. The dances are usually relatively simple and repetitive, the better to evoke the meditative mood. Joining hands in a circle, then moving step-by-step inward, lifting the hands with each step, is a typical simple dance. Some dances require gazing into the eyes of other dancers, usually speaking words that recall the love that is at the heart of Sufism.

REVIEW TIPS

- If you are interested in studying Islam from an intellectual perspective, check local universities for courses; those interested in a more religious view may find instruction through local Muslim congregations or mosques.
- If you are unwilling to study Islam and to accept its ways, real Sufi dancing is not a likely meditative practice for you. You may, however, still engage in a similar practice through the Dances of Universal Peace.
- Contact the international office of Dances of Universal Peace for information on local events.
- When you attend, dress comfortably and casually; be ready for several hours of movement. If you have limited mobility, provide that information to the leader, who can help you find ways to participate in the event.

RESOURCES

Barks, Coleman. *The Essential Rumi.* San Francisco: HarperSanFrancisco, 1995.

Barks, Coleman, translator and commentator. *The Illuminated Rumi.* New York: Broadway Books, 1997.

Breton, Denise, and Christopher Largent. *Love, Soul, and Freedom: Dancing with Rumi on the Mystic Path.* Sherman Oaks, Calif.: Hazelden, 1998.

Douglas-Klotz, Neil. *Desert Wisdom: Sacred Middle Eastern Writings from the Goddess through the Sufis.* San Francisco: HarperSanFrancisco, 1995.

Ellis, Havelock. *Dance of Life.* New York: Grossett, 1923.

Harvey, Andrew. *Light upon Light: Meditations from Rumi.* Berkeley, Calif.: North Atlantic Books, 1996.

St. Denis, Ruth. *Wisdom Comes Dancing: Selected Writings of Ruth St. Denis on Dance, Spirituality, and the Body.* Edited by Kamae Miller. Seattle, Wash.: PeaceWorks, 1997.

International Network for the Dances of Universal Peace, 444 NE Ravenna Blvd, Suite 306, Seattle, WA 98115-6467; (206) 522-4353

Threshold Society and Mevlevi Order, 139 Main Street, Brattleboro, VT 05301; (802) 254-8300

part 6
western traditions

Introduction • Western Traditions

Be still and know that I am God.

— Psalms 46:10

Although Asian traditions such as yoga and Zen most often come to mind when the word *meditation* is used, there are also a number of traditions that derive from European philosophical and spiritual roots. Some two thousand years ago spiritual movements from the eastern Mediterranean, such as Christianity and Judaism, encountered the ideas of the Greek philosopher Plato and the indigenous spiritual traditions of the Celts and other tribal Europeans. From this joining came meditative techniques that compose what is called the Western Wisdom Tradition.

Basic to this tradition is the idea of a divine force that created and sustains the universe. Sometimes this force is seen as having no gender or as being equally feminine and masculine; more frequently, the divine force is described in masculine terms, as the God of monotheistic Christianity and Judaism. Even within those religions, however, there are semidivine feminine figures who have numinous spiritual power, such as the Christian Mary and the Jewish Shekinah; although not called goddesses, these figures nonetheless may be the focus of prayer and meditation in a way that elevates them above the merely human.

Sometimes in the Wisdom Tradition, this divine force is seen as immanent, meaning within human beings, as in the "inner light" or the "still small voice." Sometimes it is described as transcendent, meaning outside humanity. Often divinity is seen as both immanent and transcendent, because that which permeates the universe would by definition have to be part of humanity as well.

Western meditative traditions usually focus on the connection between the meditator and this divine force or being. Various kinds of prayer and contemplation are common to Western religions. Often such activities are predominantly mental or intellectual, rather than being expressed with the whole body. This orientation derives, in great part, from Gnostic philosophy, which holds the spirit and body to be separate, with the former being closer to the divine than the latter. In addition, the influence of Plato is felt in the assumption that what our senses perceive is only a limited part of universal reality.

An important part of many Western meditations is the connection to action in the everyday world. So, an ethical framework — good deeds, in addition to good thoughts — is vital to Western spirituality. In some cases, as with Quakerism, this connection is explicit, for movement toward social action is expected to arise from the meditative experience; in other cases, such as the Methodist technique of spiritual journal keeping (see Part 7: Creative Meditations), the meditation is implicitly assumed to lead toward a better, more ethically sound life.

In specifically Christian versions of this tradition, a vital concept is salvation: that God's son, Jesus Christ, descended to earth and died for our sins. Meditation in this framework is understood to mean acceptance of an originally sinful state that was redeemed by this miraculous sacrifice. Some Christian traditions see salvation as a moment, an event that has occurred once and holds for all time; others see salvation, like creation, as an ongoing process in which we all participate.

WESTERN MYSTICISM

When, in the fourth century C.E., Augustine of Hippo forged a connection between dualistic Manicheanism and the radically democratic new vision of Christianity, Western religion began to suppress some aspects of human life and to exalt others. Sexuality, for instance, was pushed away as unreligious, or even evil; bodily appetites in general were defined as antithetical to spirituality. An alternative Christian vision had been articulated by the Celtic monk Pelagius, who argued that everything that God had created was good. In the Pelagian vision, it was the aim of spiritual life to learn to love all aspects of God's creation, including the body and its desires. This "happy heresy" was denounced by Augustine and his followers, whose influence won the day. Within official church doctrine thereafter, the mind was elevated over the body.

Yet a spiritual tradition survived that bonded body and soul in a grand spiritual adventure: mysticism. Despite official teachings, scores of mystics experienced a unifying vision of the divine. St. John of the Cross, St. Teresa of Ávila, Julian of Norwich, Hildegard of Bingen, Margery Kempe: they were transformed by a direct experience of the divine that shattered all limiting descriptions. As scholars of mysticism such as Geoffery Parringer and Evelyn Underhill have defined it, the mystical experience meant that the temporal body becomes the mechanism for experience that is beyond the temporal. Illumination, to use Hildegard's term for the experience, comes through despite the senses. Some of the most magnificent music, poetry, and art of Christianity derive from the spiritual visions of such mystics. So, the mystical tradition expands and corrects the dualistic vision of Augustine and his followers, and the visions of mystics have as much in common with Asian as with Western religious visions.

RECENT EXPANSIONS OF THE WESTERN TRADITION

While most Western Wisdom Tradition meditation techniques are based in Platonic Christianity, some new developments have moved beyond that source. Neopaganism, the fastest-growing religion in the United States today, draws its inspiration from pre-Christian European spirituality. Nondualistic and body-affirming, neopaganism runs counter to the general trend of Western religious tradition. Practitioners often explore even beyond European tribal religions to gain ideas for religious practices. While most derive from ancient shamanic techniques, others are more specifically rooted in Asian or other spiritual traditions. Because neopaganism is essentially a religion of active practice, rather than of scripture, such wide-ranging eclecticism does not contradict any basic texts or tenets. It has, however, been criticized as overly eclectic for its willingness to draw from many sources.

As strong as the religious impulse in the West has been, there has been for several hundred years a counterforce, in the form of scientific materialism. Although science need not oppose religion — indeed, many contemporary theorists find, in quantum physics and chaos theory, the potential to rejoin science and spirituality — the heritage of the European Enlightenment has been the separation of these two important cultural forces. Agnosticism and atheism accept a "clockwork" world, in which physical forces alone create the universe we see. This separation of science and religion has led to tremendous scientific creativity since the Enlightenment. It is no surprise, then, that technologically-mediated forms of meditation have arisen out of the Western tradition.

Chapter 20 • Contemplative Prayer

Contemplation is a simple intuition of God, produced immediately
in the soul by God and giving the soul a direct but obscure
and mysterious experiential appreciation of God.

— Thomas Merton

In Christian scripture, Jesus Christ often retired to secluded places to pray. One significant prayer experience was his retreat of forty days in the desert, before St. John the Baptist proclaimed his identity. Another, at a similarly significant moment, was his prayer in the Garden of Gethsemene, on the evening before his final passion and death.

With these stirring images in mind, Christians have long relied upon prayer as the most significant form of worship. But Christianity is not the only religion to approach the sacred in this way; indeed, all religions have some form of prayer. Some describe meditation as distinct from prayer, while others do not. When distinguished, meditation is defined as inwardly directed, and prayer as directed to something outside the self.

This is complicated, of course, when divinity is seen as immanent; does a prayer directed to an inner divinity constitute meditation? These theological questions are not necessary to answer, however, in order to use contemplative prayer as a form of meditation. It is important, however, to acknowledge that the prayer is directed to a divine being, whether defined as immanent or transcendent. Christian prayer, especially, requires the submission of the will to that of the divine force. It is not intended to be used simply as a technique of relaxation or healing, but rather as a practice that opens the heart and mind to the will and grace of God.

181

Prayer is often defined as divided into four types. Adoration acknowledges the vastness and incomprehensible greatness of divinity. Thanksgiving offers gratitude for the created world and for specific benefits we receive from it. Contrition is an apology for transgressions and an effort to bring the self into unity with divine will. Finally, petition asks for the needs of the individual to be met; at its most profound, such prayer also asks for divine wisdom in reconciling desires to reality.

The great mystic St. Teresa of Ávila defined the types of prayer somewhat differently. The first level of prayer, she believed, was the prayer of quiet, in which the soul is enlarged and the mind is stilled. Then comes the prayer of incipient union, also called rapture, in which the senses cease functioning and one feels transported to another realm of being. Next comes the prayer of spiritual marriage, in which the individual remains permanently in contact with the divine, often experienced as a flooding light; such an individual typically engages in activities of service and love. In Teresa's view, all these prayerful states are gifts; they cannot be earned, even by the most diligent contemplation and meditation.

Prayer can be either solitary or collective, vocal or silent. It can happen in places of worship or in other settings; it can be phrased in song or in speech. Contemplative prayer, by contrast, is a solitary experience, usually silent. It is a unique inner experience that cannot be shared with another, although several can pray silently in the same room.

A great insight that Christian meditation and mysticism stresses, in a way that other traditions do not, is the likelihood of periods of spiritual difficulty, which are encountered despite the most arduous prayer and meditation. The Spanish mystic St. John of the Cross named this the "dark night of the soul," and described in his autobiography his own struggles with a sense of dryness and futility that could not be banished despite continual effort. Thomas Merton, the American Trappist monk, also described periods where meditation and prayer seemed to fail him, when helplessness and desire contend and paralyze the soul. Such dark nights, in Christian belief, are eased only through grace, a divine gift that cannot be courted nor earned. However, paradoxically, continuing to pray and meditate during these dark times is necessary for the soul to be prepared for the grace that will, undoubtedly, finally come.

CONTEMPORARY USES

With the increasing attention paid to various traditions of meditation today, it is no surprise to find that Christian religious practitioners and theologians have been active in finding ways to meet the needs of their co-religionists in this regard. For more than twenty years, members of the Catholic order called the Trappists have been influential in finding a vocabulary and practices for Christian meditation. Thomas Keating, abbot of a Trappist monastery in New York, was particularly influential in this area, as was the renowned monk, Thomas Merton.

Several contemporary forms of contemplative prayer or Christian meditation are commonly practiced. One, called the Hesychast prayer or Jesus Prayer, dates to the days of the Desert Fathers, those anchorites who lived in extreme poverty and deprivation at the dawn of Christianity. This form of meditation, which involves the repetition of a short and very ancient prayer, is especially important in Orthodox (non-Roman) Catholicism; monks in Greece still pray this way for hour upon hour.

Another, more modern form, consciously joins a meditative practice with a Christian style of prayer. Although arguably part of Christian practice through the centuries, it has been given greater prominence in the last half-century, as Western (predominantly American) religious people have encountered and embraced the possibilities of Asian, especially Buddhist, routes to inner peace.

Within this movement, there are two main streams. One, called centering prayer, is associated with the Trappist monks Thomas Keating and Basil Pennington, as well as with the work of Thomas Merton. The second, articulated by the Irish Benedictine monk John Main, who served in Malaysia and learned Buddhist meditation there, is often simply called Christian Meditation; the World Community of Christian Meditation supports and promotes this form. These forms of meditation are virtually identical, relying upon the repetition of sacred words or phrases.

A special instance of contemplative prayer is the retreat — a period of time spent away from the normal bustle of daily life, usually in a convent or monastery, and often under the spiritual guidance of a lay or ordained religious person. Retreats can last from a few days to a few months. They are often undertaken at times of special need: after a death, during a major life change, when a spiritual test presents itself. During retreats, silence is usually observed. There will probably be a series of formal prayer times; at other times, the retreatant will read, pray, meditate, and meet with the spiritual director. Although one need not be a member of a specific faith to go on a retreat in their religious centers, one must be open to the beliefs and language of that faith for the experience to be successful.

How to Begin

The posture of meditation is not so much emphasized within the Christian tradition as in many others. While in a *zendo* (a Zen Buddhist monastery), meditators are given precise directions as to how to sit and how to hold their hands, however, the posture of Christian meditators varies greatly. Sitting quietly and in stillness is acceptable, as is the kneeling posture traditional to Catholic prayer. The hands may, but need not be, folded — that is, with palms resting together and pointed upward.

The Jesus Prayer — called Hesychast prayer or simply "quiet prayer" — is the repetition of the words, "Lord Jesus Christ, Son of God, have mercy on me." This prayer is repeated, over and over, the first two phrases spoken inwardly with the intake of breath, the last phrase with the exhalation. As in any mantra meditation (see chapter 9, Mantra), other thoughts will arise, sometimes related to the prayer, sometimes on other subjects. When that happens, bring your mind back, gently, to the prayer. Emotions, too, may well up; do not resist them, but do not cease repeating the prayer to focus on them. One or two daily sessions of ten to twenty minutes each is recommended for this meditation.

Centering prayer is another typical mantra-style meditation. It is the most popular of the various forms of Christian meditation currently practiced. Any word from Christian tradition can be used, including names or titles of God (*Abba, Father, Jesus,* as well as *Mary, Love, Shalom* are used); the Aramaic word *maranatha,* meaning "come, Lord," is frequently employed. As with the Jesus Prayer, the word is repeated many times, for as long as thirty minutes. When thoughts or emotions arise, they are not permitted to distract the mind, which is guided back to the chosen word.

A related practice, called the Lectio Divina ("divine word" or "divine reading") meditation, requires the selection of a passage from scripture that is then repeated silently. Unlike inspirational reading (see chapter 22), this meditation uses short passages that can be held in the mind and repeated easily. With each repetition, the practitioner allows ideas, thoughts, and images related to the passage to arise spontaneously in the mind. The intention is to move beyond wordy inner chatter into a direct, silent sense of divine presence.

In any of these forms of meditation, the visualization of moments or scenes from the life of Jesus, from Biblical tales, or from lives of the saints is accepted as a means of creating a link to the godhead. It is not ideal or even necessary — as it is, for instance, in Zen Buddhism — to utterly clear the mind, to encounter the silent void. It is rather more important to focus and concentrate the mind upon spiritual matters than to empty it entirely.

REVIEW TIPS

- Select a style of contemplative prayer that suits your beliefs and the demands of your life. Practice it regularly — daily is best — for at least several months before you alter it. Changing practices more frequently just makes it harder to attain a focused state.
- While it is not necessary to pray with others, nor to pray in a special place, some find that silent prayer in the silence of a church or in the company of other prayerful seekers deepens their concentration.
- If you experience any emotional or spiritual difficulties during silent prayer, speak to an elder or minister of your church about it. Unconscious material can surface in any form of meditation. This does not mean that you are meditating incorrectly, nor that you are being hounded by evil forces. However, such experiences can be disturbing and may require expert counsel to help you interpret their significance.

RESOURCES

Evans, Mary J. *Woman in the Bible: An Overview of All the Biblical Passages on Women's Roles.* Downers Grove, Ill.: Intervarsity, 1983.

Hammer, Reuven. *Entering Jewish Prayer: A Guide to Personal Devotion and the Worship Service.* New York: Schocken Books, 1994.

Harpur, Tom. *Prayer: The Hidden Fire.* Grawn, Mich.: Northstone, 1998.

Harvey, Andrew. *Son of Man: The Mystical Path to Christ.* New York: J. P. Tarcher, 1998.

Kelsey, Morton. *The Other Side of Silence: Meditation for the 21st Century.* Mahwah, N.J.: Paulist Press, 1995.

Merton, Thomas. *Contemplative Prayer.* New York: Doubleday, 1969.

Simsic, Wayne. *Praying with Thomas Merton.* Winona, Minn.: St. Mary's Press, 1994.

Contemplative Outreach Spiritual Network, P.O. Box 737, Butler, NJ 07405; (201) 838-3384

WCCM International Meditation Centre (John Main meditation), 23 Kensington Square, London W8 5HN UK

World Community for Christian Meditation: www.wccm.org

Chapter 21 • Candle Meditation

Light is the thread that weaves together space and time.
— Lawrence Krauss

Ancient techniques of trance induction included many that relied upon the human sense of sight. Forms of "scrying," or fortune-telling, often included the focusing of vision. Crystallomancy or crystal ball gazing is perhaps the most familiar, though just as common were gazing into mirrors (catoptomancy), water (hydromancy), wine or blood (cycliocomancy), or the polished nails of a virgin (onychomancy). All were similar in using a reflective surface to both focus and cause a slight movement of the eyes, which together induced a mild trance; in that state the adept could receive intuitive perceptions that might be unavailable in a state of normal consciousness.

Candle meditation is similar, although not so connected to precognition as are these gazing techniques. Looking into flames has been known since the dawn of time to produce a soothing, introspective mood. Until the Industrial Revolution, people tended living fires as a regular part of their daily routine; all cooking and heating came from the fire. In the long dark nights of winter, countless of our forebears found peace and relaxation watching the orange, yellow, red, and blue of the flickering flames.

Fire has been so much a part of religious ritual that its significance is sometimes overlooked. The candles decking the altar at a Catholic Solemn High Mass, those lit on the Jewish holiday of Chanukah, candles burned to ancestors on Korean home altars — all these and many others remind us that the technique of candle gazing has roots both deep and wide. While most religions use candles as part of religious services, specific instruction in using their light to induce a prayerful or contemplative mood is often lacking.

One nonreligious group has employed candle meditation consistently; the Rosicrucians (Fellowship of the Rosy Cross), a one hundred-year-old association claiming descent from an even older secret fellowship that may date to the seventeenth century. Like similar groups based in Western Wisdom traditions, the Rosicrucians employ commonly known practices that are without question effective in altering consciousness. Many of these are accessible without recourse to secret societies, but some individuals find the association with an apparently ancient order to be a spur to their practice.

Within this century, candle meditation received some bad press when Sirhan Sirhan, who assassinated presidential candidate Senator Robert F. Kennedy in 1968, claimed that he had been led to form his plot after using the technique. As with any technique, there may be a lowering of conscious control experienced during the meditation. If one is of relatively sound mind, this alteration of consciousness is not likely to be disturbing. But repressed anger, pain, or other negative emotions can be released and encountered in such a meditation. Without the guidance of an instructor or the vocabulary of a traditional spiritual way, the meditator can feel overwhelmed and confused by these emotions and ideas. They may even be perceived as arising from outside, rather than inside, the meditator's mind. Candle meditation, like any other meditation, is merely a technique, neither good nor bad of itself. Staring into candles did not cause the assassination of Robert Kennedy; Sirhan Sirhan's disturbed mind did.

CONTEMPORARY USES

Although the Rosicrucian Fellowship is still active in promoting the use of candle meditation, today it is more frequently linked with the neopagan or wiccan groups that make up the fastest-growing religion in the United States today. Sometimes called "candle magic" or "candle magick" (the latter spelling emphasizing the wiccan connection), the technique is used in many ritual circles to focus the mind and release energy, often for healing.

There is no single dogma that unites neopagan or wiccan groups today. Some derive from a 1950s British occult tradition called Gardnerianism after its founder, Gerald Gardner; he, in turn, claimed that he had transcribed previously oral traditions of the Old Religion, which had its roots in England's pre-Christian past. Others are members of some of the many pagan organizations in America, whose rituals may be predominantly Celtic or Scandinavian or eclectic. Other practitioners were brought to their religious practices through feminism; often calling themselves Dianic, after the Roman goddess of the moon, these groups are usually for women only. Yet others were brought to their worship through ecological and eco-feminist groups such as Starhawk's Reclaiming Collective; these groups join political action with their meditative and ritual work. Finally, some neopagans are drawn together by an interest in alternative lifestyles, especially ecstatic or Dionysian ones.

Called variously paganism, heathenism, neopaganism, The Craft, witchcraft, and wicca, this religion usually presents itself as growing on ancient roots: the pre-Christian past. So techniques from shamanism as well as from the Western Wisdom Tradition are often incorporated into the rituals, which tend to be based in the yearly seasonal cycle. Most, if not all, of these worshipers define themselves as following an earth-based religion, where concern for ecological well-being is more important than individual salvation.

Candle meditation forms a major part of many neopagan rituals. While the occasions may vary from a Yule candle-lighting ritual reminiscent of Christian Advent candles to a petitionary effort to bring love as represented by shaped male/female candles, the basic form of the meditation is constant: forming an intention, lighting the candle, and looking into it to effect a light trance or meditation.

How to Begin

There are two kinds of neopagan practitioners: those who practice in groups, and those who do not. The latter, called solitaries, use candle meditation as a major form of their "working," but group candle rituals are also common. In groups, however, other meditative techniques — such as toning or chanting, which frequently begin group rituals, and many shamanic techniques such as drumming and dancing — are likely to be employed as well.

If you are interested in becoming part of a wiccan or neopagan group, you can find information about groups in your area in several ways. Local New Age bookstores often serve as centers of information for local groups, called covens, who are accepting new members. Festivals such as Starwood in New York or the Priestess gathering in Wisconsin give you the opportunity to experience group ritual, and sometimes to meet others in your geographical vicinity for further work together. Finally, a number of pagan publications list groups and individuals looking for company on this path.

It is important to determine, before joining a group, what your specific needs and desires are. In general, if a group requires a heavy admission fee, consider looking elsewhere, for there is a general practice in this religion of not charging for membership (although instruction may be offered at a cost); similarly, if there are "initiation" rituals, including sexual practices or changes in lifestyle with which you feel uncomfortable, withdraw from the group rather than proceeding.

If no appropriate groups exist in your area, consider forming your own. You don't need twenty people; three or four is plenty to start with, provided a serious commitment is made to work together. There are many good books now available that guide you through the process of forming your own neopagan group. Given the rather free-form nature of such worship, you need not be worried that you'll "do it wrong." As neopaganism is an emerging religion, you can be certain that, if a meditative practice feels safe and effective to you, that you're "doing it right."

If you are interested in working alone, or if you have no access to appropriate groups, you can begin by employing candle meditation as a regular practice. Although you may find elaborate rituals including specific colors and even clothing, in general candle meditation is very simple. Find a quiet space and time. Sit or stand before a prepared altar on which you have arranged significant artifacts; these may include images of the divine in the form of statuettes or even flowers, as well as emblems of your own spiritual efforts, such as stones from a childhood home or shells from a beach where you experienced spiritual awakening. Remain quiet for a few moments while you gather your thoughts and make your mind peaceful. Then, light the candle. Look into its flame for five or ten minutes. Then blow the candle out.

Some ritualists suggest bowing to or otherwise invoking the four quadrants of the universe (north, south, east, and west) at the beginning, and then repeating that acknowledgment at the end. Others suggest specifically calling upon the divine as both god and goddess. And others promote the idea that you should determine a specific intention to hold in your mind throughout the meditation. If you plan to use that final idea, be aware that wiccan thought emphasizes the "threefold law" or the "law of return," which is that anything that you send out from your mind and soul will return amplified to you. Ethical wiccan practitioners also emphasize that any intention should always be about the self, not about controlling another's behavior or feelings.

REVIEW TIPS

- Determine if you wish to practice on your own or in a group.
- If you wish to find a compatible group, check with a local New Age center for ideas; you may also find information in publications, either national or local.
- If anything within a group's process disturbs you, withdraw from the group while you consider its practices. If you continue to find it disturbing, do not return.
- If you are practicing alone, set up an altar representing your spiritual visions and goals. Those practicing in groups usually do this as well.
- Use the altar as the focal point for your meditation. Keep it clean and orderly; replace objects that no longer express your inner self; use it regularly so that your body-mind will associate it with the meditative state.
- You don't need special candles for candle meditation, despite what some candle merchants may tell you. Anything that flickers and glows will do.

RESOURCES

Buckland, Raymond. *Practical Candleburning Rituals.* Saint Paul, Minn.: Llewellyn, 1985.
Curott, Phyllis. *Book of Shadows.* Cambridge, Mass.: Holt, 1998.

K, Amber. *Covencraft.* Saint Paul, Minn.: Llewellyn, 1998.

Malbrough, Ray T. *Charms, Spells, and Formulas.* Saint Paul, Minn.: Llewellyn, 1986.

Medici, Marina. *Good Magic.* New York: Prentice Hall Press, 1988.

Morrison, Dorothy. *Everyday Magic.* Saint Paul, Minn.: Llewellyn, 1997.

Morrison, Sarah Lyddon. *The Modern Witch's Spellbook.* Secaucus, N.J.: Citadel Press, 1971.

Priestess Gathering, Re-formed Congregation of the Goddess, P.O. Box 644, Madison, WI 53716

Starwood Festival (sponsored by the Association for Consciousness Exploration), 1643 Lee #9, Cleveland Heights, OH 44118; (800) 446-4962

Chapter 22 • Inspirational Reading

We shall not cease from exploration
And the end of all our exploring
Will be to arrive where we started
And know the place for the first time.

— T. S. Eliot

Not all religions have holy books. Some religious traditions, to the contrary, refuse to write down their myths and secrets. These "people of the word," who include the ancient European Celts and most of Native America, rely upon oral tradition to convey the deepest spiritual truths of their culture. There may be writings in such cultures, but they are not believed to be the ultimate truth, merely a personal reflection on it.

Then there are the "people of the book." Some of today's most widespread and powerful religions hold up a single book — Jewish Talmud, Christian Bible, Islamic Koran — as articulating the essential truth. Such scriptural religions often see their sacred book as divinely inspired, as the word of the supreme god. Even scriptural religions, however, acknowledge a variety of other important holy writings, usually the works of saints or masters.

Each of these religious approaches has its limitations. For the people of the word, a single generation raised in ignorance of the tradition suffices to utterly destroy it. Conveyed orally at significant moments and in specific rituals, the religious underpinnings of a culture are lost without continual and correct transmission. For the people of the book, the opposite problem holds. Overly tenacious clinging to a specific religious formulation has led to crusades and jihads, to sectarian wars and individual persecutions. Meditation through inspirational reading, then, must be considered in light of the sometimes tragic history of text-based religion.

Another part of the historical background of this form of meditation is the rise of general literacy. From the invention of writing in Mesopotamian temples almost thirty-five hundred years ago, literacy was a limited skill, often available only to those in the upper or religious classes. Through much of human history, literacy has been the exception rather than the rule, and books were rare and precious. Johannes Gutenberg's invention of movable type, and the resultant decline in the price of printed matter, revolutionized reading. But class and income were still factors in determining who learned to read and write. Even as late as the last century, laws forbade some people from learning to read — black slaves on American plantations, Catholics in Ireland — in order to maintain them in their disempowered state. This century, however, the right to literacy is virtually taken for granted in much of the world. The power of the written word, and its potential for self-transformation, is now within many people's range of experience.

CONTEMPORARY USES

The use of literature for meditation has been part of the tradition of scriptural religions for many centuries. In the Christian world, reading Biblical verses daily is the practice of untold thousands of worshipers. In some cases, this is meditation as defined in this book: it focuses and expands the mind, it puts the body in a state of calm alertness, it salves the emotions and sustains the soul. In other cases, however, the use of holy texts becomes part of an unexamined negativity toward others and toward their actions.

One can repeat the steps of a T'ai Chi form without focusing the spirit, hoping to grow more graceful and sexy. One can sit in Quaker worship, fantasizing about winning the lottery. Every form of meditation can be used for the ego's purposes. But no other meditative form has the potential for being turned against others in quite the same way as inspirational reading. Because of the power of words apparently dictated by God himself (and the God in question is invariably male), holy writ can be, and has often been, used as a way to focus on others rather than the self. Meditation with readings, however, can have the opposite effect, of permitting focus on the inner world. As such, it is practiced by many people today, whether they participate in conventional religion or not.

A tremendous growth in inspirational reading has been seen over the last two decades as a result of the increasing number of people participating in Twelve Step programs. Alcoholics Anonymous and its siblings — Adult Children of Alcoholics, Al-Anon (for families of alcoholics), Narcotics Anonymous, Emotions Anonymous, and many others — derive from a Christian tradition and, as such, are people of the book. The scripture, in this case, is the "big book," the AA manual created earlier this century by Bill W. Reading from the "big book" is a part of the spiritual practice of many involved in recovery programs.

In addition to the "big book," daily meditation books are common readings for those in recovery. The so-called "one-day-at-a-time" books derive their name from a tenant of recovery: that it is futile to try to change the future, except through changing one's behavior in the moment. So, the slogan goes, it's important to live one day at a time. To reinforce this concept, daily meditation books offer a few paragraphs of wisdom for contemplation. Hundreds of daily meditation books now exist, each devoted to a single theme. What began in the recovery movement has now spread well beyond it, so that many who use the daily meditation books may be unaware of their origins.

How to Begin

To use inspirational reading as a form of meditation requires one major tool: something to read.

And therein lies the challenge. Not everything is suitable for inspirational reading. While it's theoretically possible to read the morning paper meditatively, that's a greater challenge than even most advanced meditators would take on. Inspirational reading requires a text with the following qualities: it can be read in short sections; each section is rich enough to provide sustenance for meditation; and it reflects the general worldview of the meditator.

This last requirement is important, for silent arguing with a text is not meditation. Yet the text must be sufficiently challenging to stretch your mind and soul. Many daily meditation books fail in this regard, for their single message grows stale over a few months. When considering purchasing one of these books, read through one of the later months of the year before you approach the checkout counter. If the author's inspiration has worn thin, October or November will quickly reveal that.

Many great works of religious and philosophical literature make excellent choices for inspirational readings. Often dense and difficult when read straight through, these texts are better absorbed in small portions. Teresa of Ávila's autobiography, *The Interior Castle*, is representative of this sort of writing. Describing her intense spiritual visions, the book can be quite exhausting to read in an unbroken stretch. The *Pensées* of French philosopher Blaíse Pascal, and the writings of Simone Weil are texts that, having been written in disjunctive fashion, also benefit from being read slowly over many weeks.

Similarly, the works of great mystics, of whatever religion, often make excellent choices for inspirational readings. The poetry of the Sufi master Rumi, the songs of St. John of the Cross, the words of Hildegard of Bingen: these can provide marvelous inner images and experiences. For many Christians the best source for inspirational readings remains the holy book, the Bible; similarly, for Jews the Midrash or commentaries on the Talmud can be effective meditative tools.

Once you have selected a text or two, determine when and where you will use them. Most people who use inspirational reading as part, or the whole, of their meditative program have found it useful to ritualize their reading. Once you have become familiar with this kind of meditation, it is quite possible to use it at different times and places — on the bus, on a plane, while waiting in the dentist's office. But at first, setting up a specific time and place for reading reinforces its meditative aspects. A comfortable and quiet chair with good light and a place nearby to store your reading materials is all that you'll need. You'll also need an uninterrupted span of ten to twenty minutes, so select a time of day when you are not likely to be interrupted.

Expect to read no more than a page each day. Take a few moments to compose and focus your thoughts; it can help to close your eyes at this point. Then locate the reading for the day and read it slowly. Try to read with an open mind and heart, not arguing with or critiquing the words, but seeking their deepest meaning. Then, after reading, reflect briefly on what the passage means to your life. Let images rise like dreams if they will; experience without judging any emotional reaction you have to the text.

Then reread the text to see if your reactions change in any way. Consider the meaning a second time before concluding the meditation.

Many who use this meditation find that, over time, the readings sometimes attain a somewhat oracular quality. A morning reading on humility, for instance, can come back vividly when there's difficulty with a mistake at work. The mind can find examples in daily life of that day's reading. These experiences can be quite vivid and memorable, but the purpose of inspirational readings is not to seek foreknowledge of the future, but to deepen life in the present.

REVIEW TIPS

- Select a text or texts to read. Besides scripture, there are any number of inspirational readings you may chose. Select something that is deep and rich, and that readily breaks down into small, approximately one-page sections.
- Determine when and where you will read. Take ten to twenty minutes for an uninterrupted meditation. Because meditative reading looks a lot like ordinary reading, it is important to let others know that you should not be disturbed. Ignore the phone and the cat, too.
- Read your text once, with an open heart and mind. Reflect upon it; apply it to your life; consider its deepest significance. Then read it again.
- When you have become used to this form of meditation, you may want to carry a small text with you for those times when you have a few moments. A meditation book in the car, for delays as a long train crosses the road or other potentially irritating moments, can be a welcome refuge.

RESOURCES

The Bible.

Birch, Cyril. *Anthology of Chinese Literature.* Westminster, Calif.: Grove Press, 1965.

Bokenkamp, Stephen R. *Early Daoist Scriptures.* Berkeley, Calif.: University of California Press, 1997.

The Cloud of Unknowing.

Douglas-Klotz, Neil. *Prayers of the Cosmos: Meditations on the Aramaic Words of Jesus.* San Francisco: HarperSanFrancisco, 1994.

Hammer, Rueven. *The Classic Midrash.* Mahwah, N.J.: Paulist Press, 1995.

St. John of the Cross. *The Dark Night of the Soul.* New York: Doubleday, 1990.

The Koran.

Monaghan, Patricia. *The Goddess Companion: 366 Prayers of the Goddess.* Saint Paul, Minn.: Llewellyn Publications, 1999.

St. Teresa of Ávila. *The Interior Castle.* New York: Doubleday, 1972.

Chapter 23 • Free-Form Meditation Groups

Peace within makes beauty without.

— English proverb

Throughout history, meditation has frequently been practiced in groups. In many religious traditions, in fact, group meditation is a significant part of spiritual discipline.

Monks and nuns of cloistered Christian orders, for instance, engage in silent group prayer, usually at regularly scheduled intervals. From morning matins to lauds in the evening, the convent or monastery day is organized around group prayer. Sometimes that prayer is oral, or even sung; at other times, it is silent, as when members of the Benedictine order reflect upon a psalm or prayer whose reading begins the meditation.

Other Christian groups also employ silent group prayer. Most notable are the Quakers, whose unprogrammed silent worship looks, on the surface, very much like some of the free-form groups we will discuss below. But other Protestant denominations make a space for private, silent group meditation or prayer, although sometimes at an alternative time than the traditional Sunday service.

Those who practice various forms of Buddhism, too, engage in group meditation. Serious students of Zen gather in *zendos*, where they practice their meditation under the watchful eyes of masters. Some teachers even become punitive, should a student slide from meditation into sleep, for instance. Practitioners of the various types of Indian Buddhism, too, engage in group meditation at retreats and on specific holidays.

Many people find it easier to meditate in a group than alone. To some extent, this ease is a result of a group's social pressures; we are less likely to fall asleep when surrounded by others than when sitting in our own favorite chair. A leader can help focus a group by presenting an initiating reading or thought. And through the process of entrainment, bodies will slowly come into synchronization with each other. A group of people breathing deeply will provide subtle, almost invisible, biological cues to the beginner, with deeper breathing and more intense meditation being the result. So group meditation has distinct advantages and benefits.

CONTEMPORARY USES

While there are many opportunities for silent group prayer and meditation within various Eastern and Western religious traditions, some today wish to engage in meditation without feeling constrained to believe in any specific dogma. So nondenominational groups, that meet for the sole purpose of sharing the benefits of meditation together, have sprung up, with their number increasing especially over the last decade as meditation has become a more mainstream activity.

Sometimes such groups are formed as part of another, ongoing focus, as when a cancer wellness program offers meditation to its participants or a women's center offers space for women who wish to meditate only with other women. Such groups have the advantage of drawing together like-minded individuals. They can have the disadvantage of being overly reliant upon a single committed volunteer, whose priorities or life situation may change.

Other groups are formed by friends who wish to deepen their connection by sharing meditative space. One disadvantage to such an approach is that meditation can become less a priority than verbal sharing; it takes a certain discipline to move past everyday chitchat and into meditation. With such discipline, however, this can be an enriching experience. Similarly, families can use meditation in the way traditionally religious families use ritual and prayer, as a way of nonverbally strengthening the family's bonds.

Free-form meditation groups can meet daily, weekly, or monthly — whatever suits the members. They can meet for a brief or a longer time, again according to the members' needs. They can meet in public places or in homes, in church basements or in gardens. They can include chanting as well as silent meditation; virtually any meditation in this book is possible for a meditation group, in fact.

It would seem as though the free-form meditation group is a fail-safe, surefire way to gain the benefits of meditation without either having to adopt a set of potentially challenging beliefs, having to learn a specific physical or mental discipline, or having to find a qualified teacher. But these apparent advantages can, ultimately, become disadvantages. The wisdom of ages is encoded in traditional religious practices, and in the rigorous disciplines that derive from them. Teachers can assist the meditator in going past blocks, which can range from a tendency to snooze during meditation to mental agitation.

Finally, free-form meditation groups face challenges of interpersonal dynamics that they must work through without the guidance of a tradition or a teacher. Just because a group meets for meditation does not mean they will not face difficulties in this area. A simple framework for understanding such a development is that we all grow up in families, some of them less healthy than others. And we tend, even despite dedicated efforts, to replicate our family of origin in other groups. The family clown will try to gain laughs, the overly responsible one will become burdened and angry, the bully will demand things be his or her way. These reenactments will probably be subtle, but they hold the seeds of dissolution — even angry dissolution — of any group. Yet attending to and working through friction can enrich and empower a meditation group.

How to Begin

To find a meditation group, you can try two routes. You can locate an existing group; or you can form your own. Each has its promises and pitfalls.

To locate an existing group, check the bulletin boards at local cafes and bookstores. Read local publications that feature yoga, vegetarianism, therapeutic techniques, and alternative health care. Or, if you believe that you would benefit from a special focus, inquire at centers dealing with that area of life — women's centers, hospitals and wellness centers, churches.

Once you have located a group, ascertain that it is open to new members; call or otherwise contact the group to discover when and where it meets, how often, and what is expected of its members. Attend one or two meetings before you commit yourself to joining. At these exploratory sessions, pay attention to how you feel. If you have any sense of discomfort with the process or the people, it is likely to be a good indication that the group is not suitable for you. Even a good group can be wrong for some people. Don't try to force yourself into a group where the fit is not easy. You don't deliberately buy shoes the wrong size, so don't buy into the wrong meditation group.

If you find the group resonates with your values and is congruent to your needs, inquire about what the group expects of its attendees. Guests may not be expected to donate money, for instance, for facility upkeep, but regular attendees probably are. Or perhaps regulars always spend several hours drinking tea and discussing their interests. Before you commit yourself to the group, make certain that you are comfortable with the entire group process, not just with the meditation period.

Should you wish to establish your own group, you can either find companions among people you already know, or advertise to find compatible meditation partners. In either case, you should determine what frequency and length of meetings you wish to aim for. Do not become so wedded to your vision that you grow overbearing, but don't start without some articulated idea of what you want. You won't last long in a group that votes to meet for two hours monthly, if you want a half-hour weekly group.

Whether you ask friends or advertise in a bookstore or library for others to join you, screen the people carefully. One disruptive person can destroy a group. Don't fear to be ruthless and critical in your judgments; letting someone know they're not suitable for the group is better than having the group dissolve from internal pressures. Conversely, you'll never gather people together for a group unless you're willing to accept the wonderful diversity of human nature. Organizing a group requires walking the fine line between judgment and judgmentalism.

If you have organized your own group, establish the expectations immediately about what is expected of members. Tardiness, talking after the beginning time, relying on other members for emotional or financial support — these should be understood from the start to be unacceptable. But groups will vary in terms of whether they light candles before meditation, whether they include some period of vocal prayer or chanting, and many other aspects of meditation. Establishing these parameters early in the group's life will mean that the members know what to expect, and can commit themselves with confidence.

REVIEW TIPS

- Decide whether you want to locate an existing group or form your own.
- If you are interested in joining an existing group, plan to spend several months exploring the possibilities before you make a commitment. Locate information from appropriate centers and bookstores; make contact with the group; attend at least two meetings before you commit yourself to anything. Especially, do not agree to make more than a token monetary contribution until you have determined that the group is suitable to you.
- Once you have determined that a group is appropriate, interview several members to learn the group's customs. Only after you have this information should you make a decision about whether to join.
- If you are organizing your own group, set parameters for meeting frequency, time, and place. Determine, too, what kind of meditation the group will engage in. Then present all this information to potential members, so that they may decide whether the group sounds appropriate for them.
- Never strong-arm someone into joining a group. Whether it's a spouse or a neighbor, a hesitant joiner will remain disengaged. Groups work best when all the members have joined without guilt.
- Set a series of exploratory meetings — three is sufficient — for the group to experience each other and the type of meditation, before making a decision as to whether to continue the group. If it's not working smoothly, accept it. It is better to end it soon, rather than risk damaging relationships as people grow more and more unhappy with the group.
- If you are using more than one type of meditation — say chanting and sitting *za-zen* — it often helps to establish an order in

which they will occur. This relieves the mind of wondering what's going to happen next, and permits deeper meditation.

RESOURCES

Csikszentmihalyi, Mihaly. *Flow: The Psychology of Optimal Experience.* New York: Harper & Row, 1990.

Kenyon, Tom. *Brain States.* Naples, Fla.: United States Publishing, 1994.

Wolinsky, Stephen. *Hearts on Fire: The Tao of Meditation.* San Diego, Calif.: Blue Dove Press, 1997.

Chapter 24 • Quaker Worship

*This waiting, this not making plans, this searching the heavens, this being
silent is one of the most important things we have to learn.
The moment will then follow when we are called.*
— Carlo Caretto

More than three hundred years ago, the mystic George Fox had a
famous vision. Atop the little rise in northern England called
Pendle Hill, he saw people being freed from the prison of "steeple
houses" — his name for churches — and directly encountering the divine.
From that vision arose the Society of Friends, whose firm establishment
was greatly assisted by Fox's wife, the brilliant Margaret Fell.

Imagine the times: England was in the grip of a puritanical Christianity
that preached that our immortal souls were predestined either to salvation,
in which case we would spend eternity in bliss, or to damnation, in which
case we would suffer unspeakable agonies for all time. Neither prayer nor
good works would change our future, because the all-knowing god of the
Puritans already foresaw whatever we would do. Our fates were sealed.

It was a stern doctrine, descended from the equally stern philosophy of
Calvinism on the continent. But, to the Puritans, predestination did not
mean that actions were unimportant. Although good works would never
earn us a place in heaven if we were doomed, the lack of them was a certain
sign of damnation. Neither was it possible for humans to know the mind of
God; direct revelation was impossible. So the Puritans and their associates in
seventeenth-century England examined even the tiniest action — their own
and others' — to try to guess at who was saved, and who was damned.

Not everyone was willing to embrace this tortured vision. There were Dissenters of various sorts (who, to the Puritans, proved their lack of faith by dissenting), whose heritages remain with us in the Methodist and Congregational Protestant churches of today. Fox was one of these Dissenters, one whose message, to beleaguered natural mystics of his day, must have felt like a cool breeze on a hellishly hot summer afternoon.

From the start, the Society of Friends believed in a kind of meditative worship that permitted a direct encounter with the divine force. Divinity was not seen as entirely outside the human heart — as transcendent, in theological terms. It was immanent, "the light within," something that spoke to us in the silence of meditative prayers. From this direct encounter with the divine, spoken messages might emerge, called vocal ministry. These were frequently preceded by a sense of inner (sometimes outer) shaking, from which the Society of Friends gets its common name of Quakers.

From the start, the Society of Friends joined action to prayer, for the unplanned and uncontrived messages that spirit brought into the silence of the meetings often dealt with peace or social concerns. Early Quakers, often imprisoned for their beliefs, began to advocate for more humane treatment of prisoners. Commitment to peace and to peaceful ways of handling interpersonal conflicts was important, too, as was a radical democracy that gave rise to one of the most stereotypical of Quaker ways. At that time when the English language had two second-person pronouns (*thou* and *you*), there appeared a vogue for flattering others by using the plural *you*. Quakers, who were committed to "plainness" in speech as well as dress, continued referring to individual people with the singular pronoun *thou* long after the rest of English society had abandoned the old distinction.

This radical vision that all people are equal, because all have access to the divine within, led Quakers to be among the first to oppose slavery in America. The history of Quaker involvement in such abolitionist activities as the Underground Railroad, escorting escaping slaves to the freedom of Canada, is both stirring and moving. Women's rights were also important from the start. There were no Quaker priests or ordained ministers, with women having just as much access to the inner light as men; so women were encouraged to speak out at a time when they were barred from other public forums. In America, such nineteenth-century feminist leaders as

Susan B. Anthony, Lucretia Mott, and the Grimké sisters drew inspiration and strength from their Quaker backgrounds.

In the nineteenth century, a division split American Quakerism. At the time, Quakers were predominantly rural people, often holding to old and somewhat outmoded ways. This is the era popularized in the novel and film *Friendly Persuasion,* a time when some meetings seemed more invested in patrolling the color of ribbons in a young girl's bonnet than in encountering the source of all light. Soon, however, Protestant revivalism began to sweep the country, and the Quakers were among those affected. Some meetings changed dramatically, hiring pastors to preach and encouraging hymns and other liturgical revolutions. At the same time, a peculiarly Quaker form of revivalism occurred, called the Hicksite movement after the Long Island farmer Elias Hicks. Far from encouraging singing and preaching, the Hicksites — among whom the "good gray poet" Walt Whitman worshiped — emphasized silence as a source of divine access. There are both revivalist ("programmed") and Hicksite ("unprogrammed") Friends meetings today.

The traditional Quaker commitment to peace, called the "peace testimony," has drawn newcomers to Friends meetings in the United States during periods of international conflict. The First and Second World Wars, and the Vietnam era were times when Quaker membership grew significantly. But although the peace testimony is one of the most visible aspects of Quakerism, its roots are in worship, which continues to bond the Society of Friends no matter what occurs in the outer world.

Contemporary Uses

Some Quakers would be surprised, even annoyed, to find their worship described within a book on meditation. Meditation, they would argue, is different from worship. If someone comes to an unprogrammed Quaker meeting and sees a dozen (or a hundred) people sitting in a silence that is broken only occasionally by a spoken message, that newcomer should not assume that the Quakers are meditating. No, our argumentative Friend would say, they are worshiping.

But what is the difference?

There is a common parochial definition of meditation, often encouraged in Buddhist literature, that holds that meditation involves emptying the mind entirely. Yet many forms of meditation encourage instead filling the mind — with healing imagery (visualization), with words (contemplative prayer), with narratives (active imagination). Movement meditations encourage a shift of awareness to the body; meditations in nature encourage a similar shift, to the world around us. The point of all of these forms of meditation is the same: to move the mind away from the frenzy of everyday concerns into a point of greater stillness and serenity. By our definition, unprogrammed Quaker worship is indeed a form of meditation.

Quaker meetings in the United States are predominantly of the unprogrammed variety, although there is a significant minority of programmed meetings as well; both usually meet weekly. Some groups have buildings, while many meet in borrowed or rented spaces; therefore groups are not called "churches" or "parishes" but are named for the monthly business meeting at which organizational concerns are dealt with. Each meeting is entirely self-governing; there is no Friendly Pope or even a Friendly executive director. Meetings are organized geographically into Yearly Meetings, which in turn are connected through larger Quaker organizations like Friends United Meeting (mostly programmed) or Friends General Conference (mostly unprogrammed). Annual meetings of the latter groups bring together Quakers from all around the nation for workshops, worship, and fellowship (including that popular FGC activity, singing Broadway show tunes).

Meetings for worship are normally held on Sundays, almost invariably in the morning. Most meetings welcome newcomers, who are encouraged to introduce themselves after worship during what is called "the rise of meeting." There is no distinction, in the worship, between "attenders" and "members." A member is merely someone who has gone through the formality of joining a specific meeting or of having membership transferred from another meeting. Some attenders never join, or join only after many years of meeting attendance; similarly, a member may remain connected to a home meeting for years or decades after moving. Within the meeting for worship, such matters are not at all important.

A fellowship hour often follows meeting for worship, which is sometimes followed in turn by a special lecture or other program. Midweek meetings for worship are often found in larger urban centers; there are also study groups on Quaker history and/or social concerns sponsored by meetings of all sizes. In addition, a complex committee structure handles organizational matters for unprogrammed meetings, which have no pastor or staff. Such committees as Peace and Social Concerns, or Ministry and Counsel, offer an opportunity to serve the meeting's needs and to get to know Friends more intimately. Specially called meetings are part of the ongoing structure of each meeting. These include rites of passage such as weddings and funerals, which are celebrated within the format of the meeting for worship. Finally, special Committees on Clearness engage an individual's personal quest within the context of worship; such committees are typically constituted when an attender plans to join the meeting, when members plan to marry (and sometimes, to divorce), or when a significant professional or personal decision needs to be made.

How to Begin

To find a Quaker meeting in your vicinity, check the phone directory first. Quaker meetings are usually listed under "Society of Friends (Quakers)". However, some meetings list themselves under the name of their monthly meeting ("Northside Friends Meeting"), in which case the phone book may direct you to the American Friends Service Committee (AFSC), a social service organization, or similar Friendly group, which can often refer you to a local meeting. Call for information about times and locations of worship; you will probably get a voice mail service, for few Quaker groups have staff to answer calls.

Once you have ascertained when meeting for worship is held, plan to be there five to ten minutes early so that you can be comfortably seated when the meeting begins. Do not expect a greeting committee or other acknowledgment of your presence; you may be greeted with friendly smiles, but the beginning of meeting is generally a time in which people settle down into the silence.

There is no signal for the beginning of Quaker meeting for worship; no bell or gong, no announcement, no prayer. As they arrive, Friends will slide into their pews or chairs and close their eyes. You should do likewise.

Worship is usually an hour in length. For the beginner, it can be quite difficult to sit still for an hour, so expect at the beginning to discover that you occasionally feel restless. Unlike many forms of meditation, there is no specific posture requirement for Quaker worship; sit in a way that makes you feel comfortable, cross or uncross your legs if you need to, and breathe normally. You will find, over time, that the physical difficulties of maintaining a quiet posture for a hour lessen dramatically. At first, just relax and focus inward.

The silence will be quite palpable, almost a living thing. In the supportive silence, do not struggle with your mind and its inner actions. Let it move where it will; let ideas and worries surface and submerge; do not try to structure or control your thoughts. Rather, imagine holding those thoughts in a divine love. Some people do this through visualization, imagining an inner light that illuminates concerns and ideas. Others use a more rational process, thinking through problems in the context of ethical or moral considerations. Each Friend around you will be worshiping in an individual and unique way. Some may be praying silently; of those, some will address a Christian god, some will not. Because there is no doctrine to Quakerism, only a set of practices and testimonies, you will not — and need not — be engaged with others' forms of worship. Your own will emerge with time.

Many newcomers report periods of intense emotion in the silence of Friendly worship. Some, in fact, find themselves weeping silently, often without knowing exactly why. Do not be surprised to find emotional stirrings of this sort. Meditation need not be unemotional. If tears come, let them come. And continue to silently search for the light.

At some point in the meeting, people will begin to rise and speak. The messages are those that cause "quaking," an inner sense of urgency demanding speech. Normally newcomers do not speak, although it does sometimes occur. It is also a commonplace of Quaker worship that a "weighty Friend" — someone with many years experience of worship — will speak almost the exact thoughts of a newcomer (or of another regular member). This peculiarly Quaker form of telepathy is called "speaking to my condition" and is often a sign that the meeting is especially profound or "gathered."

During the vocal ministry, people do not debate or argue. Each verbal message appears from the silence and sinks into it again. There may be one message or a dozen; messages may be connected, although usually they are not; children may be brought in from Sunday school during this period; occasionally someone may sing or even dance as part of this shared ministry.

Often the silence reestablishes itself briefly before the rise of meeting, which is conventionally indicated by Friends shaking the hands of those around them.

REVIEW TIPS

- Find a Quaker meeting by calling meetings and/or Quaker organizations in your area. If you cannot find one, write to the Friends General Conference or the Friends United Meeting for a list.
- Arrive five minutes early. If you are more than ten minutes late, you may have to sit in a special adjacent room so as not to disturb those already in the meeting.
- Sit quietly. Don't assume a position that will be difficult to hold for an hour. If you feel the need to shift your position, do so quietly.
- Your inner experience will be unique; it may seem like thinking or weighty consideration, it may be very emotional and imagistic, or it may resemble prayer or contemplation. Whatever your inner process, seek to locate and fan the flame of truth within yourself.
- At first, you should be wary of speaking in the meeting. Occasionally a newcomer will speak, but rarely. Listen to the vocal ministry quietly and with an open heart; don't argue, don't think of exceptions, and don't resist. The message may be one you need to hear, or it may be meant for someone else. When each message ends, seek to return to your own inner work again.
- At the rise of the meeting, be ready to introduce yourself and thank the meeting for welcoming your presence there.

RESOURCES

Cooper, Wilmer A. *A Living Faith: An Historical Study of Quaker Beliefs.* Richmond, Ind.: Friends United Press, 1990.

Gwyn, Douglas. *Apocalypse of the Word: The Life and Message of George Fox.* Richmond, Ind.: Friends United Press, 1986.

Ingle, H. Larry. *First Among Friends.* New York: Clarendon Press, 1994.

Jones, Rufus. *Faith and Practice of the Quakers.* Richmond, Ind.: Friends United Press, 1980.

Loring, Patricia. *Listening Spirituality. Volume I: Personal Spiritual Practices Among Friends.* Washington, D.C.: Openings Press, 1997.

West, Jessamyn, ed. *The Quaker Reader.* Wallingford, Pa.: Pendle Hill Publications, 1992.

Wilson, Louise. *Inner Tenderings.* Richmond, Ind.: Friends United Press, 1996.

Chapter 25 • Labyrinth Walking

Few if any images of a planned path through ignorance to understanding are better than the labyrinth.

— Penelope Doob

Labyrinth walking is a kind of walking meditation. In his book, *The Complete Guide to Prayer Walking*, Linus Mundy offers this historical conjecture on how walking meditation was discovered:

> It all begins with stillness. In ancient times the practice of sitting still was held in high regard, both in the East and the West. Enlightened mystics retreated to their ivory towers or caves, removed, separate, and apart, and practiced quiet contemplation. Somewhere along the way they came to the realization that they needed to move. So these contemplative meditation masters strolled in their monasteries in rhythmic patterns, forward and back, to and fro, reciting the Psalms, uttering meditations of all descriptions, reading holy writings. Then these monk masters walked down from their towers and became teachers. Somewhere along the way they began to "institutionalize" this health-giving exercise of walking. Monasteries of contemplative men and women played a clear role in furthering, preserving, bringing forward this "modern" prayer style, which empties the mind and fills the soul.

The contemplatives of Nepal have walked meditatively in circles for so many years that they have worn paths into the bedrock of the Himalayan Mountains. The word *contemplation* means "to make a temple with" or "to make sacred." So meditative walking makes walking a sacred act. There are walking meditation forms in Korea and Japan, and there is a tradition of sacred pilgrimages in literature and myth, but these are not the same as labyrinth walking.

Medicine wheels of various spiritual traditions of Native American tribes, such as the Hopi, involve walking. It's spoken of as an Earth Walk through the stages of life starting with the East: Birth, South: Childhood, West: Adulthood, North: Dying in a general generic sense. There are meditative medicine wheels made out of colored rock in various sites. Some wheels offer death in the west. But in general, we walk through stages of life, transitions, qualities, emotions, being offered gifts at each stage. Walking the medicine wheel is a phrase that can be used as a common way of speaking.

WALKING MEDITATIONS

Meditative walking allows you to be quiet on the inside while you are moving your body. It is simple to walk with natural mindfulness. This way of walking uses the Buddhist practice of aimlessness *(apranahita)*, which means to let go of purposefulness in order to be present in the moment. Walking mindfully is a way to stitch our awareness to the world. One Zen master compared walking meditation to the fine stiches of a robe, each step perfect and complete.

Today, bookstores usually have whole sections on fitness and exercise. With all the pubic awareness of wellness, nutrition, weight management, and other health maintenance practices, one can find many books about walking for well-being. Often they emphasize race walking and the cardiovascular benefits of an aerobic style of walking. Sports catalogs sell shoes specifically for walking, as if one could not walk in any comfortable pair of shoes. But these "walking for fitness" programs deal with the body only. Walking meditation deals with the body, the mind, and the spirit.

The contact we make with the earth on our next step forward in time can give us a deep sense of joy and a sense of completeness. The calming rhythm of walking resembles the wonderful back and forth movement of a childhood swing, the up and down of a seesaw, the back and forth of a rocking chair or cradle. These predictable rhythms emulate the comforting pulse of our mother's heartbeat, which filled our senses in the womb. Meditative walking can restore that rhythm and revive inner harmony. As we walk, Mother Earth acknowledges our presence with every step. In more advanced or sensitive forms of the practice, we can imagine ourselves acknowledging Mother Earth in return. Can you imagine such an exchange of love and comfort?

LABYRINTHS AND MAZES

The words *labyrinth* and *maze* mean a path that is highly complex or convoluted in character. Mazes tend have several paths that intersect, giving you more than one choice so that you can make mistakes and get lost. In a labyrinth there is a single path that twists and turns but entails no dead ends or choices. The labyrinth provides a circuitous route to the center, reminding us that the circuitous route may be the only effective way to reach a goal.

The labyrinth walker is ignorant and confused while immersed in the process, but the design of the labyrinth can lead to enlightenment. Just as when you are walking in a maze or a labyrinth your vision is constricted, but when viewing a maze or labyrinth from above you see the whole pattern. The complex artistry of labyrinths incorporates surprises and setbacks, so the labyrinth is considered to be a metaphor, just as a pilgrimage is an allegory, for the path of life. Even the ancient circular and spiral labyrinths were symbols for the divine mother or the Goddess.

The eleven-circut labyrinth

Labyrinths of antiquity were sometimes prisons, sometimes impenetrable, and sometimes inextricable. In medieval times, the labyrinths were made of hedges or stone walls. In France, Italy, and Germany labyrinths were created on the floors of cathedrals. They were used in celebrations. The eleven-circuit labyrinth was created from the Chartres Cathedral in Paris, France, which is illustrated here. It contains a six-petaled flower shape in the center that echoes the facing rose window. The English countryside is dotted with turf and earthwork labyrinths and turf mazes that have patterns resembling the labyrinths in the French cathedrals. Presumably these were places of aesthetic delight and recreation.

A symbol of the route through worldly error, the labyrinth defines a sure path through confusion and suffering. Labyrinths and mazes can be round, square, or of any shape. They may or may not include blind alleys and baffling choices. The shifting character of the labyrinth creates confusion and change, qualities that add to the richness of the poetic metaphor of the shape. In the moral realm, the labyrinth can connote patience in adversity, or persistence in folly.

A walker gets lost or finds the way, depending on luck and skill. Experiencing a state of disorientation in the midst of a maze seems to be part of the process. There are other transformational practices such as Feldenkrais or Alexander work that produce disorientation and confuse the nervous system as a by-product of their healing process. Out of this confusion, a new perspective may be born. This is one way of viewing the rationale behind the labyrinth as a design for a meditative walk.

Being disoriented in space may be pleasant or unpleasant. That is not the point, for the pursuit of pleasure in the ordinary sense is not a main theme in meditative practices. Yes, we all want to be happy, of course. But often the pursuit of pleasure seems to impede happiness if one clings to the pleasure. By allowing yourself to become disoriented and confused in a meditation practice such as labyrinth walking you are developing the skill of restoring equilibrium after losing balance. You are also cultivating detachment so that the momentary discomfort of confusion can be viewed in a larger perspective. The architect of the labyrinth knows that a certain process is necessary if the walker is to get where the architect wants him or her to go and to learn what should be learned. The confusing and difficult process is necessary to prepare the maze walker for spiritual or cognitive transcendence.

MYTHICAL BACKGROUND

In the Bronze Age city of Knossos on the island of Crete there was a palace that was destroyed in the thirteenth or fourteenth century B.C.E. It was excavated from 1900 to 1905 and has been extensively restored. Called the Palace of Minos, it had an elaborate plan and winding corridors that may have been the reality behind the myth of the Minoan labyrinth. In the myth, a Greek mythological monster called the Minotaur (half man and half bull) was the offpsring of Pasiphaë, wife of King Minos of Crete, and a beautiful white bull. Pasiphaë had failed to offer the bull in sacrifice to the gods, so as a punishment, Poseidon caused her to fall in love with the bull. The Minotaur was kept in a labyrinth until he was killed by the Athenian hero Theseus, with the help of Ariadne, daughter of Minos. She gave Theseus a spool of thread to help him escape from the Minoan labyrinth.

CONTEMPORARY USES

After a long hiatus following the flourishing of labyrinths in medieval cathedrals, there is a renewal of interest in labyrinth walking as a meditative path. The Reverend Dr. Lauren Artress is cannon for special ministries at Grace Cathedral in San Francisco, California. She is the creator of the Labyrinth Project/Quest. The design that she chose for Grace Cathedral is that of the labyrinth on the floor of the Chartres Cathedral in Paris, France. This is the labyrinth illustrated on page 215; it may be considered an example of sacred geometry.

Made by prayer and meditation groups, labyrinths based on this pattern can be found in many places in America. At least one hospital in California has constructed a labyrinth for the benefit of its patients and guests. Dr. Artress leads labyrinth walking tours to Europe where the participants visit many cathedrals and gardens, some of them quite old, that have labyrinths one may still walk today. A Public Broadcasting Corporation videotape entitled *Labyrinth: The History of the Maze,* illustrates ancient and modern labyrinths in Europe and America. American workshops on labyrinth walking are often combined with other forms of prayer or meditation such as *vipassanā.* The resources listed in chapter 12, *Vipassanā* Meditation, can guide you to possible teachers in your area.

HOW TO BEGIN

You can make your own labyrinth by scratching the pattern of a simple spiral, or a more complex pattern from this book, into the sand at the beach. Or you can spread out large sheets of canvas and paint them with a labyrinth pattern. If you want to build your own labyrinth you can order a kit from the Labyrinth Project, Quest at Grace Cathedral, 1051 Taylor Street, San Francisco, Calif. 94108 or call (415) 749-6300. To find a labyrinth near you, visit the web site of the Labyrinth Project/Quest at www.gracecom.org.

If you can find a labyrinth to walk, then follow these instructions. Enter the labyrinth and pause. Sense your body and your breath. This kind of walking meditation assumes that there is only one path, you do not have to worry about getting lost or making decisions about how to find the correct way. Wait until the person ahead of you has made one or two turns.

There are two choices here; first, to walk with the intention of letting go of extraneous thoughts in order to arrive at a quiet mind, and second, to carry a question or a problem with you. Once you have chosen how you want to walk, simply find your own pace and walk the path. Generally it helps the quality of mindfulness to go slowly. Some people walk at an extremely slow pace, paying attention to the setting down of their feet, the moving of their weight, the lifting of their back foot, and the moving of that foot through the air. When you arrive in the center of the labyrinth it is often a surprise because the long winding path seems illogical and cannot be figured out by the linear mind. After quieting your mind in the first part of the walk, the center presents a new experience — a place of meditation and prayer. Often people at this state in the walk find insight into their situation in life or clarity about a certain problem. Hence, this stage, finding the center, is called "illumination."

The third stage begins when you leave the center of the labyrinth and retrace the path that brought you in. Many people who have had an important experience in the center feel that this third stage of the labyrinth gives them a way of integrating the insights they received, so it is called "union." This three-fold path is based on a universal understanding of meditation: to release and become quiet, to open the heart and receive, and to take what was gained back out into the world.

The best way to learn about the labyrinth walking is to walk one a few times with an open heart and an open mind. Allow your experience to tell you whether this will be a useful tool for you. A quiet mind does not happen automatically. You must gently guide your mind with the intention of letting go of extraneous thoughts. This is sometimes easier to do when walking than when sitting still.

REVIEW TIPS

- Find a labyrinth, or make one.
- Walk the path.
- Slow down slightly, or even greatly, if it helps you to be more mindful.
- Enjoy the process.
- Remain aware.

RESOURCES

Artress, Lauren. *Walking a Sacred Path: Rediscovering the Labyrinth As a Sacred Tool.* New York: Riverhead Books, 1995.

Doob, Penelope R. *The Idea of the Labyrinth from Classical Antiquity through the Middle Ages.* Ithaca, N.Y.: Cornell University Press, 1992.

Hanh, Thich Nhat. *The Long Road Turns to Joy: A Guide to Walking Meditation.* Berkeley, Calif.: Parallax Press, 1996.

Monaghan, Patricia. *The New Book of Goddesses and Heroines.* Saint Paul, Minn.: Llewellyn Publishing, 1997.

Mundy, Linus. *The Complete Guide to Prayer Walking: A Simple Path to Body-and-Soul Fitness.* New York: Crossroad Publishing Company, 1996.

Tricycle. Autumn. 1996.

Viereck, Eleanor. "Walking." *Daughters of Inanna* vol. 8, no. 8 (fall 1996).

Daughters of Inanna, P.O. Box 81804, Fairbanks, AK 99708

Labyrinth: The History of the Maze. Video. Washington, DC: New River Media, 1996.

Labyrinth Project/Quest, Grace Cathedral, 1051 Taylor Street, San Francisco, CA 94108; (415) 749-6300 or www.gracecom.org

CLASSIC PILGRIMAGE TALES

The Inferno by Dante Alighieri

Don Quixote by Miguel de Cervantes Saavedra

The Pilgrim's Progress by John Bunyan

The Canterbury Tales by Geoffrey Chaucer

Chapter 26 • Biofeedback

Everybody gets so much information all day long that they lose
their common sense.

— Gertrude Stein

The word *technology* typically conjures up images of wires and widgets, but in fact any tool that enhances, or expands the limits of the human body is a form of technology. The cart is as much a technology as the automobile, the candle as much as the biofeedback machine.

Many traditional forms of meditation employ some kind of technology: the drum, which expands the possibility of rhythm beyond hand-clapping and foot stomping; the yantra or sacred image, which externalizes and therefore focuses the mind's own image-making ability; the pen and journal, which permit the eye of the senses to witness the inner dialogue of thought. The idea of technologically expanding the possibilities of meditation is not a new one. As long as human beings have been inventing tools, we have been inventing tools to expand our consciousness.

Contemporary Uses

Biofeedback, a term coined in 1969, means simply the providing of feedback to the body, so that it can learn about itself and monitor its own processes. Before the 1940s, it was widely believed that such functions as heart rate, blood pressure, and brain activity were beyond our conscious control. But during that decade, machines were developed that permitted laboratory subjects to become self-aware of these body processes. To the surprise of researchers, it was learned that far from being out of our control, such process can be altered, when we are given clear information about what our body is doing. It was not that we are unable to control our blood pressure; we just had no way of instantaneously knowing exactly what our blood pressure was while we worked to change it. "Seeing" our heart rate on a monitor makes it possible for us to learn to change its rhythm.

In the 1950s, such technological information was brought together with the growing field of psychology; pioneers like Neal Miller and Elmer Green worked first with animals and then with human beings to design and test machines that would permit subjects to become aware of their bodies' inner processes. Since that time, the development of biofeedback has been steady. There are several different biofeedback systems now available; they monitor galvanic skin response, muscle tension, pulse, and/or temperature. The most common method, EEG or electroencephalographic biofeedback (sometimes called neurofeedback), uses sensors that read and display brain waves. EMG or electromyographic biofeedback uses sensors that read the tension of the muscles to provide the same kind of information.

Biofeedback is now regularly used to train individuals to combat attention deficit disorder, incontinence, chronic pain, sleep disorders, and seizures, as well as to relieve depression and anxiety. High blood pressure, one of the main medical reasons why people seek out meditation, responds readily to biofeedback. One study showed that 80 percent of those with essential hypertension were able to reduce or eliminate their dependence upon prescription medications. Stress reduction is also effectively handled by biofeedback; studies show that subjects are able to control their production of the stress hormone cortisol with biofeedback training. Studies are underway on biofeedback's effectiveness in treating such disorders as repetitive strain injury, phantom limb pain, and asthma.

HOW TO BEGIN

Biofeedback is the only meditation form in this book that cannot be performed by oneself. A trained practitioner, often a certified biofeedback technician, is required to hook the subject up to the monitoring equipment, and to offer training in how to interpret the information charted on the monitors. Although the actual changes in brain wave patterning are created by the subject, the preliminary steps require assistance.

The practitioner begins by taking a health history, in order to ascertain if there are any reasons not to proceed with biofeedback, and in order to learn what benefits the subject is seeking. Then a preliminary training session is held, at which time the subject learns how to read the results of the EEG. Some practitioners require a full EEG at the beginning of treatment — or training, if you prefer. The initial session usually lasts approximately two hours. Many individuals are able to pay, partially or fully, for the sessions with insurance.

After the first session, a series of regular sessions is scheduled, ranging from once a week to daily. At least ten sessions are necessary to see improvement in most cases; definite change takes as many as twenty sessions; severe difficulties require up to forty sessions. At these sessions, the subject is hooked up to the biofeedback machine: a grounding sensor is placed on each ear, then one or two on the scalp.

Alcohol is used to cleanse the skin, then a gummy substance called a conductor is applied, which assists the sensors in detecting the minute changes in brain wave activity. The sensors stay on the surface of the skin; there is no pain from the application of the sensors nor from the monitoring. Once the monitoring equipment is turned on, the subject sees signals revealing what kind of brain activity is underway. Various forms of feedback are then given, permitting the subject to train the brain to produce more or less of a given type of brain wave. Typically, the brain produces transitional waves (between alpha and beta) or beta waves, which indicate that normal, alert, conscious thought is underway. A more relaxed and meditative mental process creates alpha waves, which are charted on the computer screen and/or cause an audible tone. With practice, the alpha state can be effectively entered and sustained. Eventually the brain learns the new and sought-for brain patterns, which then become permanent.

A limitation that some have found with biofeedback is that some individuals find it difficult to sustain their meditative or alpha state without the assistance of the machine. Some practitioners taper off the use of the machine toward the end of the training sessions, so that the new meditator can learn to sustain the alpha state without feedback. Others, however, do not offer this training, leaving it to the biofeedback client to learn to engage the alpha waves without visual or auditory evidence.

Review Tips

- Determine what specific benefits you want to achieve with biofeedback.
- Locate a trained clinician in your area.
- Check to see if your insurance will cover the required number of sessions. Some clinicians offer psychotherapeutic services, with biofeedback as an adjunct; this can be covered by mental health insurance. If you are not insured, and cannot afford the lengthy training, it might be better to seek out another form of meditation.
- Be prepared to dedicate a significant amount of time, over a number of weeks, to the biofeedback process.

Resources

Csikszentmihalyi, Mihaly. *Flow: The Psychology of Optimal Experience.* New York: Harper & Row, 1990.

Kenyon, Tom. *Brain States.* Naples, Fla.: United States Publishing, 1994.

The Association for Applied Psychophysiology and Biofeedback, 10200 W. 44th Avenue, Suite 204, Wheat Ridge, CO 80033-2840; (800) 477-8892, www.aapr.org

part 7
creative meditations

Introduction • Creative Meditations

Seriousness seeks to exclude play,
whereas play can very well include seriousness.
— Johannes Huizinga

If we were to show you a photograph of a person sitting, eyes tightly closed, in the full lotus position, and ask what that person was doing, you might well reply "meditating."

If we showed you a picture of someone seated on a tripod stool outdoors, painting a mountain landscape, and asked the same question, you would probably answer "painting."

But if the point of meditative practice is to stop the mind — to focus us in the here-and-now rather than the not-yet or the already-gone or the never-to-be — that painter, immersed in contemplating the exact degree of toothy raggedness of a distant line of willows while selecting the precise mix of burnt umber and thalo blue, could be meditating as deeply as any yogi.

Virtually all arts, including most crafts, can become meditation. This is not to suggest that beauty and harmony should not be an aim of the creative meditator. However, critical judgments that intrude upon the mind during the creative act interrupt the attention given to materials and environment and inner state. It is possible that work produced during meditative moments may be less strained and self-conscious than that produced with an imagined external evaluator peering over the artist's shoulder. But the excellence or inadequacy of the work is not the point — the creative act itself is.

227

The loss of amateurism is perhaps one of the greatest losses of our modern world. Cheap and efficient reproductions make it less necessary that we make our own art and music, while holding up examples of such polished professionalism that the beginner is often immediately discouraged. Why stumble through a ballet class when you can see Mikhail Baryshnikov on television? Why pick up the brush when you can page through a lavishly illustrated book or visit a touted museum show? Why write a poem when you can read one — or have one read flawlessly to you by a great actor?

Yet the amateur — the word includes the Latin word *amo*, meaning "I love" — is a person who can enjoy art for itself, rather than for the possible professional rewards it may entail. It could be argued that only the amateur and the genius can find what psychologist Mihaly Csikszentmihalyi calls "flow" in the practice of an art form. For the amateur, once the rudiments are learned, there is the chance to create without worrying about audience approval. For the genius, who has moved so far beyond the rudiments, there is the opportunity to fully engage in the exquisite pleasure and struggle of creation.

In this section we focus on creative arts and related processes as ways of attaining a more balanced inner state. Some of the techniques are ancient, others relatively modern. What they have in common is a focus on letting go into the creative moment. Some products of that process — a photograph, a crocheted hat, a poem — may be pleasing enough to save and display, but the most important result is the illuminated mind and soul of the creative meditator.

CREATION AS BRAIN STATE ALTERATION

Creative acts, like other meditations, produce certain physiological changes in the creator. In order to understand these alterations, we must first examine the structure of the brain and the way it functions.

The human brain is actually three brains, each wrapped around the other, the innermost being the most primitive, the outermost the most developed. Nature has thriftily layered our brains so that, as humans, we benefit from the development of other species, building upon rather than losing their evolutionary advantages.

The innermost brain is called the reptilian; we share these brain structures with lizards and frogs and snakes. This sector of the brain grows out of the spinal cord, which carries the enormous amount of information provided by our nervous system, rather like a main electrical conduit carries hundreds of current-filled wires. The spinal cord enters the brain at its base, swelling into an inch-long structure called the medulla. The steady movements of the heart, pumping blood, and of the lungs, inspiring and expiring air, are controlled by the medulla. Like the other parts of the reptilian brain, the medulla does not need conscious instruction to function.

Two smaller sections of this part of the brain — the pons (from the Latin word for "bridge") and the midbrain — are connecting links to the next two layers. Wrapped around and arching over the reptilian brain is a series of brain structures called the paleomammalian, the brain of early mammal development: the thalamus, which carries most sensory information; the hypothalamus, center for sexual arousal and the autonomic nervous system; the cerebellum, which controls and coordinates movement; and the limbic system, which releases hormones and is connected to our emotional awareness and, some studies suggest, to our learning abilities.

The outer layer of the brain is the most recently developed, the neomammalian or new mammal brain. It includes the neocortex, a complex and rich array of cells that carry within them our ability to plan and to dream, to worry and to create. The two hemispheres of the neocortex have become well known in recent years. The dominant brain section (in most people, the left, controlling the right side of the body) processes language and linear thought, while the nondominant (in most people, the right, controlling the left side) is filled with images and holistic ideas. Joining these hemispheres is the important corpus callosum, a kind of rubber band of brain fibers that carries information between right and left sides of the brain, and from throughout the body.

There is significant research that suggests creativity, as it is conventionally defined, activates the nondominant sector of the brain — which we will call, for convenience and with apologies to left-handers, the left brain. Seeing things as a whole, rather than in linear parts, the left brain is the source of intuition and inspiration, of those "aha" moments when everything seems suddenly clear. It is then the project of the right brain to articulate or otherwise express these "aha" moments, to organize the details of that expression. There is evidence that the corpus callosum is vital in this process, and that continued effort in such expression actually strengthens the efficiency of the corpus.

Within these brain structures, constant activity takes place. Since the invention of the electroencephalogram machine (EEG), we have been able to chart how the neurons, the nerve cells of the brain, emit electrical impulses that carry information. The impulses are like vibrations along a tightly wound string and are described in terms of frequencies (hertz). These impulses are categorized — from lowest to highest — as delta (.5–4 Hz), theta (4–8 Hz), alpha (8–12 Hz), beta (12–16 Hz), high beta (16–32 Hz), K-complex (32–35 Hz) and super high beta (35–150 Hz). Lower than .5 Hz is considered brain death.

Not all of these brain states are understood. Some are little explored because they seem to be relatively rare. In the case of others, technological limitations have made them difficult to study; the super high beta state was only recently discovered because previously the paper installed in EEG machines wasn't wide enough for the higher frequency bands to be charted. There have been relatively few studies of the brain states over high beta — although there is some evidence that K-complex states can be connected with highly intuitive moments and that super high beta may include what are termed out-of-body experiences.

Meditators, however, only need to become familiar with the more frequently experienced brain states. We all enter delta when we sleep; very highly experienced meditators can also sometimes enter delta without falling asleep, defining it as a state of imageless, disembodied relaxation. In theta, the brain waves move approximately twice as fast as in delta; images, visual and otherwise, created in the mind in this state seem extraordinarily real and tangible. In alpha, the relaxed body is receptive to inner suggestion, but there is considerably more awareness of the physical world. The beta brain state is characterized by alertness; the inner world recedes while the outer takes precedence; this is our normal "conscious" state. High-beta is experienced as anxiety and very intense alertness.

Brain States, Meditation, and Art

It should be clear from the description above that what we call meditation is a change from a high frequency of brain wave activity, such as beta, to a lower one, such as alpha or theta. Any activity that encourages the lowering of brain wave frequency would have the same benefits as traditional meditative practices such as breathing and body postures.

Creative arts and traditional meditative practices both demand focus, and they both rely upon repeated physical actions. In many traditional practices, the focus is placed upon the breath; in other cases, as in yantra and mantra meditations, a specific object or word is made the focus of the mind's activities. Similarly, any artistic endeavor requires focus and concentration. This is often not a single focus but a double one, as though the mind is looking within and without simultaneously: writing demands focus on the words that are appearing on the page as well as those heard in the mind, drawing requires the mind's eye to be open as well as the hands to be engaged. Such complex activity is often experienced and remembered as a pleasurable intensity of mind and body working harmoniously.

As for repetitive motions, this is obvious in such practices as T'ai Chi, where the practitioner repeats a sequence of motions many times. Similarly, the repeated practice of an art offers many cues to the body-mind that concentration and meditation are to occur. The opening of the paint tubes, the soft smell of the oils, the brightness of the white canvas — all of these sensory experiences become messengers of relaxation and focus. In some creative meditations, including drumming and many needle crafts, a repetitive motion is sustained for some time, enforcing a meditative mood.

So any activity that demands focus and that involves some degree of repetitive activity lowers brain-wave frequency and therefore produces the effects of meditation. In addition, creative meditations encourage the use of both hemispheres of the brain. Rhythmic and visual creative arts like music and painting obviously tap into the nonlinear, image-filled left brain. But creative efforts in writing have the same effect, for the metaphoric nature of much poetry and similar genres demands the activation of the left brain more fully than does formulaic writing.

Creative meditations are not limited to those cataloged in this section. It is possible to imagine, for instance, the making of stained glass windows as permitting the emergence of a meditative state — or the sewing of a child's garment, or the binding of a handmade book, or the throwing of a clay pot upon a wheel. Like the mindfulness meditation described in chapter 10, creative meditations involve being entirely in the moment, entirely focused on the task at hand, entirely committed to the dance of beauty emerging into form. There is, in fact, no end to this section. Invisible chapters will appear in your own life, waiting only to be discovered, read, and employed.

Chapter 27 • Sketching from Nature

*One day I realized that the seeing and the drawing had fused
into one single individual art . . . . It changed my life.*
— Frederick Franck

The connections between drawing and spirituality may be traced as
far back as the most ancient human art. In the caves of France, some
twenty-four thousand years ago, early humans drew simple, yet breathtak-
ingly exact, sketches of the animals that occupied their world. There is
considerable scholarly contention about the purpose for this art. Some
maintain that the art was magical, meant to induce animals toward the
hunters and therefore into the cook pot. More recently, however, it has been
pointed out that few of the depicted animals were significant as foodstuffs.
So the reason for the artwork may have been spiritual or even aesthetic.

There is not even agreement about who painted the caves. For many
decades, it was assumed — with no real evidence — that the painters
were the males of the society. The possibility that the painters, or at least
some of the painters, were women has only recently been broached; in
support of this theory is the diminutive size of the palm print "signa-
tures" on some of the paintings. The most ancient artists may therefore
well have included our foremothers as well as our forefathers.

For many eons after these unknown artists painted the caves, the treasures remained hidden from human view. In the latter part of the last century, the caves were rediscovered: sometimes by accident, as when a small
dog ran into the opening of the great amphitheater of Lascaux; sometimes

purposefully, as when the riches of Niaux and Peche-Merle were located by those searching for Paleolithic treasures.

Since that time, the caves have been visited by tourist and scholar alike — so much so that the great paintings have suffered significant deterioration, mostly from microorganisms whose growth is encouraged by the moisture in human breath. A century of human curiosity has done more to degrade the art than millennia of dark silence. Some of the most significant and artistically impressive caves have been closed to all but a select few visitors. In the case of the magnificent Lascaux cave, the French government built a replica so that visitors can still wonder at the astonishing liveliness of its horses and bison.

Art has not always been connected to spirituality. Much European art for instance, has its roots in commerce, in the pleasing of rich patrons; where those patrons were church leaders, even art with religious themes was created, not as a meditative act, but for the wealth it could bring. Yet we find many traditions in which the creation of visual art is, itself, the religious act. Chinese brush painting, for instance, has as its intent not the creation of a specific object, but the creation of a state of mind. Similarly, much Tibetan art, like the sand mandalas delicately and deliberately built, color upon color, by monks, is valued for the effects of its process rather than the product — which may, to emphasize its negligible value, be destroyed as soon as it is completed.

There is no such great and elaborate tradition behind sketching from nature. Although it has been practiced virtually throughout human history, the meditative art as it is practiced today is a recent innovation, requiring the common availability of paper and drawing implements. In times past, sketching might have been done in scrimshaw, with natural forms incised quickly into bone; a stick in sand might suffice, or a bit of charcoal from the fire, on a rock. Not created to be masterpieces, such quick sketches were not saved from the elements. But given that their purpose was to train the outer eye to observe and the inner eye to remain focused, their loss is not to be mourned.

CONTEMPORARY USES

Life drawing has been important to artists for centuries; the great Leonardo da Vinci's sketches reveal his intimate observations of the world around him, and Albrecht Dürer's engravings show a similar intense observation of the natural world. But sketching for the nonartist could not emerge as a popular activity until the necessary materials became cheap and available enough to lure the amateur. This happened approximately a century ago. Sketching from nature first became widely popular in nineteenth-century Europe, especially in England, where it was a favored exercise of leisured people who enjoyed capturing the passage of seasons through the plants and animal life around them. Notebooks, often leather bound, were filled with careful sketches that showed the curlew's nest or the budding yellow gorse. Sketchbooks might be decorated with philosophical sayings or wise adages, or the drawings were accompanied by a few lines, noting the weather or other aspects of the day.

Sketching from nature remains a vital part of artistic training, but amateurs — disappearing in many other arts today as well — are less active. Some field scientists still use pencil and paper to record their observations, but many rely upon cameras. The camera, indeed, is probably the primary reason that nature sketching has diminished in the contemporary world. Faced with a splendid natural vista, it is easier to grab the camera than to sketch the scene. And while some photographers can focus their minds as well as the lens, in most cases the speed of execution eliminates the careful observation that is part of meditation in nature. Tourists have traded a series of snapshots to show back home for the vivid memories that can illuminate even the crudest sketch.

Today's offhand reliance upon the camera is unfortunate, because the careful observation of even an ordinary leaf can lead to an intensely focused state of mind. Those who do regularly practice nature sketching find that they enter an altered state of perception, seeing the most minute details of the object they are observing — or, if the object is an animal, keenly observing the gestures and movements, in a way that merely watching does not do.

When the hand joins the eye in observing, focused attention is multiplied. Drawing uses the brain's right side, where shapes and forms are processed. Whether the final drawing is especially pleasing or not — though, with regular practice, even amateurs can draw passably — the process of watching deeply while tracing the shape with the hand elicits the state of calm attention that is the hallmark of all meditative traditions.

How to Begin

Nature sketching takes more equipment than many forms of meditation — but not much more. A drawing implement, a drawing surface, and a natural scene or object are all that it takes.

While sketching is often an outdoor activity, it need not be. Sketching a houseplant, a sitting cat, or cumulus clouds can elicit the same kind of deep attention as sitting in the open air on a sunny day. Similarly, it is not necessary to look for spectacular settings. A backyard aster, or the rose covering an old shed, can hold as much fascination as the foothills of the Himalayas or the snowy tip of the Matterhorn. For the beginner, in fact, the smaller object may recall fewer pieces of great art, which, haunting the inner eye, can inhibit the hand's free flow.

Selection of setting or object can be, in itself, a pleasurably calming experience, so long as one is not hiking madly through the brush looking for "just the right" location. Sitting still in a less than spectacular site, sketching quietly, may call forth the hawk whose shadow makes the sketch especially dynamic. But whether or not the hawk appears, the sketcher's efforts should go toward observing what is actually there, rather than storming off in pursuit of an imagined vista.

The pursuit of the perfectly tipped pen or the most sleekly textured paper can similarly detract from the meditative experience. While there is no doubt that some tools are more efficient, more pleasurable to use, and more effective than others, a dime-store pencil or a crayon is sufficient. Similarly, while there are many grades of paper, some of which produce more interesting textures under the pen or pencil than others, it is possible to sketch meditatively on cardboard shirt backing. It is better to put one's effort into the process, rather than the materials.

That process is simple, yet almost infinitely variable. Study the object for awhile. Be careful to note the way that the flower, tree, or bird is irregular; don't impose regularity upon nature. You will begin to feel a slight shift when you are ready to draw — your attention has moved from self-awareness to absorption in your object.

When this shift occurs, you may continue staring at the object while your hand moves across the page; you may look at the object and then down to the paper; or you may alternate or otherwise combine these actions. The first kind of drawing is sometimes called a "gesture sketch," because it is as though you are making the gesture of the object with your hands over the paper. Looking at the object, then drawing without looking up again, is called a "memory drawing." Most commonly, sketchers look, sketch, look again, sketch again, and so forth.

A sketch can take five minutes or an hour; it can be full of detail or sparse in line. Neither time nor appearance are important in using natural sketching as a meditation. What is important is the process: focused looking, combined with hand motions that activate the right side of the brain, lead to a sense of calm, well-being, and peace.

REVIEW TIPS

- Assemble your equipment: pencil, pen, or both; paper or sketchbook.
- Find a suitable subject. This can be indoors or out; it can be as small as a chickweed flower or as large as Mount Denali. Do not beleaguer yourself over the subject. Look only until something draws your attention; then start drawing.
- Observe the object carefully before you start to draw. Try to see it as deeply as possible. Observe not only its color and shape, but the repeating patterns that compose it, the breaks in those patterns, and the chiaroscuro of its surface.
- Begin drawing when you feel yourself growing familiar with the object's appearance. Often in the drawing, you will see more than you had originally seen.
- Do not hurry the drawing. You are not a Polaroid camera. Allow yourself to make corrections when you feel they are necessary. Permit yourself to become absorbed in your task.
- When you have finished with your sketch, you can keep it or discard it. Many people like to record time, date, and place on their sketches; later examination will provoke a slight reprise of the meditative state, when it is brought to memory by such information.

RESOURCES

Franck, Frederick. *Art As a Way: A Return to the Spiritual Roots.* New York: Crossroad, 1981.

Franck, Frederick. *The Zen of Seeing: Seeing/Drawing As Meditation.* New York: Random House, 1973.

Hamilton, John. *Sketching with a Pencil: For Those Who Are Just Beginning.* United Kingdom: Blandford Press, 1991.

Leslie, Clare Walker. *Field Sketching.* Dubuque, Iowa: Kendall-Hunt, 1985.

Leslie, Clare Walker. *Nature Drawing: A Tool for Learning.* New York: Prentice-Hall, 1980.

Nicolaides, Kimon. *The Natural Way to Draw.* New York: Houghton Mifflin, 1941.

Chapter 28 • Needle Crafts

If life deals you a pile of scraps, just stitch them together one by one.
When you're done, you'll have a more harmonious life —
and a beautiful treasure.

— Dorothy Morrison

Until the Industrial Revolution, the cloth used in clothing, bed linens, even ship's sales was laboriously hand produced. Linen, for instance, was derived from a weed whose stalks were first soaked, and then beaten and combed to produce fibers that were then twisted into thread. Wool had to be sheared, carded, and combed; silk was untwisted from worms' cocoons; cotton was hand harvested, its seeds removed, and carefully cleaned.

All this labor, just to prepare the thread that was then woven into cloth or hooked in an early version of knitting or crochet. Clothing, cut from such cloth, was hand stitched; sometimes, as in smocking, the stitches formed the shape of the clothing, whereas other stitching was decorative, often relying upon ritually significant ornamentation. In the arctic, furs took the place of cloth, but delicate sewing was even more vitally important for protection against frigid weather; in many parts of the Americas, arduously tanned leather was cut and sewn into garments and tentlike homes. In Native American cultures, weaving often took the form of basket making, with the weavers producing containers for food and even, with extremely tight work, water and other liquids.

In most cultures, women were the spinners, weavers, and seamstresses; occasionally, we find evidence of men as basket makers, weavers, or other fiber workers, but mainly it was one of ancient woman's most essential contributions to society. It is likely that most forms of needle crafts were originated by women, propelled by the need to clothe and even house their loved ones — but inspired as well by the artistic influence that encouraged elaboration and decoration.

It is impossible to know with certainty what the inner state of our ancient foremothers was, as they sat by a peat fire spinning lambs' wool, or crouched in the dim light of a seal-oil lantern making sinew seams in a winter parka. But repeating the same motion, over and over, will produce a state of deep relaxation and/or concentration. And mythic traces suggest that the repetitive motions of spinning, especially, were recognized as leading to a meditative state or light trance. In more than one mythology, we find the figures of spinning women who predict the fate of newborn children — the ancient Greek Fates, the Norns of Scandinavia, even the fairy-tale witches who appear in the tale of "Sleeping Beauty" and who probably descended from Germanic goddesses of destiny.

Early needle crafts emphasized utility. Certainly, there were always ornamented fabrics and garments that gave pleasure to their wearers; there were also ritual objects such as the robe annually woven by the superstars among Athenian weavers for the statue of the city's goddess, as well as symbols of royal status like the stunningly elaborate imperial robes of ancient China. But in general, strength of fiber and ruggedness of weave were more important than a decorated surface. Later, however, this shifted. As spinning, weaving, and clothing making became specialized and mechanized tasks, a new kind of needlework arose among the leisure classes. Delicate stitching — needlepoint, bargello, silk embroidery, tatting, and the like — was an art of cultivated ladies showing, by the sheer uselessness of their work, how much wealth their families controlled. Even during this period, however, women of less privileged families were still plying their needles at quilting bees, darning socks, and making rag rugs.

CONTEMPORARY USES

While in the earlier part of this century, even women in the industrialized nations were likely to know how to wield a needle efficiently if not creatively, today such skills are less likely to be a routine part of women's lives. Mothers are more likely to teach their daughters shopping than spinning. So many traditional skills have fallen into disuse.

At the same time, however, there has been an increased attention to the spiritual nature of homely, sustaining tasks. Theologian Katherine Rabuzzi, in the 1970s, was one of the earliest writers in the women's spirituality movement to draw attention to the connection between the repetitive motions of many household tasks — including needle crafts — and such practices as turning a prayer wheel or praying a rosary. Other contemporary theologians and needle practitioners — especially quilters — have similarly stressed the meditative aspects of craft work. So at the same time there has been a decline in the actual practice of such crafts, there has been an increase in awareness of their value. While meditation centers generally do not yet teach needle craft as a spiritual path, many women and increasing numbers of men are finding their own way to this ancient wisdom.

How to Begin

Not everyone had a granny who taught Aran Island knitting patterns to her elementary school-aged grandchildren, or an aunt who wielded sharp scissors and a flying needle to create magnificent quilts — or even a mother who could sew on a button firmly. Even if one were blessed with such a teacher, it is likely that the needle crafts offered in youth were limited. So learning needlework sufficiently well to use it as a meditative practice must usually be the first step.

It is important to stress that beginners will, in needle craft as in other meditative forms, generally not receive the benefits they seek immediately. It is hard to relax while trying to balance two knitting needles for the first time. Only practice will permit the motions to become almost automatic, allowing the mind to relax into the moment.

Before learning a needle craft, one faces the task of deciding which one to learn. If you have never done needlework before, it may help to know that most needleworkers learn multiple crafts — knitting and sewing and embroidery, for instance. But one or two will tend to stand out as the most suitable to the crafter's temperament. You should be aware that you may well have to try several crafts before you find the one that produces the meditative effect you desire.

The primary needle craft is spinning, which can be done either by hand (with spindle and whorl) or with a spinning wheel; this is one of the most rewarding crafts in terms of its meditative potential, but it is also rather difficult to master. Other crafts you can consider include those that use yarn to create fabric (knitting, crocheting, tatting, lace making), those that create a fabriclike surface on canvas (needlepoint, bargello), and those that decorate a fabric surface (silk embroidery, crewel, cross-stitch). Most needle crafters will report that mending (especially darning) and hand quilting can be quite restful, while the varying demands of assembling a garment make sewing less monotonous, and therefore less meditative as well.

There are those, especially visual learners, who can teach themselves needle crafts from printed instructions. Many fine books and magazines exist that can launch such a budding needleworker. But visual learners are outnumbered by auditory learners, who learn when people describe something verbally, and kinesthetic learners, who learn by watching and following what someone else does. For such learners, a teacher is important. Many craft shops have short classes that can provide basic instruction. Remember, however, that the purpose of such classes is to sell products, so thrift will not be encouraged. While our foremothers made patchwork quilts of worn-out clothing, today's craft shops sell prints by the yard, ready to be cut with templates. Classes at shops, however, are for many people the only access they have to craft instruction.

If you can locate a friend or relative or acquaintance who practices a needle craft, you might ask him or her to teach you the craft. Be aware, however, that skill with the needle may not translate into patience with a clumsy beginner. Negotiate in the beginning for how many lessons you feel you will need, whether your teacher would accept payment (in coin or in barter) for the instruction, how often and for how long you will meet, and over how many days or weeks the instruction will extend. Courtesy, including arriving on time and leaving promptly, will endear you to your teacher.

Once you have learned the basics, select an extremely simple project that, however, is large enough to occupy you for some time — a simple knit sweater, a needlepointed pillow, a set of embroidered place mats, for instance. Tiny kits (for change purses and sachets and the like) are often available that encourage the learner by being quickly finished. If, however, your aim is not to fill the world with evidences of your newfound skill, but instead to use the craft as a meditation, it's better to select a larger project.

Yes, it will take longer, but what's the rush?

As we have said before in this book, it is possible to turn anything into work. Needle craft offers a profound temptation to those who are overly task-oriented. That scarf becomes not a way to move rhythmically with bright yarn and shiny needles, but something that has to be completed by a certain day in order to wear with a certain hat. Rushing not only leads to dropped stitches and other mistakes — it eliminates the meditative benefits of needlework. Never set a deadline for completion of a project if you want to meditate while crafting.

Most crafters find that portable crafts like knitting permit the attainment of calm meditation even in unlikely settings, like the crowded waiting room of a dentist's office. Conversely, the body-mind responds well to cues of setting, so having a knitting basket or embroidery bag near a favorite chair will often create a setting that will encourage you to settle into meditation more quickly. While working, let your mind drift. You may find yourself worrying, or fantasizing, or even praying. Even if you're fussing mentally over a problem, the rhythmic actions of your craft — the thread rising and falling, the crochet hook dipping in and out of the wool, the needles sliding past each other — will alter the inner experience. Worrying while sitting still (or worse, lying in bed) often creates more worries, but fretting while crafting often releases anxiety instead. Sometimes, in fact, the more relaxed state even permits a new answer to the problem to appear in the mind.

A final word: crafting while watching television is not meditation.

REVIEW TIPS

- Determine which craft you will begin with. Select one that seems neither too simple (and so will soon bore you) nor too complex (which will discourage you).
- If you are a visual learner, locate some books or magazines with clear instructions as to how to proceed. If you are an auditory or kinesthetic learner, locate a teacher either through a crafts store or through your friendship network.
- Select a first project that is neither tiny (encouraging rapid completion) or huge (encouraging a closet hiding place for the

"impossible to finish" project). Purchase sufficient materials to complete the project without having to resupply.

- Beginners usually benefit from doing all their craft work in one setting, usually a comfortable chair under good lighting. As you become more advanced, portable crafts permit you to take your meditation anywhere.

- Soft music in the background can enhance your meditative experience. Conversation and television, however, will not.

- Let your mind drift, as you work, to whatever subject it wishes. Just keep moving, using the rhythmic motions of the craft as the focus of your attention.

- Avoid rushing. Avoid setting deadlines for project completion and pushing yourself to do more than you feel like doing in a single sitting.

RESOURCES

Campanelli, Pauline. *The Wheel of the Year: Living the Magical Life*. Saint Paul, Minn.: Llewellyn, 1989.

Gostelow, Mary, ed. *The Complete Guide to Needlework: Techniques and Materials*. Atlanta, Ga.: Chartwell Books Inc., 1982.

Hangen, Eva C. *Symbols: Our Universal Language*. Wichita, Kans.: McCormick-Armstrong Company, 1962.

Hochberg, Bette. *Spin Span Spun*. Santa Cruz, Calif.: Bette Hochberg, 1979.

Hower, Virginia G. *Weaving, Spinning, and Dyeing — A Beginner's Manual*. New York: Prentice-Hall, 1976.

Johnson, Mary Elizabeth. *Star Quilts*. New York: Clarkson Potter Publishers, 1992.

McRae, Bobbi. *The Fabric and Fiber Sourcebook*. Newtown, Conn.: The Taunton Press, Inc., 1989.

Morrison, Dorothy. *Magical Needlework*. Saint Paul, Minn.: Llewellyn, 1997.

Ryan, Mildred Graves. *The Complete Encyclopedia of Stitchery*. New York: Doubleday, 1979.

Znamierowski, Nell. *Step by Step Weaving*. New York: Western Publishing, 1967.

Reader's Digest Complete Guide to Needlework. New York: Reader's Digest Association, Inc., 1979.

Chapter 29 • Haiku

Images, like our lives, are meaningful only as they stand in
relationship to nature. The themes of haiku recognize this truth.
— Clark Strand

The Japanese verse form called haiku derives from Zen spiritual practices. Like Zen walking, brush painting, calligraphy, and the tea ceremony, it challenges the practitioner to keep the meditative center while performing an action. In the case of haiku, this is made exponentially more challenging by the fact that the mind, rather than clearing itself, actively engages in verbal thought.

The name, as well as the form, comes from China. It was the first verse in a linked sequence called a *renga* chain, often composed by groups of poets working together. After the first verse, which was ideally the entire poem in miniature, the *renga* elaborated and expanded the images of that verse, the *hokku*. So the haiku easily became a form in itself, about three hundred years ago. It is part of a larger group of Japanese verse forms based on the three-line *katuata*, which asks a question and then provides an emotionally appropriate, though often not logical, response.

Because Japanese is an agglutinative language, whose words are formed by putting together small syllables, the counted-syllable form of the haiku and other verse styles is very well suited to the language. The haiku is traditionally three lines, with five syllables in the first and last, and seven syllables in the middle. More specifically, the haiku is a five-syllable phrase and a twelve-syllable phrase, with either one of the following occurring first: a seasonal image or word, called in Japanese a *kigo,* and an expanding or contrasting phrase. The image conjures the subtle feel of the season evoked, surprising us with insight into the nature of the universe (this is as distinguished from the similar senryu, which shows us something about the nature of humanity).

So much for the technical background. The spiritual background — haiku's connection to Zen — is somewhat harder to trace. It is likely that it arose in the "capping phrase" *(jakugo)* exercises, wherein a koan or puzzle is offered to the student. ("What is the sound of one hand clapping?" is the koan best known to the non-Zen audience today.) After the student offers an appropriate response — it can hardly be said to be an answer — to the koan, it is time to move onto the next stage of training. From a collection of thousands of capping phrases in a book made for this purpose, the student selects, the one exemplifying the spiritual states she or he has attained. Such capping-phrase books as the *Zenrin Kushu (Zen Forest Anthology)* are classics of Zen literature — and many of these phrases, composed in Japanese, were in the haiku form.

One of the greatest poets of Japan, Matsuo Basho, was a master of the haiku and a Zen master as well. Born in 1644, he is still beloved today. In his hands, the haiku became an extraordinarily flexible tool for revealing the essence of ecstatic moments in nature. One of his most famous poems, composed as the master poet embarked upon the strenuous journey that formed the subject of his famous book, *Narrow Road to the Deep North,* reads:

> yuku haru yu
> tori naki uo no
> me wa namida

"Spring is passing by," Basho says, "/Birds are calling on the wing,/In the eyes of fish, tears." Such sharp vision and intense emotion, combined with such precise language and imagery, is the ideal of the haiku poet.

CONTEMPORARY USES

Is there an American child who has not been subjected to the creation of haiku in poetry class? And how many are forever discouraged from making any more poetry because of that experience?

Syllabic verse, relatively easy in the Japanese language, is extremely difficult in such a highly accented language as English. So the experience of counting syllables and trying to cram them into the tight little foreign verse form is often perplexing at best, discouraging at worst, to the American student.

Yet the kind of insight that can be gained from the meditative art of haiku can be satisfying to even amateur poets, if the process rather than the product is emphasized. The great American poet William Carlos Williams urged poets not to have ideas, but to embody their poetic insights in images: "No ideas but in things." The haiku requires the same from its practitioner. Finding the exact expression for a fleeting insight, clothing it in natural images, is a rewarding activity even when language and form seem to struggle against each other.

In Japan, haiku societies still flourish, with an estimated six million poets actively engaged in the art. Some American poets, often those intrigued by poetic form, have written syllabic verse, including haiku. But for the most part, with the exception of Zen students, haiku has been relegated to the classroom and seen as a kind of short, therefore easy, poem for children.

This is unfortunate, for the haiku offers a fine meditative discipline. Unlike those meditations that ask you to empty your mind, writing haiku requires a quite different skill: the ability to focus utterly on the moment and to allow images to well up to meet it, followed by the patience to find exactly suitable language without losing the meditative connection to the moment. Practiced regularly, haiku can be a remarkably mind-clearing endeavor, a kind of intellectual cold shower, bracing and envigorating.

HOW TO BEGIN

How this art begins:
in the depths of the country,
a rice-planting song.
— Matsuo Basho

Any writing can become a form of meditation if practiced with that conscious intent, for letting go of the "monkey mind" that Zen points out is always clambering around with worry and agitation permits the release of the "wild mind," that soaringly creative aspect of our selves. The challenge in writing as meditation is to focus on the process of writing, and to let go of the desire to craft an excellent product. Not that a fine product cannot result, but it must not be the main object. Those who joke about the Japanese Olympic archery team that studied Zen deeply, but failed to hit their targets, are pointing out that external results are not the goal of Zen practice. If the arrow hits the target, the arrow hits the target. If it does not, it does not. Similarly, if a fine haiku results from meditation, a fine haiku results. If it does not — it does not. The product does not define the quality of meditation.

Letting go of the desire to control, to make an excellent, product of a creative act, is extremely difficult. But real joy is found in that vivid moment in which an experience resounds in the depths of the soul, then is brought forth in an image that, dreamlike, expresses it precisely. Letting go of the ego's demand for a perfect product becomes easier each time we experience that creative joy.

To begin a haiku practice, determine a time and place for your meditation. Just as sitting on a meditation pillow or unwinding a meditation shawl can help focus the body-mind into the meditative state, so too will having a regular time and place for haiku writing assist the process. Expect that considerable practice will be necessary to learn this technique; once learned, however, it can be practiced less regularly. Like bicycle riding, haiku writing is a skill that will last, ready to be called forth when occasions demand.

A special notebook and comfortable writing implement (pen or pencil) will be necessary, as well as between thirty to forty minutes. Make yourself comfortable and still your mind. Let your senses become aware of the world around you, and of your inner world as well. Do not reject or judge either. If it is cloudy and humid, and your mood is pained and sad, these are simply the way things are at that moment. The weather, interior or exterior, is neither bad nor good; it simply is. Permit yourself to experience and acknowledge those weathers.

Avoid articulating at this early stage. Especially, do not label your emotions. "Goodness, I'm sad" is not actually what you are experiencing; it is a name we give to a complex collection of physical and spiritual interactions. Instead, attend to your body. Are your shoulders slouched, your chin heavy on your chest? Is your breathing shallow and strained? This is what you know, before you label it "sad." Stay with the feelings, rather than the words for the feelings.

After a time, you will sense images lurking, ready to make themselves known. When images emerge organically in this way, a dreamy feeling often results. In this meditation, you have relaxed sufficiently that the "wild mind" is beginning to provide you with information, which arrives in the form of images rather than words. Let the images emerge, like dolphins from the deep, until one grabs your attention more thoroughly than the others.

As you begin to write, you will be moving into the more difficult part of this meditation, for it is easy to let the "monkey mind" take over, putting down words, crossing out words, and generally being a busy little pest. Rather, let your mind stay empty and focused on the image as you write a few words to capture it.

Most people find that working carefully, line by line, leaves the door open for the "wild mind" to enter. Rather than writing a three-line poem and then returning to the first line for revision, perfect the first line before you move to the next. Speed is not the point; do not rush to finish your haiku. Instead, keep focusing on the moment and on your inner senses, and proceed slowly through the tiny space of the poem — which will, when approached like this, reveal itself to be vast as the ocean.

Another way to compose haiku is less sedentary. Once the basics have been learned, haiku walks or even strenuous hikes can bring together a kind of meditative movement with focus on the natural world. Even the process of searching for — by not searching for — the subject of the haiku becomes a part of the meditation, as well as the inner composition of the verse, which is then written down upon return.

REVIEW TIPS

- Find a quiet comfortable place and time for this meditation.
- Provide yourself with a notebook and writing implement.
- Clear your mind. Let go of daily cares. Attend to the information your senses provide you. Look, listen, smell, and otherwise open yourself sensually to the world.

- At the same time, open your awareness to your emotions and spiritual condition. Do not judge or reject; merely observe.
- Allow images to surface without judging. Do not begin writing until one image becomes predominant as an expression of both your inner and the outer seasons and weather.
- Remember to mention the season or to employ a seasonal image. Traditionally, for instance, autumn haiku mentioned chrysanthemums, which are common in Japan in that season. Your haiku need not employ such timeworn emblems; derive your own from the land you occupy. Sweet corn might symbolize summer for you, or blueberries, or mangoes. Focusing on the season helps bring you into the moment.
- Wait until an image arises that expresses your inner reality. Do not analyze and never label your emotions and spiritual states. Grief may be a wrenching in the chest or a sense of tearing. Concentrate on the feeling, not the emotional label.
- Cast your work in the traditional three lines, in the five-seven-five syllabic pattern. When possible, the final line should provide a delightful surprise.
- Haiku writers don't win a lot of fame, or even infamy. They virtually never get movie contracts for their work. Let go of all ambition as you write. Just concentrate on the moment and let the words pour forth to express it.
- Once you have learned the form, consider writing haiku in your mind in natural surroundings: the garden, the path through a park, a mountain trail. This can immeasurably enrich your practice.

RESOURCES

Aitken, Robert. *A Zen Wave: Basho's Haiku and Zen.* New York: Weatherhill, Inc., 1978.

Blyth, R. H. *Zen in English Literature and Oriental Classics.* New York: Dutton, 1960.

Bownas, Geoffrey, and Anthony Thwaite, trans. *The Penguin Book of Japanese Verse.* New York: Penguin Books, 1964.

Downer, Lesley. *On the Narrow Road: Journey into a Lost Japan.* Loveland, Ohio: Summit Books, 1989.

Goldberg, Natalie. *Writing Down the Bones.* Boston, Mass.: Shambhala, 1986.

Shigematsu, Soiku. *A Zen Forest: Sayings of the Masters.* New York: Weatherhill, Inc., 1981.

Shigematsu, Soiku, trans. *A Zen Harvest: Japanese Folk Zen Sayings.* New York: North Point Press, 1988.

Strand, Clark. *Seeds from a Birch Tree: Writing Haiku and the Spiritual Journey.* New York: Hyperion, 1997.

Turco, Lewis. *The New Book of Forms. A Handbook of Poetics.* Hanover, N.H.: University Press of New England, 1986.

Ueda, Makota. *Matsuo Basho, the Master Haiku Poet.* New York: Twayne Publishers, 1970.

Chapter 30 • The Body Scan

Your body image gives you your identity, self-assurance, security
in your movements, and clearness in your orientation in space.
— Gerda Alexander

Sweeping the body with one's awareness is a meditative technique for gaining a sense of embodiment and for improving relaxation skills. This technique is a part of the Buddhist *vipassanā* tradition, and is sometimes called body sweeping or body scanning. It is also part of the German practice of Eutony, which is a Western version of yoga whose the goal is to experience the unity of the total person. This feeling of integrity liberates creative forces. Another goal of the body scan is an improved contact with one's own body that allows for better contact with others in the environment.

In the philosophy of Eutony there is a wide range of muscular states from very soft and loose (hypotonia) to very hard and tight (hypertonia). The suffix, *tonia,* refers to the tonus of the muscle, which is the amount of tension in the muscle. In Eutony, a muscle can be either hard or soft, depending on which state is appropriate. Many, if not most, bodies are chronically hypertonic or chronically hypotonic or even chronically average with no possibility of great strength or great stillness. Eutony allows one to experience the full range of muscular states.

So the goal is not a "hard body" or a "soft body" but a body with a wide variety of available responses and states. The adaptable body is capable of both speed and stillness, it recovers quickly from illness or disease, it acknowledges pain but does not cling to dysfunctional states, and it has a lot of aliveness. And recall that Joseph Campbell defined spirit as aliveness. The goal of the body scan is to increase the spirit of the body.

CONTEMPORARY USES

The body scan is appropriate for anyone. A body scan meditation is often included at the end of a hatha yoga session as part of the relaxation practice. It can be practiced in bed before going to sleep, after a hard workout, or even if you are in a hospital bed and experiencing a great deal of pain. In fact it can be combined with many of the meditations in chapter 35, Meditations for Pain and Grief. You might assume that directing your awareness to a painful region of the body is a bad idea. Strangely enough, a body scan sometimes works to alleviate pain. The process works on the principle that the only way out is through. Of course there are limits to this approach. Sometimes the pain may be overwhelming. Maintaining a regular meditation practice gives you better skill at remaining quiet in the face of disturbance and pain. You learn to just be still with it.

HOW TO BEGIN

In a simple body scan, you use both focused attention and physical movements such as stretching to increase your body awareness. After you have practiced for some time you will notice the sensation of your body even when you do not make a special effort to be aware of it. The body scan will improve your ability to relax and give up your defensive posture. When you give up your defense mechanisms you become more and more receptive to the relaxation process of opening and releasing. Your breath moves right through you without any effort as you observe the spreading of the breath wave. Any sound that comes to your attention can be used to relax and release further.

To practice the body scan, lie on your back in a comfortable, relaxed posture. If it is necessary to support your knees with a pillow or a bolster, then arrange the cushions so that you are as comfortable as possible. Becoming conscious of your body starts with focusing on the sensation of how your back and other parts of your body are touching the ground. This sensation of touching the ground will lead to a greater consciousness of your inner space.

As you lie quietly and comfortably, observe all the different areas of your body, one at a time. Observe the details of your body's sensations without doing anything to change your body. This method of directing your attention to each part of your relaxed body in turn is a screening technique whose aim is to allow you to see things as they are.

Any old unresolved emotional states that are stored in your body tend to dissolve under the beam of awareness. These stuck emotions often manifest themselves as physical pains and tight places. The sweeping technique can bring release and quiet. You learn to observe these feelings with a witness consciousness instead of reacting. When you react to a sensation, you create more feelings.

This practice trains you to remain quiet. It will reduce your craving, your wanting. Your wants and desires are going to continue to arise, but you develop skill in experiencing aliveness without succumbing to the addictive pull of your wants and desires. When you direct your attention to a particular area of your body, you activate of your brain cells and trigger a change in bodily reactions. Each thought has a biochemical component. Each time you focus on one particular area of your body, you create a new center of perception and that part of your body feels alive. You activate a new interaction between specific brain cells and the cells of that specific physical area. This creates a sense of where your muscles and bones are in space and is called your proprioceptive sense.

Body Scan Exercise

1. For the best results, record these instructions on an audiotape, which you can then play back while you practice. Be sure to pause between each instruction to allow time to become aware of the new sensations. Or you may find someone to slowly read the instructions out loud as you practice.

2. Lie on your back on a blanket or pad and get comfortable. If needed, place a pillow under your knees. First bring your attention to the toes of your left foot. Experience any sensation that you detect such as coolness or tingling. Or, if there is no sensation at all, then experience the absence of sensation. Try to sense each toe separately. It is okay to move your toes slightly if necessary before you settle into stillness. Then direct your attention to the top of your left foot and ankle. See

if you can feel any pressure or other tactile sensations. Now go to your heel. It is usually easy to sense the point at which the left heel makes contact with the ground.

3. Now move your attention to your left lower leg. Detect which part of the skin is touching the floor. What is the shape of that contact area? Which part of the skin of the lower leg is not touching the floor? How much space is there between the back of your knee and the floor? Sense your whole lower leg, from the skin to the bone, from top to bottom. Now sense your left thigh. Experience the shape of your thighbone as it extends from your hip socket to your knee. Feel the muscles and skin hanging loose from the thighbone. Does the back of your thigh touch the ground?

4. Now move your attention to your right toes. What do you feel there? And to the top of your right foot and ankle, do you experience any sensations at all? What part of your right heel makes contact with the floor? Is it the same as the point at which your left heel makes contact or are your heels asymmetrical? Direct your interest to your right lower leg, your right knee, and your right thigh, and experience whatever sensations you find. Your sense awareness of your legs may change as you do this. Examine your hip joints at the base of the pelvic bone. Imagine they are little balls of air and that your two legs are abandoned on the floor.

5. Direct your attention to your pelvis. There is a flat, bony plate at the bottom of the lower spine called the sacrum. The sacrum may lie flat on the floor or it may be tipped so that the tailbone pokes down into the mat. See if you can imagine that the area of contact between your lower back and the floor is growing larger and softer.

6. Move your attention to your upper back. Notice that the portion of your spine at the waist does not touch the floor. This is the lumbar curve. There is also a portion of your spine at the back of your neck that does not touch the floor. This is the cervical curve. Experience how your upper back makes contact with the floor. Notice those vertebrae that touch the floor and notice how far out to the side the ribs contact the floor. Is it the same on the right and left sides?

7. Notice your belly and chest and observe how they move with each breath. See if you can be the witness of your breath, and not the director. Let the wave of your breath move naturally. Then examine the sensations in your left palm and fingers. Feel where your hand touches the floor. Experience your wrist and imagine there is space between the bones of the wrist. Feel your lower arm, your elbow, and your upper arm, and observe whether you can detect any little tugging movement in your upper arm as you breathe. As your ribs and chest move with your breath, you may detect your arm responding. Now examine your right palm, fingers, wrist, arm, elbow, and upper arm in the same careful way, alert but detached. As you do, remain interested, moment to moment, in your own kinesthetic awareness.

8. Finally consider your head as it presses down into the floor. Are you still trying to hold your head up or can you allow the floor to support it? Experience the base of your skull as if it were broad and open. Experience your upper eyelids pressing down like curtains. Notice the line between your upper and lower eyelids; does it seem to extend farther out to the sides as you relax? Notice the line between your upper and lower lips. Does it also grow longer as you relax? Feel the skin of your face pressing down on the bones of your cheeks. Rest for a moment and absorb the sensations of relaxation.

9. To return to normal consciousness and awareness, slowly open your eyes, sit up, and take a deep breath. Feel good about the fact that you have spent time dwelling in this deep inner space, your healing center.

THE BODY SCAN LITANY

Let my legs be crossed without moving.
Let my knees be lower than my hip joints.
Let my spine rise up straight.
Let my buttocks be parallel and balanced on the cushion.
Let my thighs descend.
Let the skin of my thighs spin toward the center.
Let my coccyx move deep into my body.

Let my anus face the floor.

Let my inner pelvic rim move up.

Let the wave of each breath rise and fall evenly.

Let me feel the fire of energy for the practice.

Let me feel no dullness.

Let my head feel light.

Let my neck be easy.

Let my eyes be closed softly.

Let my lips widen out toward my ears.

Let my jaw be peaceful.

Let my tongue not touch the upper palate.

Let my shoulders hang down.

Let my knees be happy.

Let my armpits be directly above my anus.

Let my lower ribs move back.

Let my iliac crests rise.

Let my lower lumbar spine move forward.

Let my abdomen move in and out quietly with my breath.

Let my back be flat like a leaf, never collapsing.

Let there be space between each veterbra.

Let my hard inner belly support my back.

Let my sternum rise like a balloon.

Let the inner sternum be well lifted, but not the outer part.

Let my shoulder blades be parallel, never rising.

Let the back of my arms hang down heavily.

Let me feel the distance from my bent elbows to the ground.

Let this distance not go up or down with the breath wave.

Let my back be alert.

Let my waist dance like a snake.

Let my back skull feel broad.

Let my ears be receptive.

Let my muscles be elastic.

Let the pores of my skin be open.

Let the skin of my face hang down.

Let my nostrils feel the flow of air.

Let my eyebrows lengthen out to the temple.

Let my breath move smoothly and slowly.
Let my heart feel the joy.
Let my thoughts know the radiance.
Let my mind capture innocence.
Let my intellect be subtle.
Let my memory let go of pain.
Let my desires and aversions dissolve in the moment.
Let my higher wisdom speak to me.
Let me know what I am doing.

— Eleanor G. Viereck

Review Tips

- Body scan meditation can be practiced before bed, after a hard workout, or even in a hospital bed.
- Maintaining a regular meditation practice gives you better skill at remaining quiet.
- Focus your attention and physical movements to increase your body awareness.

Resources

Alexander, Gerda. *Eutony: The Holistic Discovery of the Total Person.* Great Neck, N.Y.: Felix Morrow Publisher, 1985.

Denison, Ruth. *The Body Scan.* Wendell Depot, Mass.: Dharma Seed Tape Library, 1997. Audiotape.

De Peyer, Katia. *Dancing with Myself: Sensuous Exercises for Body, Mind, and Spirit.* Willow Springs, Mo.: Nucleus, 1991

Geissinger, Annie. "Toward the Unknown. An Interview with Janet Adler." *A Moving Journal,* vol. 5, no. 3 (fall-winter, 1998).

Kabat-Zinn, Jon. *Guided Body Scan.* Worchester, Mass.: University of Massachusetts Medical Center. Audiotape.

part 8
meditations in life

Introduction • Meditations in Life

I follow nature as the surest guide, and resign myself,
with implicit obedience, to her sacred ordinances.

— Cicero

The early practitioners of Tantrism pioneered development of meditations that could be done in the midst of any activity. Homemakers, artisans, and laborers of all types were taught how to transform their awareness in the midst of their daily occupations. Miranda Shaw writes in *Passionate Enlightenment: Women in Tantric Buddhism,* "A jeweler could meditate by envisioning that everything is as pure and radiant as shimmering gold; a winemaker might picture herself as distilling bliss from the grapes of experience; a shoemaker could imagine that he was sewing the leather of passion with the thread of freedom to produce shoes of enlightenment." Vietnamese Tibetan monk and author Thich Nhat Hanh has taught many meditations for particular moments in daily life, such as brushing one's teeth, washing, eating, answering the phone, or stopping at a red light. In each case you use the experience to remind you to be aware and attentive in the moment with a spirit of appreciation.

There is a law in physics called the Weber-Fletcher law that states that information is a function of the amount of noise. This means that the more environmental noise there is, the larger the information signal must be in order to hear it. In lifting weight, this same law explains why, if you are holding a heavy bag of groceries, you can't feel the weight of a paperclip if it is added to the bag, but you can feel the weight of a paper clip if you are holding it in your hand instead of the grocery bag. The weight of the grocery bag in this case is the noise. The significance of this principle for bodywork is that you sometimes need to stop working so hard in order to be more sensitive to the signals of the body that give you information about the most efficient way to do whatever task you are engaged in. In terms of meditation in daily life, this means you need to stop working so hard and being so busy. This small poem can help you remember:

Stop!
Innocently
Joy is.

Chapter 31 • Sports As Meditation

Enlightenment is an accident,
but some activities make you accident prone.

— Krishnamurti

If it seems too difficult to find enough time to meditate and also practice your fitness regime, don't worry, because you can work out and meditate at the same time. In fact, the famous "runner's high" is very similar to being in a state of meditation. The euphoria of the runner's high and the euphoria of meditation produce similar physiological changes, such as an elevation in the level of hormones correlated with a positive mood state. Since both exercise and meditation produce a state of euphoria, you might want to know how to add awareness to your running or walking in order to enhance this effect and make it more deliberate.

In the West, the connection between philosophy and the athlete began when athletes ran in the original Olympic games in ancient Greece. In indigenous cultures, the running traditions of Native American tribes have long combined a practical and spiritual function. They ran, and still run, to carry messages and to hunt, but also to cultivate spiritual visions using visualization techniques. The Sufi dervishes use whirling as a meditative technique to induce a trance state and a oneness with the divine. They also use deep breathing exercises and drumming.

Whether your practice is formal sitting meditation, a moving meditation, or a sport such as running, you experience mediation by feeling your body. You acknowledge the reality of your body by means of the physical sensations that arise within it. Experiencing physical sensations is of central

importance in the practice of most meditation sytles. You need to actually
work out, exercise, train, and do the practice. Just reading about it is not
enough. The following story on swimology by William Hart illustrates this
fact.

Once a young professor was making a sea voyage. He was
a highly educated man with a long tail of letters after his name,
but he had little experience of life. In the crew of the ship on
which he was traveling was an illiterate old sailor. Every
evening the sailor would visit the cabin of the young professor
to listen to him hold forth on many different subjects. He was
very impressed with the learning of the young man.

One evening as the sailor was about to leave the cabin after
several hours of conversation, the professor asked, "Old man,
have you studied geology?"

"What is that, sir?"

"The science of the earth."

"No, sir, I have never been to any school or college. I have
never studied anything."

"Old man, you have wasted a quarter of your life."

Next evening again as the sailor was about to leave the
cabin, the professor asked him, "Old man, have you studied
oceanography?"

"What is that, sir?"

"The science of the sea."

"No, sir, I have never been to any school or college. I have
never studied anything."

"Old man, you have wasted half of your life."

With a still longer face the sailor went away: "I have wasted
half my life; this learned man says so."

Next evening once again the young professor questioned
the old sailor: "Old man, have you studied meteorology?"

"What is that, sir? I have never heard of it."

"Why, the science of the wind, the rain, the weather."

"No, sir. As I told you, I have never been to any school. I
have never studied anything."

"You have not studied the science of the earth on which you live; you have not studied the science of the sea on which you earn your livelihood; you have not studied the science of the weather which you encounter every day? Old man, you have wasted three quarters of your life."

The next day it was the turn of the old sailor. He came running to the cabin of the young man and cried, "Professor, sir, have you studied swimology?"

"Swimology? What do you mean?"

"Can you swim, sir?"

"No, I don't know how to swim."

"Professor, sir, you have wasted all your life! The ship has struck a rock and is sinking. Those who can swim may reach the nearby shore, but those who cannot swim will drown. I am so sorry, professor, sir, you have surely lost your life."

You may study all the "ologies" of the world, but if you do not learn swimology, all your studies are useless. You may read and write books on swimming, you may debate its subtle theoretical aspects, but how will that help you if you refuse to enter the water yourself? You must learn how to swim.

— William Hart

The Art of Living: Vipassanā Meditation As Taught by S. N. Goenka

CONTEMPORARY USES

The elegant forms of T'ai Chi, Qigong, and yoga present time-tested opportunities to combine movement with meditation. Sports can do the same thing. In recent years health promotion programs have incorporated mind-body exercises that combine physical activity with different kinds of mindfulness training. This training has an internal focus that produces a self-contemplative mental state during the course of the physical exercise. Since the debut of *Zen and the Art of Archery* by Eugene Herrigel in 1989, many books have been written about the inner game of sports. Sports have a lot more going for them than just scores and skill. In sports, as in life, the sacred currents run deep, and, despite ourselves, we still feel their insistent pull.

Sports may no longer be about transcendence, but they retain the power to intensify experience and awaken within us a larger sense of being. Sports continue to give expression to primordial forces that in other times were called gods, and today might be called archetypes. These archetypes still constitute the primary themes and motifs of art, philosophy, and psychology. (This Warrior archetype is one of the most conspicuous in sports.) This inner life is the hidden dimension of sport.

IN THE ZONE

For the contemplative athlete who is combining a sport with meditation, the primary value of the sport lies in the inner experience. Baseball legend Yogi Berra observed, "Ninety percent of hitting is mental. The other half is physical." One indication of this inward focus is the advent of the phrase "in the zone."

The "zone" originally signified an optimal mental, emotional, and physical state, but the phrase now means more than that. The word calls up imagery of the supernatural (*The Twilight Zone*) and carries an implicit connection to altered states of consciousness (zoned out). The zone is a place, but a map won't get you there. When in the zone, one experiences a state of profound joy, acute intuition, and a feeling of effortlessness in the midst of intense of exertion. One also experiences increased mastery and heightened concentration.

When an athlete is in the zone, all his or her actions are efficient, skillful, and joyful. Being "in the zone" is a thing that happens when a runner gets a second wind. It leads to nearly miraculous throws, hits, and catches. Calmness, confidence, and perceptual enhancement are other benefits of being in the zone.

Coaches, athletes, and sports team owners would all love to bottle the zone. And a trip to the bookstore will show that quite a few authors claim to sell such a bottle. There are "inner game" books about many sports and arts, and even business. However, you cannot reach the zone by snapping your fingers. There are exercises in meditation, martial arts, and relaxation therapies, along with conventional methods of athletic training, that will help an athlete get to the zone more frequently. Or will they? Some sports psychologists believe that the zone experience cannot be intentionally cultivated. It happens when it happens, and thinking about it just gets in the way of it happening at all. Self-transcendence, a characteristic of the zone at its most profound, cannot be produced by a force of will. As any med-itator, musician, or martial artist knows, when the self tries to go beyond itself, it just creates more, well, self. The bootstrap principle doesn't apply here.

Andrew Cooper, author of *Playing in the Zone: Exploring the Spiritual Dimensions of Sports*, writes, "Mastery of one's craft and relaxed concentration are necessary, but they are not sufficient. Visualization, meditation, counsel-ing, progressive relaxation, and the other techniques of sports psychology can enhance one's physical and mental abilities, but they cannot produce self-transcendence. This is the paradox of intuition. You must work and work some more, but the golden moment cannot be produced through an act of will. The unpredictability remains. The mystery prevails. In spiritual pursuits you come up against this paradox in a number of guises."

The zone is a kind of meditative state. One can be in the zone in all aspects of life, not just during sports. It is also called type C behavior. If the type A person tries too hard and the type B person is too sluggish and dull, then the type C person has the quality of using just the right amount of energy for the task at hand.

In both sitting meditation practice and sports, certain experiences rep-resent a qualitative leap in consciousness that is discontinuous with the preparation leading up to it. The state of satori in Zen is analogous to the state of being in the zone. In both satori and the zone experience, you depart with a deeper and richer sense of the inner landscape through which you travel. They are not end points. They are good in and of themselves.

One difference between sports and meditation is that in most sports the goal is to win the game or improve the skill, and little attention is given to the moral or ethical values of the athlete. Ernest Hemingway once called Ty Cobb "the greatest of all ballplayers — and an absolute shit." The meditative paths and spiritual traditions, however, have the goal of per-sonal illumination combined with a sense of responsibility toward others. Meditation is not a selfish path because it includes the cultivation of com-passion.

Another difference between the sports zone and satori is the mood. Sports thrive on enthusiasm, whose meaning is derived from a Greek word meaning "possessed by a god." This results in an ecstatic, communal sensi-bility. The meditative path cultivates equanimity and detachment. Still, in both there is happiness through absorption. The player is so absorbed in the game that he or she becomes the game, as in meditation when the observer becomes the breath. Both sports and meditation join consciousness to excellence in form. They are autotelic — worth doing for their own sake. They may or may not make us better people, but at least they show us the place within the swirl of action where we find what poet Rainer Maria Rilke called the "stillness like the heart of a rose." The term "flow" is used by author Andrew Cooper to mean very much the same thing as "in the zone." The flow experience occurs when you encounter a task that is challenging without being too stressful, a task in which there is a merging of action and awareness, a high degree of concentration, an absorption, and a sense that time seems to move in slow motion. The elements of concentration and absorption occur when one is content within oneself and in one's relationship to the divine.

How to Begin

Your fitness regime can serve as your meditation. It is possible to cultivate the meditative state while walking, swimming, biking, skiing, or jogging. Other repetitive sports are suitable for the combination of meditation and sport. A sport where you have to respond to the unexpected moves of an opponent, such as tennis, is not so suitable, although there are strategies for playing the inner game of tennis. The first thing to do is to cultivate the intention to practice both the inner and the outer sport. Second, you have to find instruction in your chosen sport. Third, you need to practice regularly.

Most people do not realize that the ability to focus one's mind like a laser beam and be in a state of deep relaxation at the same time can be developed through action. A common obstacle is the tendency to tense up at the first onset of an uncomfortable sensation. Activities such as running or skiing can cause pains that are warning signals to stop and protect one's body. These are the danger signals. However, there are other kinds of pains, often associated with a long-unused muscle that is stiff or weak. These pains are slightly uncomfortable, but not dangerous, and one needs to learn to distinguish between the two kinds of pain. Old stuck pain generally involves an emotional block or a physical habit. For example, one may have a habit of tensing the muscles of the body in situations where there is a fear of falling. This is very common in beginning skiers or skaters. This tension causes pain. The old habit of rigidity needs to be transformed into a new habit of a more relaxed awareness. Old stuck pain, which will go away naturally, can cause damage by tensing up in reaction to the pain. The great art is to learn to experience discomfort without clamping down on it.

When you are in the zone there can be exhaustion and pain but it is not stuck, it is flowing. You maintain equanimity even while sweating. You discover a way to stop wasting energy fighting the pain. As in many kinds of "dis-ease," one's own tendency to fight the problem aggravates the problem. It is natural for the body to work efficiently, even in the face of a bit of fatigue or discomfort.

REVIEW TIPS

Shinzen Young, author of *Meditation in the Zone,* has described eight steps to make your fitness workout a meditation.

- Before you work out, take ten minutes or so to get settled. Remain quiet and cultivate the quality known as repose when your body is still. Lying on your back with your knees bent, simply relax and observe your body.
- Do a grounding exercise. For example, focus on your breath, let go of distractions, and feel your mind and body grow calm.
- Have a strong intention that you will use your workout to develop your skills of focusing attention.
- When you get up from grounding try to keep the quality of quiet.
- During your workout:
    a. Remain aware of your breath.
    b. Mentally note the places where you feel strong sensations in your body.
- Constantly practice focusing your attention.
- Keep soft eyes, which is a way of looking through things instead of directly at them. It is an "out of focus" seeing used in the martial arts.
- After the workout, lie down and observe the repose and stillness, enjoy the runner's high.

RESOURCES

Alon, Ruthy. *Mindful Spontaneity: Moving in Tune with Nature.* Garden City Park, N.Y.: Avery Publications, 1990.

Cooper, Andrew. *Playing in the Zone: Exploring the Spiritual Dimensions of Sport.* Boston, Mass.: Shambhala, 1998.

Cooper, Andrew. "The Man Who Found the Flow." *Shambhala Sun* (September 1998).

Cooper, Andrew. "The Secret Life of Sport." *The Inquiring Mind: On Art, Sport, and Idleness,* vol. 13, no. 2 (1997).

Galway, W. Timothy. *The Inner Game of Tennis.* New York: Random House, 1997.

Hart, William. *The Art of Living: Vipassanā Meditation As Taught by S. N. Goenka.* New York: Harper, 1987.

Harte, J. L., G. H. Eifert, and R. Smith. "The Effects of Running and Meditation on Beta-Endorphin, Corticotropin-Releasing Hormone and Cortisol in Plasma, and on Mood." *Biological Psychology,* vol. 40, no. 3 (June 1996): 251–265

Herrigel, Eugene. *Zen and the Art of Archery.* New York: Vintage Books, 1999.

La Forge, R. "Mind-Body Fitness: Encouraging Prospects for Primary and Secondary Preventions." *Journal of Cardiovascular Nursing,* vol. 11, no. 3 (April 1997): 53–65.

Murphy, Michael, and Rhea White. *In the Zone: Transcendent Experience in Sports.* New York: Penguin, 1995.

Schulteis, Rob. *Bone Games.* New York: Breakaway Books, 1996.

Solberg, E. E., K. A. Berglund, O. Engen, O. Ekeberg, and M. Loeb. "The Effect of Meditation on Shooting Performance." *British Journal of Sports Medicine,* vol. 30, no. 4 (December 1996): 342–346.

Young, Shinzen. *Meditation in the Zone.* Boulder, Colo.: Sounds True, 1996. Audiotape.

Chapter 32 • Gardening

The garden is a metaphor for life,
and gardening is a symbol of the spiritual path.
— Larry Dossey

No one really knows when humans began gardening. For countless ages, our forebears wandered their territories, gathering seasonal plants, fishing, and hunting that probably had meditative effects on them. Only within the past five thousand years has our species deliberately planted, cultivated, and harvested food plants. And for even less time has gardening been a meditative way of connecting with nature. As long as food was scarce and every grain stalk was looked at with urgent hunger, there was little opportunity to perform gardening activities without being driven by the need for a successful harvest. And, as we have seen, such a focus on productiveness works counter to meditation.

But with the rise of cities, made possible by agriculture, leisure classes emerged who were able to enjoy gardens in a meditative spirit. Several great landscape traditions arose, in widely separate and climactically different lands, that emphasized the spiritual aspect of the garden. The gardens of Japan, deriving from a mixture of Zen Buddhism and the animistic indigenous religion called Shinto, were designed to encourage leisurely strolling and contemplation. Not far away, in the jungles of Vietnam, a tradition of creating tiny container gardens to represent the vastness of nature evolved. In the dry lands of Persia and Arabia, walled gardens were designed in which two streams joined in the middle — gardens that give us their name, *paradise*, to indicate a realm of joyous connection and peace. In Europe, the great traditions of landscaping had less to do with spiritual concerns than in Asia and Persia; landscaping was a form of architecture, emphasizing the drastic alteration of nature to create ornate parks in which castles were set like jewels. The tradition of the herbal monastery garden, however, tended by monks and nuns for the healing the plants would produce in both themselves and in their patients, shows that awareness of the spiritual value of gardening was not absent from Europe. In the nineteenth century, the great outpouring of Romantic thought brought this sensibility to the fore; gardens were redesigned in terms of the exaltation they would produce in the viewer. Whether those who tended such sublime landscapes felt their spiritual power is not, however, generally recorded.

CONTEMPORARY USES

If gardens have been created and sustained for centuries as meditative retreats, we know little of the inner feelings of gardeners of generations past. Perhaps they were meditative gardeners; perhaps they were merely exhausted and underpaid laborers. (It is generally easier to meditate while performing a chosen activity, for focus on power and productivity are usually antithetical to the meditative state.) It is only within the last several hundred years that gardeners have shared, primarily through writing, the profound spiritual effects that they experience while working with plants, sun, and soil.

Not all gardeners are meditative. In fact, many gardeners are quite the opposite, driven to compete for the greenest lawn, the most floribundant rose, the biggest collection of hosta. Such gardeners do not need tomatoes to feed their children, but they will compete furiously for first prize at the fair; they do not need to sell flowers to live, but they drive themselves into hypertension to win a flower show award. Just as it is possible to knit demonically, aiming at finishing an object on a deadline (see chapter 28, Needle Crafts), so it is possible to view a garden as an obsessive project rather than a place of solitary or companionable meditation.

The meditative gardener, by contrast, emphasizes the process of gardening rather than the product. The perennial beds may look quite as healthy as the ones next door, but that is not the point. The intention of the meditative gardener is to lose the sense of time's rushing passage, and to enjoy the momentary pleasures and challenges that the garden presents.

In the past decade, gardening has become the most popular leisure time activity in the United States, with more than half of surveyed gardeners claiming that they engage in the activity for the peace and serenity it provides. At the same time, a number of books have been published that emphasize the spiritual, rather than the material, rewards of gardening. Workshops and seminars on spiritual approaches to gardening have recently begun to be offered; some of these provide ideas for building gardens in which to engage in static meditation, while others offer insights into how to use gardening chores as movement meditations. So, those who find the garden a meditative place or gardening a meditative activity will find common ground with many other gardeners today.

How to Begin

It is possible to make anything into work, and it's possible — though difficult — to make anything a meditation. Anyone who has tried to turn a mundane chore like dishwashing into a meditation knows how difficult it can be. Some forms of labor, by contrast, lend themselves readily to meditation. One of these is gardening. The tasks themselves rarely require much conscious thought. Weeding, deadheading flowers, double digging beds — once these tasks are begun, the work itself is relatively monotonous. So the mind is free. It need not puzzle out where next to place the shovel or the hoe. Enough attention is demanded that some types of thinking are difficult; abstract rationalizing, for instance, is difficult while retiring weeds from the vegetable patch, if only because part of the mind is engrossed in sorting which seedling is weed, which lettuce. So the activity of gardening provides enough stimulation to keep the "monkey mind" busy, while at the same time providing a rhythmic and repetitive action (which, granted, changes from day to day and season to season) that serves as a kind of heartbeat for the "wild mind."

Gardening is a sequence of meditations, changing with the seasons and the weather. Spring is the time for planting meditations; summer, for cultivating; fall, for harvesting; winter, for planning. The latter is without question the hardest season for the meditative gardener. Seed catalogues come, bearing their temptations to turn the garden into a zone of conspicuous consumption. But many gardeners report that paging through the glossy booklets, circling possible additions, and dreaming of gardens to be, is a refreshing form of meditation. However, the outdoor work of the other seasons offers more obvious opportunities for meditation.

It is possible to use houseplants as a substitute for outdoor gardening, if land is not available, physical limitations are encountered, or personal taste mitigates against outdoor gardening. Carefully attending to the needs of a window box can create the same attuning to the natural cycles that a larger outdoor space encourages. Some indoor gardening traditions, like the creation and tending of dwarf bonzai trees or the maintenance of glassed-in terrariums, are especially suitable for meditation. Again, it is important to focus on the process, rather than the product in indoor gardening; this world sees as many obsessive African violet growers, intent upon forcing the greatest floral display in time for the annual competition, as it does giant-cabbage growers. Anything can be work. Anything can be meditation.

Review Tips

- Determine where you will engage in your meditative gardening. If you do not have land to plant, determine if your community has gardening space available in vacant lots and other waste space; or consider indoor gardening.
- Be frank with yourself about your reasons for gardening. If you are highly competitive at work, you may turn gardening into another stage for competition — this time with the neighbors. Such an attitude will make meditation while gardening unlikely if not impossible.
- Rely as little as possible on machines. The hacking sound of the small internal combustion engine discourages meditation. The swish of a nonmotorized lawn mower, however, can be very soothing.
- Be aware that you are not able to control the weather. Unlike many meditations, gardening is one that you may engage in for four hours on one day, then be held hostage indoors for the next two days while the heavens water your yard. If you are meditating for medical reasons, you may wish to have an alternative form of

meditation available for those rainy days.

- Don't compare. Every rose is an incomparable witness to nature's beauty. Even a slug-munched cabbage is singularly alive. Eden is a myth. No garden is ever perfect. Your garden is just one of those perfectly imperfect creations.

RESOURCES

Davidson, A. K. *The Art of Zen Gardens: A Guide to Their Creation and Enjoyment.* New York: J. P. Tarcher, 1987.

Gilmer, Maureen, and Jerry Pavia. *Rooted in the Spirit: Exploring Inspirational Gardens.* New York: The Taunton Press, 1997.

Glyck, Vivian Elisabeth. *12 Lessons on Life I Learned from My Garden: Spiritual Guidance from the Vegetable Patch.* Emmaus, Pa.: Rodale Press, 1997.

Handelsman, Judith. *Growing Myself: A Spiritual Journey through Gardening.* New York: Dutton, 1996.

Lacy, Allen, and Cynthia Woodyard. *The Inviting Garden: Gardening for the Senses, Mind, and Spirit.* New York: Holt, 1998.

Messervy, Julie Moir, and Sam Abell. *The Inward Garden: Creating a Place of Beauty and Meaning.* New York: Little Brown & Co., 1995.

Monaghan, Patricia. *Magical Gardens: Myth, Mulch & Marigolds.* St. Paul, Minn.: Llewellyn, 1997.

Ray, Veronica. *Zen Gardening.* New York: Berkley, 1996.

Chapter 33 • Pilgrimage

*Centuries of travel lore suggest that when we no longer know where
to turn, our real journey has begun. At that crossroads moment,
a voice calls to our pilgrim soul.*

— Phil Cousineau

There is perhaps no form of meditation with a longer pedigree than
pilgrimage, which has been a part of spiritual and religious traditions
for as long as history has been recorded, and doubtless was practiced for
many centuries, even eons, before that. At the root of pilgrimage is the idea
that some sites, or times of the year, are especially spiritually powerful,
calling forth a deepening of the soul and an opening of the heart. Often
pilgrimage destinations are physically significant: towering mountains,
ceaselessly flowing springs, thermal waters, huge fallen meteorites. Others
are significant for historical reasons: Christ's birthplace at Bethlehem and
India's Bodh Gaya, the site of the Buddha's enlightenment. Yet others are
the sites of specific annual rituals, as the summer climb up Ireland's pyra-
midal Croagh Patrick. And some sites combine all of these, as in Islam's
Ka'aba, a massive black meteorite that has for many centuries been the destination for Moslems making the *haij*, the once in a lifetime Ramadan pilgrimage to Mecca.

Pilgrimage traditions are found throughout the world, but none is as
complex and compelling as that of the walkabout practiced by the
Aboriginal peoples of Australia, often as a coming of age ritual. Their land,
they believe, is covered with invisible song lines, spiritual patterns that tie the
physical world together with the spiritual dimension called the Dreamtime.

Human connection with the Dreamtime is vital for personal, social, and ecological health. And it is important to continually reinforce this connection by walking the song lines, singing the ritually correct songs that tell how Dreamtime beings acted and spoke at each of the sites along the route. So the Australian pilgrimage tradition knits personal development, social cohesion, spiritual power, and ecological concern in one continually-enacted ritual. Few pilgrimage traditions are as rich and evolved as Australia's.

While polytheistic religions like those of Australia often have multiple pilgrimage sites, monotheistic religions tend to focus on a single site, usually related to the primary narrative. So Christian pilgrimage historically centered on the scenes of Christ's birth and death, and it was the limitation placed on such pilgrimages that gave the excuse for medieval crusades. Islam's great pilgrimage site is Mecca, scene of pre-Muslim pilgrimage as well, for the great black stone was recognized as a goddess site long before Muhammed.

Growing from the pilgrimage tradition is an awareness of life as a continuing movement toward divinity, to so-called "Pilgrim's Progress." The pilgrim's journey becomes a metaphor for life itself, with its adventures and its challenges. It was this vision that inspired the English Protestants who called themselves Pilgrims and who, at odds with the established English church, settled in great numbers in North America's New England. Their stringent Calvinism may have put a dour face on the word *pilgrim,* but the history of pilgrimage offers many alternative visions.

CONTEMPORARY USES

There are two kinds of pilgrimage in today's world. The first derives from established religions and follows patterns traced over centuries. The most famous of these is the annual Islamic pilgrimage to Mecca, but other major religions have similar traditions. Shinto believers travel to Ise, the huge wooded shrine of the sun-goddess Amaterasu; Hindu pilgrims travel to bathe in the Ganges, the watery substance of the goddess herself.

Today's Christian pilgrimage is predominantly to sites associated not with the male divinity but with the Virgin Mary, mother of Jesus. Such sites as Knock in Ireland and Lourdes in France have been recently eclipsed by Mejegordie in the former Yugoslavia, where the Virgin is said to regularly appear to a peasant woman and pilgrims in attendance on her. In the United States, too, there are a number of significant Marian pilgrimage sites, including the sanctuary church of Los Remedios in Texas.

In Ireland, Christian pilgrimage sites are dedicated to saints but incorporate pre-Christian rituals, some dedicated to Celtic gods or goddesses, others with roots in the dim pre-Celtic past of two thousand years ago and more. Such pilgrim sites include many shrines dedicated to Saint Bridget, most impressively the holy well near Kildare, which allegedly leapt forth from the ground when the saint dug there, and the spiral walk dedicated to the same saint at Liscannor near the spectacular Cliffs of Moher. Ireland's most significant site of pilgrimage is appropriately dedicated to Saint Patrick, but the pyramid-shaped mountain named Croagh Patrick was a Celtic pilgrimage site as well. The midsummer climb up the steep mountain, performed today by the Catholic faithful, has been practiced regularly for as long as two thousand years.

In addition to these traditional religious practices, there is another kind of pilgrimage today, with destinations ranging from Stonehenge and Machu Picchu to an anonymous wayside shrine in a lovely virgin grove. Awareness of the spiritual and meditative significance of pilgrimage has grown significantly in recent years, fueled in great part by literary works such as those of Jean Shinola Bolen and Scott Peck that recount deep experiences at ancient spiritual centers and on the route there. There is, in fact, such substantial interest in pilgrimage that many companies now operate tours devoted solely to the needs of the spiritual traveler.

But true pilgrimage cannot be purchased at a group rate. It is an extended meditation that leads the pilgrim to greater awareness of self and of the powers outside the self, whether those be experienced in a specific holy form or as the power of the earth itself. While it is possible to work one's way through a checklist of the world's most important power places, spending substantial amounts of time and money doing so, real pilgrimage may not result. A weekend hike near home may, in fact, have more of the meditative effects than a round the world journey.

Party pilgrims have probably been around for as long as real pilgrimage has occurred, as Chaucer attests in *The Canterbury Tales*. And who knows? Perhaps the Wife of Bath on the bus next to you, who seems only to be rattling on aimlessly, may be the truest pilgrim of the lot.

How to Begin

Pilgrimage begins, not at embarkation, but at the first moment that you imagine the journey. The very process of deciding to go forth upon a pilgrimage is part of the experience, as is the decision of where to go, the preparation for the trip, and, upon return, the reentry into your usual life. Using all these various points as meditative, centering experiences will deepen your pilgrimage's effect upon you.

In most religions, pilgrimage is a once in a lifetime experience and is often the cornerstone of a rite of passage occurring at a major life transition. Most religions, however, emerged at times when lives were shorter, travel more hazardous, and resources more limited. Today's pilgrim could conceivably take one or more lengthy journeys each year. But pilgrimage is more than sacred sightseeing. A visit to an old church in your neighborhood can be more truly meditative than a month at Stonehenge. Ultimately, pilgrimage is an internal journey, which reflects and is reflected by the outer one.

The first step in beginning a pilgrimage is to assess your reasons for considering one. Is this the right time in your life to make a commitment to the inner change that pilgrimage will bring? Are you willing to open yourself to the challenges of the experience itself? Are you willing to let go of control, to let the experience speak to you? If not, you may wish to simply travel, without weighting your trip with the expectations that it be a spiritual pilgrimage.

If, however, you decide that pilgrimage still calls to you, you face two decisions: where to go, and whether or not to travel with a tour group. To make the first decision, you must rely upon your deepest inner promptings. Just because a friend had a spiritual experience at Lourdes does not mean that it's the right destination for you. Let your heart and your dreams speak to you. Be open to even the unusual images or ideas that arise, for they may bear your personal truth. Your true pilgrimage may be to a nearby or unknown spot, or to one of the historically important power places. Remember, it is the journey as much as the destination that makes up your pilgrimage.

Once you have committed yourself to a pilgrimage, the journey has already begun. Journaling, reading, discussion with others on spiritual issues, creative arts — all these can be part of your preparation for the pilgrimage. Preparation, both inner and outer, is necessary. Just as you must take appropriate clothing for the weather, you also must decide what "baggage" you need to take with you and what to leave behind, in your emotional and spiritual life.

As part of this process, you should consider whether you should travel with others, in a tour group, or alone. Group travel, especially with strangers, has its own dynamic. While this can enhance the pilgrimage experience — which does not necessarily mean make it easier or more pleasant — it can also provide so many distractions that you fail to satisfy your soul's purpose in making the journey. Conversely, having the details of residence and transportation taken care of can free you to concentrate on your inner experience; this can be especially helpful if your pilgrimage site is located in a country that speaks a language other than your native tongue.

Once you have embarked upon your journey, you should use each moment as part of the meditative process. Continue the searching that began before your departure. Many pilgrims find that simple rituals — lighting a candle every night, writing in a journal each morning, praying or meditating in specific ways and at specific times — deepen their experience. Meditation is the art of living in the present; distancing yourself from your daily routine makes this both more difficult and easier. You may easily become absorbed in the challenges of travel itself, fretting endlessly over something you cannot control; conversely, the changed setting can serve as a reminder that, indeed, we only pass this way once.

Finally, remember that pilgrimage is not intended to be an easy path. Many early pilgrims made the journey more difficult by traveling barefoot or otherwise in discomfort. You will, assuredly, have some difficult, even miserable, moments on your journey. In the great myths of the hero's journey, there are always "guardians at the gate," threatening beings who must be dealt with before the adventure can proceed. The annoying roommate, the bus that breaks down, the disorganized guide: these may be your guardians. You can focus on them and your distress, thereby trapping yourself in the negative moment. Or you can accept their presence as a part of your pilgrim's learning, and in your struggle with them learn and grow.

REVIEW TIPS

- Assess whether this is an appropriate time for you to embark upon a pilgrimage. If it is, examine your most heartfelt dreams and desires in order to ascertain what destination calls to you.
- Begin the pilgrimage immediately by employing as many meditative techniques as appropriate: pray, read inspirational literature, do creative arts, write in your journal, record your dreams, talk with spiritual advisors. The journey begins as soon as the journey is imagined.
- Determine whether you will travel in a group, with a loved one, or alone. In making this decision, let your inner guide call to you. You may not generally enjoy traveling in a group, but the spiritual lessons that you need to learn may require it. Conversely, you may dislike being alone, especially in distant places, but you may have spiritual lessons that only loneliness will teach you.
- Before leaving, do everything you can to ensure that, during your pilgrimage, you will not be interrupted by demands from your usual life. Do not plan to return email or access voice mail while away. Pilgrimage is not travel. You cannot attend to your deepest spiritual needs while also managing the details of business.
- When on pilgrimage, set up daily meditative rituals. Even something as simple as praying before a meal can take on a deeper meaning when performed on pilgrimage.
- Find a relic, a souvenir, a reminder of your pilgrimage. Bring your pilgrimage home into your daily life this way.
- Know that the pilgrim's path is not always an easy one. You will be tested in some way; otherwise it would not be a pilgrimage. Your learning lies as much in the difficult times as in the splendid, transcendent ones.

RESOURCES

Aitken, Molly Emma. *Meeting the Buddha: On Pilgrimage in Buddhist India.* New York: Riverhead Books, 1995.

Bolen, Jean Shinola. *Crossing to Avalon: A Woman's Midlife Pilgrimage.* San Francisco: HarperSanFrancisco, 1995.

Clift, Jean Dalby, and Wallace B. Clift. *The Archetype of Pilgrimage: Outer Action with Inner Meaning.* Mahwah, N.J.: Paulist Press, 1996.

Coleman, Simon, and John Elsner. *Pilgrimage: Past and Present in the World Religions.* Cambridge, Mass.: Harvard University Press, 1997.

Cousineau, Phil. *The Art of Pilgrimage: A Seeker's Guide to Making Travel Sacred.* Berkeley, Calif.: Conari Press, 1998.

Franck, Frederick. *Fingers Pointing Towards the Sacred: A Twentieth Century Pilgrimage on the Eastern and Western Way.* Junction City, Ore.: Beacon Point Press, 1994.

Jarow, Rick. *In Search of the Sacred: A Pilgrimage to Holy Places.* Wheaton, Ill.: Theosophical Publishing House, 1986.

Justice, Christopher. *Dying the Good Death: The Pilgrimage to Die in India's Holy City.* Albany, N.Y.: State University of New York Press, 1997.

Mitchell, John Hanson. *Walking Towards Walden: A Pilgrimage in Search of Place.* Portland, Ore.: Perseus Press, 1995.

Nolan, Mary Lee, and Sidney Nolan. *Christian Pilgrimage in Modern Western Europe.* Chaptel Hill, N.C.: University of North Carolina Press, 1992.

Peck, M. Scott. *In Search of Stones: A Pilgrimage of Faith, Reason, and Discovery.* New York: Hyperion, 1995.

Peters, F. E. *The Haij: The Muslim Pilgrimage to Mecca and the Holy Places.* Princeton, N.J.: Princeton University Press, 1996.

Robinson, Martin. *Sacred Places, Pilgrim Paths: An Anthology of Pilgrimage.* New York: HarperCollins, 1997.

Rodgers, Michael, and Marcus Losak. *Glendalough: A Celtic Pilgrimage.* Harrisburg, Pa.: Morehouse Publishing Company, 1997.

U.S. Catholic Conference Staff. *Catholic Shrines and Places of Pilgrimage in the United States.* U.S. Catholic Conference, 1994.

Vest, Douglas. *On Pilgrimage.* Boston, Mass.: Cowley Publications, 1998.

Wolfe, Michael, ed. *One Thousand Roads to Mecca: Ten Centuries of Travellers Writing about the Muslim Pilgrimage.* New York: Grove/Atlantic, 1997.

www.luckymojo.com/sacredlandindex.html

Chapter 34 • Nature

If all the beasts were gone, we would die from a great loneliness of spirit, for whatever happens to the beast, happens to us all. All things are connected. Whatever befalls the earth, befalls the children of the earth.
— Chief Seattle

The tradition of earth-based spirituality, which was developed by indigenous cultures around the world, goes back more than twenty thousand years. The early native hunters would start each day reading the sky and weather in order to judge how best to go about their lives of hunting, gathering, and traveling. The shamans of the indigenous traditions carefully studied their natural environment for information to use in their healing. They listened to the voice of the earth. Today if you listen to the voice of the earth you may be locked up in a mental institution because this animistic vision of the world is opposed by both Judeo-Christian doctrine and scientific objectivity.

Twenty-five hundred years ago Hippocrates wrote in the treatise *Airs, Waters, Places* that we must study the environment of the patient in order to grasp the totality of his or her medical problem. He believed that treatment of the inner conditions requires attention to the outer. St. Francis of Assisi introduced the Christian world to the idea that wild creatures are part of the spiritual whole of the world, and that mind and nature are inseparable.

The earth-based religion of India, Hinduism, reconciles the life-giving and life-destroying forces of nature, in contrast to Western religious traditions that cast the natural forces in the roles of good and evil. The spirit of India grows out of nature; the Western spirit is opposed to nature, although this is changing. The Buddha was guided and inspired by nature, so it was under a tree — with his hand on the earth to ground himself as he faced temptations — that he attained liberation. It was in a deer park that he gave his first sermon.

The Buddhist tradition includes the concepts of interbeing and dependent co-arising. These ideas suggest that we are connected, that we are made of the same stuff that animals and plants are made of. These teachings fill us with a strong sense of association with other beings and with the planet as a whole. They give us a sense of belonging.

Engaged Buddhism works to find ways to create harmony and balance in the external world. Instead of analyzing separate factors, the vision of interdependence sees that no constituent element can be understood in isolation. It is similar to the concept of deep ecology, which recognizes the intricate relationship of mutual causality between us and the rest of the world. It acknowledges that all beings and nonliving forms on the planet sustain each other; the spotted owl and I are one. In order to be fully human, we need a connection to the natural world. We need to open our senses and awareness to that natural world and experience the reality of the seasons and the cycles of nature.

CONTEMPORARY USES

After centuries of viewing the land as lifeless and inert, today there are environmental ministries in Christian churches that are discussing planetary stewardship and creation spirituality. A new "earth and spirit" movement is exploring the possibility of a religiously based love for living things. Until recently, we in the West have repressed our empathy with nature; we have suffered a numbing of our awareness of the natural world until, as famed psychoanalyst Sigmund Freud wrote, "our ego-feeling is only a shrunken residue of a much more inclusive, indeed an all-embracing, feeling which corresponded to a more intimate bond between the ego and the world about it." The new field of ecopsychology may embody a growing refusal to settle for that "shrunken residue."

Environmental philosophers and ecopsychologists draw upon the Gaia hypothesis developed by James Lovelock and Lynn Margulis. These scientists postulated that the biota, oceans, atmosphere, and soils are a self-regulating system that plays an active role in preserving the conditions that guarantee the survival of life on Earth. The word *Gaia* is the name of the ancient Greek Earth Mother goddess. Perhaps the use of the mythic name Gaia is responsible for the fact that this hypothesis has been adopted by quasi-mystical ecofeminists and New Age visionaries. Most proponents, however, are members of the mainstream Western biomedical-scientific community that acknowledges the self-regulating nature of the planet in which ecological interdependence bonds all living things genetically and behaviorally to the biosphere.

Most of us start our day by reading a newspaper, watching the news on television, or listening to the radio report on traffic conditions. According to Joseph Meeker, author of *Minding the Earth,* "A morning that begins with numbers, words, or machines is likely to turn into a day filled with the same things. When a scanning of sky, trees, and birds begins the day, it could still turn out to be dominated by words and machines, but at least there would be a natural perspective to provide the larger context. A day that starts with a recognition of living processes can't be all bad." This quote points to the feeling of alienation that results when one ignores the more than human world.

Where does the psyche stop and matter begin? For Freud the deepest levels of the psyche merge with the biological body, and for Freud's colleague, Carl Jung, the deepest levels of the psyche merge with the physical stuff of the world. So an individual's pilgrimage to seek harmony with his or her own deepest self is not only a trip to innerspace but also a journey to the world "out there." The deepest self cannot be confined to "in here."

There is great uncertainty about how and where to make the boundary between self and not-self. We do distinguish between ourselves and our environment, however, it may be no coincidence that living in a chaotic world seems to cause distress and discomfort to the person. *Ecopsychology* is the name used for this synthesis of mind and nature. Ecopsychology proceeds from the assumption that the psyche is bonded to the earth. It suggests that our tendency to abuse the planet has a relationship to our collective state of mind and soul and that, if we are to revision the world, we must relearn the *genius loci,* the spirit of the place. This means to learn to sense that the divine in nature is also the divine within us. As poet Henry David Thoreau advised, "Read not the times, read the Eternities."

How to Begin

Go out of doors. Even if you live in a city, you can find some plants, animals, and sky to enjoy. Take a slow, mindful stroll or find a place to sit quietly and feel that diffuse, open, sensitive quality of awareness that occurs when you are outside. If it is a pleasant day and you are in a very beautiful, natural setting so much the better. Spending time in a natural environment can nurture your ability to recognize your connection to all of creation.

Natural settings often provoke peak experiences. And one of the hallmarks of a peak experience is a sense of belonging. As we begin to develop our sense of communion with the natural world, we grow to cherish nature. We find ourselves making visits to certain spots, letting the birdsong fill our mind, or feeling drawn to observe the daily progress of a flower coming out of its bud.

Cosmic Ceremonies

Your nature meditation may honor either place or time. On this planet there are certain sacred places where we can align ourselves with its primordial energies. Often these places are sites of ancient temples. Sometimes the places are famous for their healing powers; sometimes they are unknown. Find a place of your own that feels quiet and spacious where you can go to meditate.

There are also special times for nature meditations that connect you with the cosmic cycles of the planet. A meditation time may honor the turning of the planet and the circling of the moon, such as watching a sunrise or a moonrise. The sun is a symbol for meditation in ancient Yogic and Buddhist traditions. As the giver of life it is usually either the divinity itself or a symbol of the divine. Even in the Christian world, the sun is a favorite allegory for Christ.

Noticing the moon and the stars in their various cycles is another splendid way to gain a meditative perspective. Sufi teacher Pir Vilayat Khan says the nighttime is a metaphor for the meditative mind. Just as we can only see the stars at night, we can only meditate and see more deeply when the light of busy thoughts is quieted and dimmed.

Throughout human history, many people have discovered or created ceremonies of cosmic celebration, especially at the solstices and equinoxes. Marking the longest and shortest days of this year and the two times when day and night are equal, the solstices and equinoxes were celebrated in pre-Christian Europe as natural seasonal markers. The midpoints between these four holidays were celebrated as well.

Finding a Meditation Site

You may be lucky enough to find a spot by a river, lake, or ocean where you can meditate. Water, the source of life, plays an important part in the allegories of both Christian and Eastern traditions, and is a favorite symbol for the unconscious in dream interpretation. Or you may go deep into the bowels of the earth in a cave and find your Eleusinian mysteries there in the tradition of the ancient Greek mystery school.

But while the Eastern mind seeks to sink down into the soul, the Western mind seeks to be lifted up into spirit. Mountains are spiritually as well as geographically high places. Dolores LaChapelle, author of *Sacred Land, Sacred Sex,* states that many of the major spiritual traditions of the world were founded on a mountaintop. If you have the strength and skill to climb a mountain you can combine your meditation with the glorious feeling of reaching the summit.

If you are going alone into nature to seek a meditation site, you should employ common sense to ensure your safety. To begin, simply take a walk in a park or wilderness area. If you can, make your own trail. Walking slowly and mindfully, allow your attention to dwell on each step and each sensation, moment by moment. Drop the past and the future, insofar as it is safe to do so without getting lost. Enjoy the way that you respond to the inner and outer ecology, the inner and outer wilderness.

There are many guides and teachers now who take individuals or groups of people into the wilderness for vision quests, which are modeled on the practices of the indigenous people of North America and the walkabouts of Australian Aborigines. Some of the trips are by kayak, some include hiking, while others emphasize remaining in one place. Drawing on their knowledge of the local terrain, these guides have the skill to protect you from the various hazards of being in the wilderness. The guides can also protect you from the psychological hazards of the vision quest that can arise during periods of solitude and fasting. It can be a profoundly transformational experience, one that gives you a whole new perspective on life.

As author Joseph Meeker writes, "We respond to wilderness because it has its counterpart within us. Wilderness is not only a place, it is a state of being. It is a state characterized by freedom, self-organization, extravagant variety, complex order, grandness of scale, continual change, orientation in time, and beauty."

THE SHAMBHALA WARRIORS: A PROPHECY

While nature can help you heal yourself, it can also help you develop the wisdom and strength you need to make the world a better place. Joanna Macy, author of *World As Lover, World As Self*, tells a story that arose in Tibetan Buddhism over twelve centuries ago about the coming of the kingdom of Shambhala, which exists only in the human heart

The story tells of a time when life is in great danger and the kingdom of Shambhala begins to emerge in the hearts and minds of the Shambhala warriors. The warriors go into the territory of the destructive forces to dismantle their weapons. The warriors know that the weapons were made by human minds and can be unmade by other human minds. The battleground is the arena of human decisions, values, and attitudes.

The warriors train in the use of two weapons. These weapons are compassion and insight. Compassion gives you the power to act as you face the pain of the world. Insight gives you the wisdom to know that the conflict is within every heart, to know that we are all connected. These two weapons are gifts for us to claim now as we train to become Shambhala warriors in the struggle to heal the world.

In hatha yoga the spirit of the Shambhala warrior is embodied in the warrior pose. In this pose, you extend your arms to each side, turn one foot out 90 degrees, and bend that knee in a 90-degree lunge (see chapter 6, Yoga Asanas). It is a powerful pose modeled on a peaceful, not a violent, warrior. In order to combine the physical energy of this vigorous hatha yoga pose with a powerful healing image, imagine that you are training to be a Shambhala warrior. As you hold the pose, turn your palms up and imagine that your left hand holds compassion and your right hand holds insight. These are the weapons and the gifts of the peaceful warrior. You can use them to bring the world into your heart and cultivate your intention to serve the needs of the world.

REVIEW TIPS

- Take a walk out of doors for thirty minutes.
- Walk slowly. You might walk only a hundred yards.
- As you walk, become aware of all the life around you.
- When you notice something in nature, let your attention go out to it.
- Get a sense of your own awareness and the world around you simultaneously.
- Let yourself know what the earth is like.
- Get close to the inner life of the beings you meet.
- Let yourself sense when it is time to move on.

RESOURCES

Berman, Morris. *Coming to Our Senses.* New York: Bantam, 1990.

Eshana. "Earth Yoga." *The Web of Life Global Newsletter of the Council of All Beings,* (Linsmore, Australia) 4 (October 1997).

Jung, C. G. *Psychology and the East.* Bollingen Series XX. Princeton, N.J.: Princeton University Press, 1978.

LaChapelle, Dolores. *Sacred Land, Sacred Sex.* Skyland, N.Y.: Kivaki Press, 1992.

Macy, Joanna. *World As Lover, World As Self.* Berkeley, Calif.: Parallax Press, 1991.

Meeker, Joseph. *Minding the Earth.* Alameda, Calif.: Latham Foundation, 1987.

Roszak, Theodore, Mary E. Gomes, and Allen D. Kanner, eds. *Ecopsychology: Restoring the Earth, Healing the Mind.* San Francisco: Sierra Club Books, 1995.

Snyder, Gary. *The Practice of the Wild.* San Francisco: North Point Press, 1990.

Spretnak, Charlene. *States of Grace.* San Francisco: HarperSanFrancisco, 1991.

Chapter 35 • Meditations for Pain and Grief

Those who know their pain and their grief most intimately seem to be the lightest and most healed of the beings we have met.

— Stephen Levine

Throughout the ages, the goal of most spiritual traditions has been the alleviation of human suffering. The word *patience* is derived from the word *suffering*. Suffering is messy and raw. Suffering hurts the heart and the body. The people who are adept at compassionately sharing in our suffering are our spiritual leaders. In fact, it is out of their own suffering that their compassion was born. The deepest forms of meditation have occurred in the face of failure, suffering, and loss. The prayers and meditations of altruistic and visionary saints and sages include wishes for the peace, happiness, and well-being of others. But hard times keep coming around no matter what we do.

Pain can be a suffering in the physical body or it can be a suffering in the mind. Grief is a suffering in the mind, merciless, filled with loss and fear, manifesting as self-judgment. As Stephen Levine, author of *Guided Meditations, Explorations, and Healings*, writes, "Grief is the rope burns left behind when what we have held to most dearly is pulled out of reach, beyond our grasp." The bodily suffering and the mental suffering are connected.

Contemporary Uses

Much suffering is caused by resisting the original insult. Outside obstacles and impediments will continue to hinder us; but the naturally flowing river of our lives is only partly obstructed by these inevitable stumbling blocks. We tend to aggravate the problem by pushing and pulling with too much force when the situation might have righted itself without intervention. In other words, well-meaning rescuers and strategies to help oneself can often do more harm than good. This phenomenon is so well known in medicine that it has a name, iatrogenic disease, which is a physical disease caused by the cure for a prior disease.

There is a similar phenomenon in mental illness which occurs when a remedy does more harm than good. A meditative approach to mental and emotional pain has the advantage of being safe, gentle, and quiet with time for contemplative observation of the consequences of the practice. If the practice is aggravating the situation you can change it. Meditation is not just a comforting escape, it is a maker of diamonds. It is a crucible where your transformation can occur. The broken heart becomes the open heart. When you are thriving, it is easy to maintain the illusion of separateness, but when you fall, you see that the self-sufficiency you felt in success was a mirage.

Research has shown that meditation can help alleviate physical and mental pain. You must be careful, however, before you attempt to use meditation to banish pain. First make sure that the pain is not caused by a disease or injury that requires medical attention. After you have decided that you have done all that you can do with external pain-relieving measures, then it may be safe to try to release the pain with meditation. If you feel that your pain is stress related, then the practice has a lot of potential for good results. Research has shown that a ten-week program of mindfulness meditation practice caused a significant reduction in pain, negative body image, inhibition of activity because of pain, physical symptoms, mood disturbance, anxiety, and depression in ninety chronic pain patients. A comparison group of pain patients did not show significant improvement in these areas after traditional medical pain medications and therapies.

How to Begin

You do not have to go far to find suffering in your life. When you are experiencing emotional pain or when you have a physical injury, you can learn to allow your pain to become your teacher. These hard times are not the death knell of your meditation; they are a gateway to self-discovery. Although pain is unpleasant, it can serve a useful purpose.

PHYSICAL PAIN

Physical pain is a great handicap to meditation, and yet meditative practices can help to alleviate pain. Meditative approaches to pain release are particularly successful in cases where the pain is aggravated by chronic tension. Relaxation therapy can do wonders in such cases. Often the original physical pain is aggravated by protective muscle contractions, worries, anxieties, and the desire to be free of the pain; so, there the original pain and then a whole host of subsequent problems and suffering that arise in response to the pain. "Relax, and it won't hurt so much" is a folk adage that addresses this issue. Actually, there is wisdom in this adage, just as there is in many cliches and aphorisms. If you have a regular meditation practice you are likely to be much more skillful at relaxing when you need to deal with pain.

Shower of Relaxation Exercise

1. If you are experiencing any pain, try the "shower of relaxation" technique, which involves a step-by-step tensing of the entire body and a step-by-step release of tension to produce a state of relaxation. Lie down in a comfortable position and focus on your breathing. First tense your feet, making fists with your toes. Then tense your ankles, calves, and thighs. Study the tension. Hold it so tightly the muscles quiver. Continue on up your torso; then make fists with your hands and tense your arms and shoulders. Finally, tense your face. Squeeze it into a little prune, clenching your teeth. Study the tension.

2. Now imagine a shower of tension-releasing water washing over your head and down your neck, arms, torso, thighs, legs, and feet as you relax your muscles in reverse order. Study the relaxation and observe your breathing now that you are relaxed. Repeat the shower of relaxation technique at a faster pace and then again at an even quicker pace.

3. Now that you are relaxed, get comfortable and decide that you are going to spend some time using a meditative approach to pain release. This intention and mental preparation will improve the success of your practice. Then note where you feel tension or pain in your body. Imagine that the space around the tension or pain is full of liquid. This kind of image helps to soften the whole area surrounding the pain and

often alleviates suffering. Or you can imagine that your exhaled breath is blowing the pain away. Try these visualizations, and if other images come to mind that might help you, try them, too. One visualization that is often used is to imagine breath coming into the affected area as you inhale, and then imagine the pain leaving your body with your breath as you exhale.

EMOTIONAL PAIN

We all experience difficult or negative emotions from time to time. It is inevitable that we will suffer some sort of emotional pain due to anger, fear, sadness, guilt, jealousy, or grief. Or we may suffer from a combination of them all at once. If we cannot escape from the circumstances that caused the emotion, we can escape into it. As the saying goes, the only way out is through.

Denying an emotion or boxing it in often makes it worse. It becomes an old stuck pain and can cause a variety of neurotic symptoms. The first step to healing emotional pain is to stop and be present with the situation. This means that you have to see it as it is rather than denying it or rearranging it. If you are angry, afraid, jealous, or resentful then you can choose to work with the emotion. This requires maturity and courage, and it is an opportunity for real growth because negative emotions can be a vehicle for contacting our higher self.

The English word *feeling* can refer to either physical or mental experiences. This connection between mind and body also appears in the word emotion, which means "an intense mental state that arises subjectively rather than through conscious effort and is often accompanied by physiological changes; a strong feeling," according to the *American Heritage Dictionary*.

So, in order to tell if you are experiencing a thought or an emotion, look for a physical component to the sensation. If your body is responding to a thought with some kind of biochemical or physiological change, then it is probably an emotion. The physical sensations may be pleasant or unpleasant — perhaps your breath is suddenly very rapid or stops altogether in the wake of certain emotions. A gasp of surprise, a nervous laugh, or a big sigh of relief are all examples of how emotions affect the body and breath. Many of the physical elements of emotion are impossible to sense. Actually every cell of your body can respond to a strong emotion with chemical or electrical changes.

Emotions

An emotion is a combination of thought in the mind and sensation in the body. Learning to deal with difficult negative emotions can help you develop your ability to work with pain. You do not need faith of the kind defined by science fiction writer Sir Arthur C. Clarke, who said that faith is believing in something that you know is impossible. You only need to experiment with your negative emotions with a meditative attitude. To do this, you watch the emotion as it arises with a sense of detachment and dispassion. You might say to yourself, "Ah, so! Here is a negative emotion again. I remember this one."

Instead of wallowing in self-pity or developing further negative feelings by reacting to the initial emotion, you stop and watch your experience of the emotion with no particular goal for or judgment about it. Simply note what you feel the same way you note your sense experiences and thoughts during an untroubled meditation. If you have been practicing meditation regularly during the relatively stable times of your life, then when the difficulties arise you will have more skill at dealing with them. It takes consistent practice to be able to keep your equanimity in the face of an emotional onslaught, but this is a psychomotor skill that does improve with practice. In order to practice successfully you need to study and observe what is happening to you.

MEDITATING ON EMOTIONS

According to Shinzen Young, author of *How to Deal with Difficult Emotions*, there is a sequence of steps you go through when resolving negative emotions that includes four challenge levels, depending on the intensity of your emotional level and your ability to respond.

Resolving Emotions Exercise

I. First, experience the emotion and note its physical and mental aspects. Open your heart to the mind's pain and be merciful with yourself. Go gently. If you can simply experience the emotion without adding to it you will be making great progress. For the most part, when people have a difficult emotion they aggravate it by reacting with self-pity and fear. Simply see the emotion as it is and let it be. Do not try to make it go away. This both requires and creates equanimity, which is a paradox that occurs often in mind-body training when the skill you wish to cultivate is also required in order to participate in the practice.

2. Second, practice letting go of any temptation to interfere. This is letting go with a sigh. This is "not doing" and it leads to equanimity, which means a radical noninterference with the natural flow of thought and feeling. At first, however, it may be quite a roller-coaster ride as the emotion runs its course. Just let it flow without trying to stop it. Forgive yourself. At times you may gasp for air, but this process will teach you that the best way out of an emotional state is to go right through it. If you must "do" something, then send compassion to yourself.

Practicing meditation during times when you are not overwhelmed gives you a greater capacity for equanimity in times of crisis. Your regular practice becomes a resource. It is like putting money in the bank. The meditative approach to life requires only that you be willing to experience your life, as it is, moment by moment.

3. Third, after you have watched the emotional drama for a while you will discover that it changes. Naturally, and with no effort on your part, it will pass away. It may arise again. But it will once again disappear. If you pay attention to the impermanence of the emotion, you will find that its power to hurt you begins to dissolve. You will still suffer fear, sadness, or other negative emotions, but they will have a tendency to melt away. In contrast to physical injuries, which require a doctor's care to heal, your emotions can be experienced as an aspect of your nature.

4. The advanced spiritual person can transform negativity into love. However, you cannot take a negative emotion and change it directly into a positive one. First you must transform the negativity into a neutral energy. For instance, when you experience grief as a kind of "energy" you see that energy can be positive as well as negative and can be transformed by compassion. A saint or sage can go one step further and change hate directly into love.

Your pain may be telling you that you need to take action or do something differently. Sometimes you need to change your behavior to prevent harming yourself or others. Using meditation to work with your pain can lead to a better understanding of its cause, its nature, and its resolution.

MEDITATING WITH SOMEONE WHO IS DYING

Eventually, we all have to face death, whether our own or that of someone we love. Meditation can help you prepare for and cope with that moment when it arrives. In his book, *A Year to Live*, Stephen Levine describes how the contemplation of death can lead to a greater appreciation of life. The technique of meditating on your own death in order to understand impermanence has been used by many teachers as part of the training for developing an attentive heart.

All the work you have done to be capable of being present with pain and fear and grief will give you the strength to remain aware and sensitive when you are sitting with someone who is dying. This is a superb opportunity to deepen your own practice; in fact many people work with dying patients in part for their own spiritual growth.

In order to attend the dying, you must be accepting and compassionate and ready to listen with an open heart. You are not there to convert them or preach to them. You are there simply to provide comfort and support.

To expand your capacity for acceptance and compassion practice this soft-belly meditation by Stephen Levine:

Taking a few deep breaths, feel the body you breathe in,
Feel the body expanding and contracting with each breath.
Focus on the rising and falling of the abdomen.
Let awareness receive the beginning, middle, and end of each
     inbreath, of each outbreath expanding and contracting the
     belly.
Note the constantly changing flow of sensation in each inhala-
     tion, in each exhalation.
And begin to soften all around these sensations.
Let the breath breathe itself in a softening belly.
Soften the belly to receive the breath, to receive sensation, to
     experience life in the body.
Soften the muscles that have held the fear for so long.
Soften the tissue, the blood vessels, the flesh.
Letting go of the holding of a lifetime.
Letting go into soft belly, merciful belly.
Soften the grief, the distrust, the anger held so hard in the belly.
Levels and levels of softening, levels and levels of letting go.

Moment to moment allow each breath its full expression in soft belly.

Let go of the hardness. Let it float in something softer and kinder.

Let thoughts come and let them go, floating like bubbles in the spaciousness of soft belly.

Holding to nothing, softening, softening.

Let the healing in.

Let the pain go.

Have mercy on yourself, soften the belly, open the passageway to the heart.

In soft belly is the vast spaciousness in which to heal, in which to discover our unbounded nature.

Letting go into the softness, fear floats in the gentle vastness we call the heart.

Soft belly is the practice that accompanies us throughout the day and finds us at day's end still alive and well.

Meditating When Someone Criticizes You

Suppose your boss or spouse or another family member is berating you, reading you the riot act, or criticizing you. Usually this causes a lot of discomfort. Your adrenaline level probably goes up, your blood pressure may rise, and other symptoms of distress may appear. These symptoms can include rapid breathing, shallow breathing, tension in the shoulders, and tightness in the gut.

In the moment, you can create an emotional distance from your critic by directing your attention to the way his or her voice rises and falls or the phrasing of the sound, rather than the meaning of the words. Use your meditation skills to pay attention to only one thing at a time. Other aspects of the voice may also be interesting to use as a focus for your attention. Perhaps the voice reminds you of a yowling cat or an alligator thrashing in the mud. It may be useful to focus on humorous images such as these in order to protect yourself from having a knee-jerk response to the criticism.

Just as the sense of vision dominates the auditory sense, mental activity often draws our attention from our hearing. If you need to pretend that you are listening in order to practice your focused awareness, do so while you keep an attentive expression on your face. You may even find yourself laughing at the cosmic joke of being criticized by a person who is probably under the influence of irrational anger. If your laugh comes from a deep authentic place, it is a far more useful and wholesome response than to yell abusive or defensive things back at your critic. Accepting the fact of the verbal abuse is healthier than ignoring it because trying to ignore someone who is being offensive to you can cause you to repress your irritation and suppress your instinct to defend yourself. You sublimate or postpone your feelings and, instead of getting angry, you get ulcers.

In China anger is considered to be a remedy for depression because anger has more energy than depression. Humor is considered to be the remedy for anger. How you get from anger to humor is a personal journey that benefits form the wisdom of meditation. One goal of meditation is surely to prevent suffering and to increase happiness. This meditation practice is intended to prevent suffering when others are hostile and verbally abusive. As the children's rhyme says, "Sticks and stones may break my bones, but words can never harm me." Folk wisdom also appears in the children's reply to a taunt: "I'm rubber and you're glue, whatever you say bounces off of me and sticks to you."

REVIEW TIPS

Depression can be frightening and disorienting. You seem to feel that you have no way out. At this point it may be useful to do nothing. This is the essential practice of meditation.

- When your back is against the wall simply stop and practice the basic practice of quieting your mind of all thoughts.
- Do not judge the depression as bad or praise any other fantasies about healing yourself as good.
- Simply observe what is and be quiet with it.
- Do not give in to your depression.
- Let yourself learn from the process of maintaining stillness.
- Do not run away from your feelings. If you run from the feelings they may grow stronger. If you try to fit your emotions into a framework of belief or moral judgement you may grow more guilty.

You can do as Buddha did and look at things as they are. Philip Martin, psychotherapist and Buddhist scholar, writes in this book, *The Zen Path through Depression*, "We can look compassionately at what is happening to us in depression. We can examine ourselves without running, without fighting, without preconceptions, before any thought of a solution." In this self-awareness there may appear a glimmer of release or relief. It is like grace. It is like the breeze coming in through a window. All you can do is open the window, you cannot cause the breeze to blow or the healing to flow.

RESOURCES

Adair, Margo. *Working Inside Out: Tools for Change: Applied Meditation for Intuitive Problem Solving.* Berkeley, Calif.: Wingbow Press, 1986.

Kabat-Zinn, J., L. Lipworth, and R. Burney. "The Clinical Use of Mindfulness Meditation for the Self-Regulation of Chronic Pain." *Journal of Behavioral Medicine*, vol. 8 (June 1985): 163–190.

Levine, Stephen. *A Year to Live: How to Live This Year As If It Were Your Last.* New York: Bell Tower, 1997.

Levine, Stephen. *Guided Meditations, Explorations, and Healings.* New York: Anchor Books/Doubleday, 1991.

Martin, Philip. *The Zen Path through Depression.* San Francisco: HarperSanFrancisco, 1999.

Macy, Joanna. *World As Lover, World As Self.* Berkeley, Calif.: Parallax Press, 1991.

Palmer, Parker J. "Thirteen Ways of Looking at Community." *Inner Edge*, vol. 1, no. 3 (August/September 1998): 5–7.

Thanas, Katherine. "Hearing the Voice of the Body." In *Being Bodies.* Boston, Mass.: Shambhala, 1997.

Young, Shinzen. *How to Deal with Difficult Emotions.* Boulder, Colo.: Sounds True, 1998. Audiotape.

Chapter 36 • Listening

Music, the perfume of hearing, probably began as a religious act,
to arouse groups of people.

— Diane Ackerman

The Gospel of St. John begins, "In the beginning was the word . . ."
Before that there was silence. Is it possible that in ancient cultures the
sense of embodiment, of the union of spirit and body, was so natural that
the experience of the void or silence was not threatening? Indigenous cultures today often have a different relationship to silence than so-called
advanced cultures. They are comfortable with long silences. We are not. Is
it because we are running from silence and from genuine somatic experience? Does this lay bare the nature of our culture? Is most of the talk you
hear during the day a substitute for real embodiment and groundedness? Is
it true that we spend much time and effort trying to fill or to mark the
emptiness we feel inside?

Hearing is one of the senses that requires no effort. You do not have
to reach out with your ears to touch something. You do not have to open
your ears. Your ears are always ready to receive any sounds that occur
around you. What we call sound is a series of pressure waves, which are
caused by an initial physical action that radiate out through air and water.
The initial movement can be something like a flutist's breath hitting the lip
of the flute or a woodpecker's beak striking a tree. This shakes the nearby
air molecules and the molecules next to them begin trembling as the sound
wave moves through the air. Then the sound waves hit the eardrum, which

responds to the waves by vibrating like a drum, and the vibration is transferred to three bones called the hammer, the anvil, and the stirrup, which are the smallest bones in the body. The vibration is then transmitted to the fluid-filled cochlea of the inner ear, which has nerve cells that relay the message to the brain, allowing the sense of hearing to bring information to consciousness.

Hearing, like the other senses, can be used to become more aware of oneself as a living being. A person who is truly grounded in his or her body does not need the usual trappings of accomplishment and success to feel that his or her existence is validated. For the healthy person, one who is embodied and balanced, life has its own meaning and primary satisfaction. Most of the people in the West do not have this experience of innate primary satisfaction from simple sense awareness, so they turn to the secondary satisfactions of addictions, busyness, or even climbing the ladder of success.

Having a sense of hearing, like other senses, means that we are sentient (from Latin *sentire*, "to feel"). Diane Ackerman, poet, essayist, and naturalist with a Ph.D. from Cornell University, writes that absurdity means "not being able to hear" in the Arabic language. "A 'surd' is a mathematical impossibility, the core for the word 'absurdity,' which we get from the Latin *surdus*, 'deaf or mute,' which is a translation from the Arabic *jadr asamm*, a 'deaf root,' which in turn is a translation from the Greek *alogos*, 'speechless or irrational.' The assumption hidden in this etymological nest is that the world will still make sense to a person who is blind or armless or minus a nose. But if you lose your sense of hearing, a crucial thread dissolves and you lose track of life's logic."

Contemporary Uses

Music can be used during meditation to enhance relaxation and exalt the spirit. Every religion has its own sounds, chants, hymns, and liturgies that are intended to cause a meditative response, whether the listener understands the words or not. Hymns such as "Amazing Grace" seem to enlarge one's spirit. Although it started out as a Christian hymn written by the captain of a slave ship who turned his ship around after he experienced a religious conversion, this gospel song is often performed by popular and gospel singers alike. The chants of the Benedictine Monks from Spain and the songs of Hildegard of Bingen have become bestselling CDs in the United States recently. We can understand the meaning of music without knowing the language of notes and rhythms.

Practicing yoga or meditation while listening to appropriate music can enhance the physical experience, just as dancing, walking, or exercising to music is generally more pleasant. The music is a prop, and, like all other props, it can help you achieve the desired state, but it can also become addictive and it can be repressive if it prevents you from practicing in a rhythm that is natural to you. If you use music as an aid to your meditation, then it might be good to occasionally try it without music in order to explore the difference.

Today the air is filled with sound blaring from speakers in houses, cars, elevators, offices, and concert halls. The decibel levels in most cities are so high they are a health hazard, and people run the risk of hearing loss because of exposure to sounds such as loud jet engines, gunshots, or high-volume rock music. We are so overexposed to sound that we have lost our sensitivity, and sometimes our tolerance, for quiet.

How to Begin

As with most meditative practices, the first step is to stop and clarify your intention to connect your inner and outer worlds. Begin by relaxing and focusing on your breath. In order to relax, ensure that you are safe and make yourself comfortable. Then allow your breathing to become naturally smooth and even. In order to accomplish this, you can simply count to four while you inhale and count to four while you exhale. This will bring your breathing rhythm into a state of balance. Let the whole process be easy, gentle, and comfortable.

When you are ready, direct your attention to the symphony of sound that is around you. If the sounds are harsh, loud, or unpleasant, you may wish to postpone the listening meditation. However, if you pay attention to those sounds with a nonjudgmental attitude you may find that they are not really bad. Sometimes it is your own reaction to them that causes stress.

If the sounds are soothing and pleasant, close your eyes, allow your thoughts to settle. When you close your eyes you can hear better.

LISTEN TO THE SMALL SOUNDS

If you are in a quiet place, you may enjoy directing your attention to the sounds at the limit of audibility. You may hear the blood coursing through your ears or the sound of your heart beating. Many people hear whistling or hissing noises that are usually obscured. Listen to these small sounds and any other faint noises in the pauses between the louder sounds. Listen to the silences. Just as directing your attention to the clear sky reminds you of your clear mind, directing your attention to the silence helps to quiet your mind. Meditation quiets the mind for the purpose of knowing those small things that are usually hidden by the louder thoughts.

REVIEW TIPS

Practice listening to a piece of music that inspires you to a quality of mind that you feel is desirable. This could be relatively quiet or energetic depending on your needs for peace or vitality. In order to practice the art of listening to music, find an undisturbed place to play the piece on a stereo or perhaps listen in a concert hall.

- Sit and make yourself as comfortable as you can.
- Relax your eyes, jaw, and neck.
- Allow your breathing to be soft, slow, and deep.
- Listen with your whole self.
- Come back to the sound when your attention wanders.
- Any visual or emotional experiences which may arise can be noted and then allowed to pass away.
- Keep going back to the music.

Alladin Mathieu, musician, author, teacher, and Sufi choir director describes the practice this way: "Nothing is needed except awareness and your desire to let the music be your whole reality. With the regularity of a heart beat, keep returning to the sound and the sound alone. Be starved for it — let it be starved for you."

RESOURCES

Ackerman, Diane. *A Natural History of the Senses.* New York: Vintage Books, 1991.

Berman, Morris. *Coming to Our Senses.* New York: Bantam, 1989.

Hudson, John. *Instant Meditation for Stress Relief.* London: Lorenz Books, Anness Publications, 1996.

Mathieu, W. A. *The Listening Book: Discovering Your Own Music.* Boston, Mass.: Shambhala, 1991.

Pfister T., C. Berrol, and C. Caplan. "Effects of Music on Exercise and Perceived Symptoms in Patients with Chronic Obstructive Pulmonary Disease." *Journal of Cardiopulmonary Rehabilitation,* vol. 18 (May 1998): 228–232.

Stirling, John, ed. *The Bible: Authorized Version.* London: The British & Foreign Bible Society, 1954.

part 9
active imagination

Introduction • Active Imagination

What you believe is what you get. If a person has been introduced in some external way to a particular form that he is supposed to look for, then the spontaneous experiences become limited by those previous beliefs. That is why we eschew all spiritual belief systems.

— Jack Rosenberg

Renowned psychologist Carl Jung, founder of analytical psychology, first used the term "active imagination" in 1935 to describe a technique he had been experimenting with for at least fifteen years. Based on a practice used by alchemists of ancient Egypt and medieval Europe, it is similar to techniques for hearing the still small voice within that are used in many traditions. Developed as a method for integrating the many aspects of the psyche, this method is based on the natural healing function of the imagination.

Edward F. Edinger, a founding member of the Carl G. Jung Foundation for Analytical Psychology in New York and the author of many books on Jungian psychology, describes active imagination as "a process in which the imagination and the images it throws up are experienced as something separate from the ego — a 'thou' or an 'other' — to which the ego can relate and with which the ego can have a dialogue."

In active imagination it is important to know *to whom* one is speaking, and not take every voice as uttering the inspired words of the Holy Ghost! Most of the inner figures have positive and negative sides and they may interrupt one another. Remember to avoid thinking of good and evil as absolute opposites.

Authentic active imagination typically includes a mixture of several

313

elements. There are the conventional viewpoints of the ego and also genuine autonomous expressions of the deeper layers of the unconscious. As Edinger writes, the process of using active imagination as a tool to gain access to these deeper layers of the psyche "requires the alert, active participation of consciousness which leads to real dialogue and not just a passive acceptance of whatever the unconscious says."

Active imagination is a waking way of accessing the unconscious. This can be done in several ways such as dialogues with self, images, or movement. These ways of active imagination are described in further detail in their sections on the following pages. Active imagination is a process in which the individual becomes aware of a silent observer or witness consciousness in the mind which is separate from the chattering, moving, image-making portion of the consciousness. You practice active imagination by allowing your attention to direct itself toward the screen of the upwelling of words, images, or sensations. The idea of Jung was that the conscious mind looks on, participating but not directing, while the unconscious is allowed to speak or draw or move in whatever way it likes. The language of the unconscious may be biblical or it may be inconsistent.

Although Jung used this technique, he did not invent it. If anything, he rediscovered it, for it is one of the oldest forms of meditation. It has been used since the dawn of history as a way of learning to know God, the Buddha Mind, or the gods.

The method may be strictly verbal or include forms of dance, painting, sculpting, drama, or music, as one expressive form leads to another. This process facilitates communication between different parts of the psyche; and it serves to mediate between opposites and resolve paradoxes. This symbolic play allows the imagination to soar. But it also is serious work that can help a person recover from overwhelming experiences.

RESOURCES

Edinger, Edward F. *Ego and Archetype: Individuation and the Religious Function of the Psyche.* Boston, Mass.: Shambhala, 1992.

Chapter 37 • Dialogues with Self

We know that the mask of the unconscious is not rigid —
it reflects the fact we turn towards it.
Hostility lends it a threatening aspect, friendliness softens its features.
— Carl G. Jung

Active imagination is a technique for creating wholeness and a method for exploring the unknown. While Eastern methods of meditation may try to create a clear mind by obliterating its psychological contents, active imagination allows these contents to come forth and engage in an imaginary dialogue whose purpose is to integrate the various parts of the psyche into a unified whole.

The dialogue with self assumes that there is a portion of the mind that is a clear mind, a witness consciousness, an observer. To practice a dialogue with self, it is first necessary to direct your awareness to this clear, quiet mind. This will require a few moments of relaxation. It requires a quiet and comfortable posture, as in any form of meditation. Then it requires that you direct your attention to some question or image for a starting place. An image from a recent dream is often used. It is not a good idea to use the image of your spouse or significant other because the emotional involvement is too intense and complicated.

While a passive fantasy such as a daydream usually occurs sponta-neously, in active imagination you consciously and intentionally engage in a dialogue with the symbols or images that appear. When you turn your attention toward the unconscious with an expectation of dialogue, you are better prepared to reflect on and evaluate the experience. Sooner or later, you will encounter feelings that you do not approve of. Just remember, the only way out is through, and you will learn more by exploring the negative feelings than by avoiding them.

Jung used the term *individuation,* meaning to make oneself whole, to describe the process of integrating the levels of the mind. He speculated that this is the same as the enlightenment of Eastern traditions such as Buddhism or Yoga. Active imagination can promote the development of this desired state of self-realization. This process includes the acknowledgment of the dark side of the psyche, which Jung called the shadow. Individuation can be described as the surrender of who you think you are to the true self. This encounter with the higher self is essentially a mystical experience.

CONTEMPORARY USES

Reading of tea leaves, divinations with cards, and other kinds of oracular prophecy are types of active imagination because the intention of the medium or mystic is to gain knowledge that is not available through ordinary rational means.

Counselors and therapists often ask the client a question which begins a dialogue with self. This is not guided imagery because there is no script. The dialogue occurs within the mind of one individual who has to allow one part of their mind to have a conversation with another part of their mind or body. For example, a client may have a back pain. The counselor suggests that the patient ask their back "What do you want from me?" The answer is often a request to change one's lifestyle and protect the back from stress. For example, the client may actually hear a voice saying something like, "I want you to take it easy."

HOW TO BEGIN

When engaging in a dialogue with the inner self, the conscious mind has the job of focusing your attention and keeping the object of the fantasy from disappearing. In the dialogue it is the "I" who observes, asks questions, and listens to the images or symbols. While there is no recipe for putting this into practice, there are some guidelines that can help you to invite the image to appear and to come to terms with its message.

Active Imagination Exercise

1. Begin by being silent. In order to hear the voice of the inner self, the mind must learn to be silent. It is absolutely necessary to reach this condition of silence before any technique of active imagination can begin to work. Marie-Louise von Franz, author of *Alchemical Active Imagination*, calls this "emptying the ego mind." This process is similar in many forms of meditation and involves suspending the chatter of the mind. In this state of mental silence, one simply lets things happen in what is known as the witness consciousness.

2. After you have quieted your mind, you invite an image to appear or you may decide to use an image from a dream, a fantasy, or your life. If you are obsessed by a nagging worry or thought, select an image that represents that thought. Another method for finding an image is to visualize yourself walking along a forest path, a beach, or some other setting, and describe the scene in great detail. You may have a setting of your own that is provocative. Suggest to yourself that you are going there to meet someone or something. (It is wise to avoid using the image of your spouse or other loved ones for active imagination if you are currently feeling anger toward that person.) At some point an image will appear. You know when an image has arisen from the unconscious because you have a sense that "I" did not create it. You will wonder where it came from. You need to relinquish control over it and invite the image to move or speak on its own.

3. Enter into a dialogue with the image. You need to keep the image or the voice from changing while you talk with it. If you allow your attention to digress and wander off the chosen image, then you are not engaged in active imagination. You need to stick with the original image. This process requires you to balance right brain and left brain functions because emotional feelings and analytical thoughts both have a role to play. Avoid controlling the image, but at the same time do not worry if it seems that you are making it up.

4. Now bring your analytical mind to bear in order to judge the value of the information you receive from the image. As you do, do not

abdicate your ethical standards; the unconscious is amoral so it may present dangerous and destructive attitudes.

When the unconscious has revealed some piece of information during active imagination, it must be remembered somehow, otherwise it will slip back into the unconscious the way a dream sometimes escapes from memory. One way to remember the information is to write it down. It may be difficult to write the revealed information in ordinary language, so poetry or storytelling can be used to express the message. The message may also be expressed in a physical ritual using drama, movement, or art if that is appropriate.

Analyze the information you've received from the image with wisdom and compassion. Sometimes it is actually best not to bring images from dreams or active imagination in to analysis in too harsh a light. It may be wise to simply remain with the mystery and to reside with the image from the dream or the unconscious and allow it to communicate in its own terms. Often the information is non-verbal. For example, many people experience a sense of tightness or contraction in their solar plexus when the message is negative. They notice a sense of bouyance and expansion when the message is positive. If you are one of these people, then when you contemplate a question or an image you may be wise to notice your own kinesthetic reactions.

This is similar to the way you get information that is called a gut feeling or reaction. It is a mode of knowing the intuitive mind. It is a path of insight. It is different from the path of mechanistic, materialistic, or rational logic. However, you need to examine any information from the inner realms in the light of ordinary common sense. Believing in psychic predictions or conditions is like listening to gossip from a drunk at a party. You may learn something that you never would have learned from a sober person. But you had better check the validity of the facts with a sober mind, too. You are integrating the head and the heart. In making decisions or getting information, you need both the mind and the compassionate heart.

The way you judge the ethics of a situation from the unconscious is the same way you judge the ethics and morality of a situation in your ordinary life. The ten commandments of non-harming or the moral precepts of other religious traditions are good guidelines. They generally include non-harming, non-stealing, and non-lying.

According to Robert Johnson, author of *Inner Work: Using Dreams and Active Imagination for Personal Growth,* the four steps of active imagination are: (1) invite the unconscious, (2) dialogue and experience, (3) add the ethical element of values, and (4) make it concrete with physical ritual.

The hazards and dangers of active imagination include feelings of panic, being overwhelmed by powerful and frightening images, or being stuck. The best safeguard against these feeling states is to maintain a friendly attitude toward the inner work. If panic arises, then stop and do some yoga exercises to calm your emotions. Another hazard involves failing to bring the insights and knowledge gained from active imagination into one's ethical life. The messages of the inner self can generate wholeness, but ignoring them will maintain feelings of separation and loneliness. The advantage of dialoguing the inner self is that it does not require another person to guide you. However, it does require a certain amount of maturity and strength.

In active imagination, as in ordinary life, one may suddenly be the recipient of a very powerful, visionary spiritual experience like an awakening. Do not go looking for this, do not try to achieve it, simply remain humble and continue your inner work. These awakenings can be transformational, but they can also lead to ego inflation or even unpleasant physical symptoms, so you need to protect yourself by staying grounded. It is wonderful to see the unity of all things, but not while driving down the freeway.

REVIEW TIPS

- Empty the ego-mind.
- Imagine a pleasant setting and invite an image or figure to appear.
- Dialogue with the image.
- Add the ethical element.
- Integrate the imagination back into daily life.

RESOURCES

Chodorow, Joan, ed. *Encountering Jung on Active Imagination.* Princeton, N.J.: Princeton University Press, 1997.

Hannah, Barbara. *Encounters with the Soul: Active Imagination as Developed by C. G. Jung.* Santa Monica, Calif.: Sigo Press, 1981.

Johnson, Robert A. *Inner Work: Using Dreams and Active Imagination for Personal Growth.* New York: Harper & Row, 1986.

Jung, C. G. *Psychology and Alchemy,* vol. 12. *Collected Works.* Princeton, N.J.: Princeton University Press, 1968.

Von Franz, Marie-Louise. *Alchemical Active Imagination.* Boston: Shambhala, 1997.

Chapter 38 • Visualization

When we create something, we always create it first in thought form.
— Shakti Gawain

In the 1930s, psychotherapist Robert Desouille used guided imagination techniques to help his patients face difficult emotions and learn to create a more harmonious relationship with them. A contemporary of Desouille, German psychotherapist Carl Happich, interpreted specific symbols to reveal the state of the patient. If he asked a patient to visualize a meadow, the balanced and happy person would invariably populate the meadow with children, flowers, or images of spring, while the unhappy or depressed person was more likely to visualize dying vegetation or a barren landscape.

This same phenomena can be seen in how the artwork of children reveals the way their self-image is affected by the attitudes of their parents, as in the instance of the American school teacher who inquired into the home life of a six-year-old student whose drawings were appallingly gruesome. She discovered that when the child brought her drawings home, her mother used them to catch the droppings at the bottom of the bird cage.

In addition to providing clues as to the state of a person's psyche, visualization is also used proactively to promote good health. The new field of psychoneuroimmunology, which studies the relationship of the mind to the immune system and the nervous system, is accumulating evidence that a positive attitude can have a beneficial effect on the ability of the human body to resist disease.

Michael Murphy, co-founder of the Esalen Institute, writes about the use of imagery practice healing and growth in his book, *The Future of the Body*. In the 1890s, French psychiatrist Pierre Janet showed that one image in a hysterical patient could be changed into another by suggestion. Freud evoked images in his patients and stimulated imagery by free association and emphasis on early memories. Jung regarded mental imagery to be a creative aspect of the psyche that was resource for cure and personal growth. Psychologist Alfred Binet, famous for his intelligence tests, encouraged patients to converse with their visual images. He called this state provoked introspection. In the 1920s a German psychologist named Happich stimulated imagery by suggesting specific scenes such as a chapel or a meadow to his patients. This would be an example of guided imagery, since the image is suggested by an outsider. Robert Desouille developed dream drama and Hans Carl Leuner called his method guided affective imagery. All of these therapists used extended fantasies to obtain information about their subject's motivations, conflicts, perceptual distortions, self perceptions, and early memories. This is not saying that if you get sick it is all your fault for not having a positive attitude. That fallacy simply brings on more guilt. The situation is more complicated, but visualization can allow a patient to feel that he or she has more control over the recovery process.

The Silva Mind Control® method, which is a form of meditation, was created by José Silva and Philip Miele. The technique is to practice first thing in the morning by closing your eyes and looking upward, behind your eyelids, at a 20-degree angle. Then, slowly, at about two-second intervals, count backward from one hundred down to one. This practice tends to produce the alpha state of meditative consciousness. Set an alarm to go off after fifteen minutes. When the alarm rings, you bring yourself back out by counting from one to five as you open your eyes and return to normal awareness. This is a meditation similar to many others. It is a fairly passive and it includes relaxation and produces a stillness of mind.

There are active or dynamic meditations that have the purpose of improving one's life or healing some illness. They are visualization exercises that include the practices of guided imagery and affirmations. The "mind games" of Robert Masters and Jean Houston are two of the more well-known approaches of the guided imagery technique.

Houston has developed many applications of guided imagery in different countries throughout the world where she integrates visualization with the guiding myths of the country's culture or with the classical Greek myths that are still a guiding force in our lives. For example, she will describe an imaginary journey to a client or student who is in a receptive meditative state. The journey may be to a cave in a mountain where the student meets a wise being. The student would ask the wise being a question and wait for the answer.

Guided visualization is not the same as active imagery because active imagination has no script; you allow the story to unfold. In guided imagery there is a prepared script that you read or hear and follow in your mind's eye.

CONTEMPORARY USES

Guided imagery or visualization does not require a belief in an external or spiritual force. This distinguishes the technique from prayer in which the practitioner is exhorting a deity or invoking the support or help of a spiritual power. The practitioner of visualization does presume, however, that mind can influence the physical world and even affect its own process of thought and emotion. Anyone who has cured themselves of a bad habit knows how this mental self-adjustment works.

Your imagination is just like the muscles in your body. If you use it, then it will be more fit and responsive. Imagination is a function of the right side of the brain, which also governs emotions, creativity, intuition, and a sense of rhythm. The left side of the brain determines our capacity for logic, analysis, language, and reason.

Often people say that they cannot visualize, they cannot "see" anything in their mind's eye. It is true that some people are naturally better at visualization than others. Here is a simple test to ascertain whether you have a natural ability to visualize. Imagine a cube floating in space, about one inch on each side. It is painted red and made of wood. Imagine that this cube is sliced into three even layers that are separated so that you can see the red paint on the original outer surface and the bare wood on the surfaces that have just been sliced. Now slice this cube into nine sticks by imagining that a saw makes two equidistant cuts on a plane perpendicular to the first layers. Finally, slice the cube by turning the saw so it faces the long side of the nine sticks and make two equidistant cuts. Now you should see twenty seven small cubes floating in space.

The test is to answer this question, "How many of the cubes are painted red on three sides, how many cubes are painted red on two sides, how many on one side, and how many of the twenty seven small cubes are not painted red at all?" The score of the test is not the important issue. The important thing is to observe how you got the answer. A natural visualizer can "see" those cubes so clearly that he or she can reach out with an imaginary finger and count the red surfaces and the wood surfaces as if they were real. Other types of thinkers, the more logical ones, get the correct answer just as well but by other, more analytical methods. If you do not "see" anything and cannot get the answer to this kind of a thought problem, do not despair. You can still visualize, and remember, practicing visualization will improve your skill.

How to Begin

The following four exercises can help you improve your visualization skills.

Visualization Exercises

1. Select a common object such as a bowl or a spoon, put it on a table and sit facing the table, looking at the object. Study it carefully in great detail. Memorize it. Then close your eyes and imagine the object. What can you remember? Some of the information you get with your eyes closed will be memory, some will be from your imagination. At this point notice your feeling state. Are you frustrated by this exercise or does it give you a feeling of pleasure? Do you have any other emotions?

2. Close your eyes and imagine another object, something familiar that is available in the room. Then open your eyes, go find the object, and look at the real thing. How is it different from the image that you created when you tried to remember what it looked like? Once again, inquire within as to your emotional state.

3. Now try to remember and visualize some similar object from your childhood. How clearly can you recall what it looked like? How many details can you include? Can you place it in its surroundings? Does this memory include emotions that you can identify?

4. Finally, imagine a bowl or similar object that you have never seen before. Create it in your mind's eye. You can design the texture, the ornaments, the size, the shape, and other details of color and weight. What is it used for? Do you have any emotions toward it?

As you practice you will improve your ability to direct your attention toward imaginary objects. You are the creator of these mind pictures, so you can change them if they do not suit you. Later in this chapter, you will learn that many of the emotions that cause you distress can be changed just as easily as you changed the texture of your imagined bowl.

RELAXATION TECHNIQUE

Relaxing the Body

If you can visualize yourself in a relaxed state, then you are going to be much more skillful at relaxing. This can be extremely useful when you are under stress and feeling that your mind and body need to take a rest. (See chapter 6, Yoga Asana for instructions on how to relax in the posture of lying on your back. Chapter 30, The Body Scan, gives a slightly different way to approach relaxation.)

To begin, get comfortable, either lying down or leaning back in an easy chair, and imagine that your body is an ice cube melting on a hot sidewalk. Feel yourself softening, flowing, and growing calm. Dwell on the image and allow your whole body to respond to it. Remember, your body does not speak English, or any other language, but it does respond to images. Continue to focus on the melting ice cube image until you are fully relaxed.

Relaxing the Mind

After your body is quiet and calm, imagine that you are underwater. When thoughts arise, see them enter a bubble and watch the bubble rise slowly to the surface of the water. Wait in peace and stillness until the next thought arises. Acknowledge the thought, note it, and place it in another bubble and watch it as it floats away toward the surface. Eventually there will be more space and time in between thoughts. You will be residing in a thought-free meditative state.

Affirmations

You can use affirmations as a kind of visualization. An affirmation is a positive statement or visualization about some outcome you wish to achieve. It is important to use positive statements because a negatively phrased statement may be misinterpreted by the mind. For example, if you use an affirmation such as "I am not fat'" the word *not* may slip out of the field of attention and the affirmation could end up being absorbed as "I am fat." Rephrased as a positive statement, it would be "I am thin." An affirmation can also be a visual image or a feeling.

Visual affirmations are often used by athletes. In coaching athletes who are preparing for competition, the visualizations tend to combine kinesthetic awareness with visual awareness. Some racers are so skillful that they can remember a five-kilometer race course in enough detail to imagine each stride and each turn in their mental practice. By going over the race in their "mind's eye," the racers can add a sense of euphoria, ease, and skill.

Affirmations can also be used to calm your mental state. Simply repeat to yourself, either out loud or silently, "My mind is quiet. My mind is at peace." Or use the famous healing affirmation, "Every day, in every way, I am getting better and better." Affirmations can be used at any time during waking hours or right before bed. Simply choose a positive statement and repeat it to yourself either aloud or silently for a minute or so. If you feel heavy, depressed, or blue, you may enjoy using affirmations that incorporate symbols of ascent such as a ladder, staircase, or flying chariot, which produce a feeling of tranquillity and composure.

Visualization and Anxiety

Visualization can be useful in calming feelings of anxiety. If there is a specific situation that causes you to feel anxious, imagine ten different scenarios of the situation ranging from mildly to extremely anxiety-provoking. Imagine yourself encountering the first or easiest level. During this scenario, monitor your body for feelings of anxiety. Since emotions do manifest in the body, it is the best place to look for signs of unease. The breath in particular is sensitive to emotional states; as soon as you begin to lose your calm, your breathing will become less regular.

If you can encounter the first scenario without losing your tranquil state of mind, then move to the next, more difficult level. Visualize yourself in that situation and once again monitor your breath and body for any signs that your relaxed state is beginning to change. If it does, then practice at this level until you can imagine yourself in the scene and at the same time maintain a relaxed breathing pattern.

You are training yourself to keep cool under stress. You are not doing this by giving yourself an order to "chill out." You are using a positive approach that includes images, which the emotional brain responds to much more efficiently than it does to words. The images can be expressed in words, of course, but they include something more that is perceived only by the visual, auditory, or kinesthetic senses. It is a more holistic approach than the intellectually-based technique of guided meditation.

Here is an example. Suppose you are afraid of an upcoming interview with your boss. Create ten scenarios and start with the easiest one. In this scenario, you imagine yourself meeting your boss and everything going swimmingly well. Put in sensory details. What are you wearing? How does the room smell? What temperature is the air? Then when your boss asks you a question, imagine that you know the right thing to say and he or she compliments you. Feel the joy of accomplishment and confidence.

If your breathing and body remain calm, you can escalate the difficulty of the situation. Introduce a slightly more difficult question or a tiny tinge of doubt and uncertainty in your boss's reaction. Then examine your breathing and check to see if you are handling this level of difficulty without symptoms of distress. If it is easy for you, then escalate the difficulty again and continue, step by step.

If you only make it to level three, that is just fine. You may have created scenarios that are too challenging. If you make it all the way to level ten, and you can imagine yourself facing the maximum amount of uncertainty and failure with no signs of anxiety in your breathing, then you are becoming skillful at detaching yourself from the outcome. The cultivation of detachment is an important aspect of the meditative path.

Types of Images

The following images reflect symbols that resonate to universal human experiences. They are commonly found in dreams, art, and poetry. They can be used either as an object of meditation (see chapter 9, Mantra), as an image for an active imagination meditation (see chapter 37, Dialogues with Self), or as catalyst to elicit responses from the unconscious.

- A bubbling fountain suggests the source of life itself. This image can be a kinesthetic one in which you imagine the fountain is bubbling up from the base of the spine through the torso, neck, and head. This image helps to promote healing.
- A well represents the source or wellspring of life as a deep, still place.
- A rock connotes the stable essence of earth.
- A flower generally brings a sensitive, sensual, and sexual beauty to mind.
- A ticking clock can bring anxiety or it can bring a sense of the orderly progression of time.
- A quiet room is a well-known image for a sanctuary to which you can retreat when you need to feel secure.
- A cave is similar to the quiet room, but in a wilder and more natural setting. Creatures that emerge from caves may represent undeveloped or repressed qualities.
- The ocean serves as the archetypal symbol for the unconscious. It can be frightening if one has a fear of drowning. But the advice which serves many people well is: Don't drown, dive!
- Mythical beasts often embody fears. If you encounter one, feed the monster or ask what it wants.
- A mountain may be stable and enduring or it may erupt as a volcano.
- A dark cloud can represent fear. See yourself connected to the dark cloud by a long thin cord, and watch the cloud float away, grow small, and disappear as the cord breaks.
- A tunnel can signify a transition or passage from one state into another. Near-death experiences often include a tunnel.
- A chapel is a symbol of a religious attitude, the sacred center of being.
- A house can symbolize the self. If you need to cultivate a sense of nourishment, you might imagine a glorious kitchen and dining room with abundant stores of nutritious food.

- Animals have had many qualities ascribed to them including hostility, love, and strength.
- A rose is usually interpreted as a symbol for love and sex.

If the images are used as an object of meditation, one does not invite them to change or respond. They often tend to shape shift or metamorphose into other symbol. The meditator is instructed to go back to the original symbol. Hindu and Tibetan Buddhist practices include meditating on a deity in this way. If the images are used as a starting point for active imagination, then the meditator allows them to evolve and interact up to a point. One does not drift off into tangents or indulge in irrelevant fantasies. When the attention wanders (as it inevitably does in any meditative practice), you bring it back to the image although you allow the image to speak. This is the way the image serves as a catalyst to elicit responses from the unconscious.

REVIEW TIPS

- Find a safe, quiet place and relax in a comfortable posture.
- Choose one of the images from this book or from your imagination.
- Allow the image to enter your awareness.
- Keep the image in your field of attention, even though it may change.
- Monitor how you feel physically and emotionally for clues as to your unconscious response to the image.

RESOURCES

Dossey, Larry. *Be Careful What You Pray For: You Just Might Get It.* San Francisco: HarperSanFrancisco, 1997.

Drury, Nevill. *Music for Inner Space: Techniques for Meditation and Visualization.* San Leandro, Calif.: Prism Press, 1985.

Gawain, Shakti. *Creative Visualization.* Novato, Calif.: New World Library, 1995.

Houston, Jean. *The Hero and the Goddess: The Oddyssey As Mystery and Initation.* New York: Ballantine Books, 1992.

Houston, Jean. *Life Force: The Psycho-Historical Recovery of the Self.* Wheaton, Ill.: Theosophical Publishing House, 1993.

Houston, Jean. *The Possible Human: A Course in Extending Your Physical, Mental, and Creative Abilities.* New York: J. P. Tarcher, 1997.

Houston, Jean. *The Search for the Beloved: Journeys in Sacred Psychology.* New York: J. P. Tarcher, 1989.

Markham, Ursula. *The Elements of Visualization.* Rockport, Maine: Element, 1991.

Murphy, Michael. *The Future of the Body: Explorations into the Future Evolution of Human Nature.* New York: J. P. Tarcher, 1993.

Silva, José, and Miele, Philip. *The Silva Mind Control Method.* New York: Simon & Schuster, 1977.

Chapter 39 • Kinesthetic Meditations

While traveling the path, change begins to take place inside our being
and also in our bodies. We begin to see and experience life
from a greater vantage point, or from a greater depth of meaning,
from an inner place of belonging.

— Jack Rosenberg

The word *kinesthetia* means awareness of the body and its movements. Kinesthetic meditations are transformative, somatic practices in which the body is allowed to move in its own way. These practices include therapeutic dance, spiritual dance, authentic movement, continuum exercises (the self-healing movement created by Emilie Conrad-Da'oud), body-releasing movements, embodiment training, somatic exercises (the sensory awareness work of Charlotte Selver), the moving cycle techniques of Christine Caldwell, and other therapeutic movements. Improvisational dance differs from these somatic meditations if the goal is performance rather than awareness. Kinesthetic meditation does not include yoga, T'ai Chi, Qigong, or the martial arts where the movement is structured and learned.

The movements of kinesthetic meditation are created by the person in the moment. Often the practitioner will use an image to elicit or evoke a specific movement. Kinesthetic meditation also allows the practitioner to expand his or her spiritual experience through body awareness. Taken together, these therapies and meditations can be called the kinesthetic arts.

Since Neolithic times shamans and members of their tribes have engaged in trance dancing for the purpose of healing, entering an altered state, aligning themselves with the forces of the universe, or communing with spirits (see chapter 2, Trance Dancing). Sufi dervishes have whirled for centuries as an expression of the oneness with the cosmos, as a means of entering trance states, and as a form of spiritual celebration. In modern times, meditative body movement has taken a more therapeutic form and is similar to the spoken, artistic, or musical expressions of active imagination in which you let the unconscious move you. Renowned psychologist Carl Jung describes how a patient of his colleague, dance therapist Toni Wolf, danced a mandala from a drawing she had made. The patient said, "When I was in analysis with Miss Toni Wolf, I often had the feeling that something in me, hidden deep inside, wanted to express itself; but I also knew that this something had no words. As we were looking for another means of expression, I suddenly had the idea: I could dance it. Miss Wolf encouraged me to try. The body sensation I felt was oppression, the image came that I was inside a stone and had to release myself from it to emerge as a separate self. The movements grew out of the body sensations. This very freeing event was much more potent than the hours in which we only talked." This was an outward expression of an inner experience that used what Jung called "active imagination," only here the body became the instrument of expression. Often in active imagination it is the hands that can draw or sculpt figures that are unknown to the ordinary conscious mind. In body-centered meditation the whole body is the medium for the work.

CONTEMPORARY USES

Most meditative forms of bodywork start with the premise that life is fluid and constantly changing — which is indeed true — and so is the human body, which is 85 percent water and in a constant state of change. Some kinds of spiritual dance or therapeutic movement such as T'ai Chi or yoga use movements that one learns. Other forms of movement meditation aim to develop a body intelligence rather than adopt a structured movement form, so they are unstructured.

The goal of all meditation is the integration of mind, body, and spirit. This occurs when you are centered, aware in the moment, and moving from your body's core. In this state, you can learn in a relaxed, easy way. Instead of using your will to move your body, you learn to use a spatial intelligence that gives you a peaceful power.

Lulu Sweigard, Ph.D., wrote a thesis called "The Human Movement Potential" for Columbia University and the Julliard School of Music, in which she verified the effectiveness of using imagery to achieve postural improvement in the body. Sweigard found that if a student uses his or her willpower to achieve a given posture, they only impose their own neuro-muscular habits on the body and they interfere with the body's ability to organize itself. Furthermore, if they tried to force the body into a given position, (e.g., tuck the buttocks under) this only resulted in a corre-sponding deviation of some other part of the posture. She demonstrated through the use of experiments and X rays that students who merely imag-ined various kinds of body movements were changing the structure of their bodies. She also found that merely imagining a movement can improve one's ability to make that movement. This work gave credence to the idea that the mind can change the body merely by thinking.

Charlotte Selver, one of the founding foremothers of the tradition of somatics, developed a technique that she called "sensory awareness" whose goal is to enhance personal integration through the awareness of the physi-cal sensations of the body in various postures and movements. The underly-ing premise of the Selver technique and many other kinesthetic meditation methods is described by author Katherine Thamas in her essay "Hearing the Voice of the Body": "The deep attending to hard knots of holding is a pow-erfully compassionate act; a turning toward rejected parts of our being. As this newly compassionate observing occurs, the object of observation, the body-self, is transformed, and we move from denial to acceptance, from rejection to inclusion. This is the beginning of metta practice, lovingkindness for the self."

Joan Skinner, former professor of dance at the University of Washington and the founder of the Skinner releasing technique, uses imagery to help the student discover how the mind and body work together in movement. The releasing technique involves a lot of refining and fine-tuning of perception and movement. Instead of merely trying to perceive a given movement, you become the perception. Instead of noticing your per-ception of the movement, you notice the movement of your perceptions. This delicate process begins in a state of stillness. Then, from the stillness, an involuntary movement, a dance, arises. Although some Skinner releasing classes are filled with dancers who intend ultimately to perform, their goal in the releasing work is to align themselves with the forces of the universe.

Kinesthetic meditation is based on the idea of body awareness, which means that the mind is perceiving the body. It is a process in which one goes to the body for answers when one does not understand the issues or problems in one's life. This process includes two main themes. The first theme stresses the importance of training the body to be quiet. In her essay, "Grounding and Open" in *Being Bodies* by Lenore Friedman and Susan Moon, Anne Klein, professor and chair of the department of religious studies at Rice University, writes, "In cultivating mindfulness the attention is trained to be steady, but it is as jittery as a handheld laser pointer. Such an instrument is volatile and weak. If the laser light is anchored to a table it will be steady. For stillness of mind, stillness of body is crucial." The second theme is the power of movement awareness to clarify and heal issues of mind and body. This healing movement is spontaneous and improvised, but it is also a movement with a special kind of attention and awareness. It can be fast or slow, but the intention of the movement is to heighten consciousness and seek wisdom rather than to gain dance or sports skills.

Other methods of kinesthetic meditating include "somatics," which studies the body as perceived from within by first-person perception; and "authentic movement," which is a form of dance meditation developed by Mary Starks Whitehouse. Osho, a meditative master, has developed a series of meditative dance forms with a variety of original music, which is available on CD (see Resources).

How to Begin

If you enter the practice of kinesthetic meditation in a worried and fearful state, you will undercut the experience. You must let go of your thoughts and judgments and abandon any fears and goals. You do not need to try to look like a dancer. You can even move very awkwardly. Remember that meditative movement is not only something you do, it is something you are. You can move any way you want to, just as long as you are not trying to impress anybody. This is not a performance.

Find a place where you can move that is private and safe and has a clean floor. It is important to wear loose, comfortable clothing. You may use music if you wish. You can invite a friend to be there as a trusted witness if they are wise enough to refrain from interfering with your process, although you do not need to have a witness. This is a solo practice, not a partnership dance. If you practice in a group, however every member of the group dances and witnesses simultaneously.

Kinesthetic Exercise

There are four steps to the kinesthetic meditation process:

1. Focus your awareness on your body. Try to find something in your body that you can feel. Allow the sensations of your body to come more fully into your awareness. Do not try to relax or correct your posture at all. Just experience your body as it is in this moment.

2. As your body awareness grows, allow your body to move and express the sensations you feel. See if you can enter the shape of the tightness (or whatever feeling you have) and begin to give it form with a movement. Get in touch with the feeling of your body and consciously inhabit this feeling. Join with it as a participant. (Your witness may even provide drumming or music if that is appropriate.)

3. Now focus on allowing something to change. You were made to move, and now you are moving in a way that is appropriate for your body, moment to moment. The tight place may get tighter or looser, or a shift may occur somewhere else in your body. Each time your body moves, you inhabit the new shape, get in touch with the feeling of your body, and then allow your body to change again and again. You are not trying for any specific outcome; you just approach your body with gentleness and love. This dance often generates loving feelings, perhaps more than you are used to. You have to allow yourself time to feel whatever presents itself.

As you proceed, you may begin to sense the presence of the inner critic. This is the voice in your head that says, "I'm stiff. I do not have enough strength. I am too fat. I am too thin. I am too old. I have no talent." Since you created this critic, you can also create a supportive coach who says that you are fine. Give that coach power, muscle, and courage, but don't make him or her belligerent. The coach knows that this best way to fight the critic is to concentrate on positive thoughts and beliefs. Those persons with a spiritual tradition often have a metaphor for this coach. They call her goddess or the divine power.

In this process as you allow your body to change spontaneously, rather than attempting to direct it, you begin to melt the boundary between your sense of self and your own body. Usually some sort of transformation occurs. This simply means seeing anew. It is a nonverbal experience that acknowledges that our mind-body has an inner core of energy.

4. The fourth step is action. It is fine to enjoy a breakthrough of body-mind awareness and freedom in a studio. But then you need to walk out the door and proceed with your life in a way that allows the new insights, freedom, and love to operate. Self-discovery through movement allows you to enjoy a transformation that will be very personal and unique to your own needs. You will discover what parts of your body are not available, do not move, cannot feel.

Mary Starks Whitehouse is one of the leaders of this authentic movement technique. In her article, "The Tao of the Body" which is reprinted as a chapter in the book *Authentic Movement*, edited by Patricia Pallaro, she tells the following story of a woman's first experience with authentic movement:

> Together we went out to the studio [My teacher] said she wanted to see me walk and to see how I was built and how I moved. I walked and as I see myself now, it was as if my body did not belong to me — the very fact of being alone with someone watching me brought a little light to the surface. Putting my feet together was a new experience and I never shall forget the feeling of wholeness my hands expressed when I put them together, thrusting them out into space. Perhaps I did not know it, but my hands contained all that my body did not.
>
> Later she wrote, "Something inside of me jumped for joy when I discovered I have something to work with instead of something working with me."
>
> Mary Whitehouse continues, "The kinesthetic sense can be awakened and developed in using any and all kinds

of movement, but I believe it becomes conscious only when the inner — that is, the subjective — connection is found, the sensation of what it feels like to the individual, whether it is swinging, stretching, bending, turning, twisting or whatever."

Review Tips

- Find a quiet place and stand, directing your attention to your body.
- Get in touch with the feeling of your body.
- Join the feeling and participate in it with your whole mind and body as you express the feeling with movement.
- Allow the sensations of your body to move and change.
- After the movement has come to its conclusion, integrate the new freedom and love you've experienced into your life.

Resources

Alon, Ruthy. *Mindful Spontaneity, Moving in Tune with Nature: Lessons in the Feldenkrais Method.* Dorset, England: Prism Press, 1990.

Caldwell, Christine. *Getting in Touch: The Guide to New Body-Centered Therapies.* Wheaton, Ill.: Quest Books, 1997. http://members.aol.com/caldwellmv/faq.htm

Davis, Bridget Iona. *Releasing into Process: Joan Skinner and the Use of Imagery in the Teaching of Dance.* Chicago: University of Illinois Press, 1970.

Feldenkrais, Moshe. *Awareness through Movement: Health Exercises for Personal Growth.* New York: Harper & Row, 1977.

Friedman, Lenore, and Susan Moon. *Being Bodies: Buddhist Women on the Paradox of Embodiment.* Boston, Mass.: Shambhala, 1997.

Geissinger, Annie. "Toward the Unknown: An Interview with Janet Adler." *A Moving Journal,* vol. 5 (fall–winter 1998).

Johnson, Don, ed. *Bone, Breath, and Gesture.* Berkeley, Calif.: North Atlantic Books, 1995.

Murphy, Michael. *The Future of the Body: Explorations into the Further Evolution of Human Nature.* Los Angeles: J. P. Tarcher, 1993.

Ogden, Gina. "Continuum's Wakeup Call: About Emile Conrad-Da'oud." *New Age* (November–December 1998).

Rosenberg, Jack L. *Body, Self, and Soul: Sustaining Integration.* Atlanta, Ga.: Humanics Ltd., 1985.

Sweigard, Lulu. *The Human Movement Potential: Its Ideokinetic Function.* Lanham, Md.:
    University Press of America, 1988.

Thanas, Katherine. "Hearing the Voice of the Body." In *Being Bodies: Buddhist Women
    on the Paradox of Embodiment.* Boston, Mass.: Shambhala, 1997.

Todd, Mabel Ellsworth. *The Thinking Body.* Pennington, N.J.: Princeton Book
    Company, 1980.

TRAINING

Antioch New England Graduate School, 40 Avon Street, Keene, NY 03431-3516.

The Institute for the Study of Authentic Movement, Ste. 309, 526 West 26th Street,
    New York, NY 10001. ZOE1815@aol.com

TAPES

Osho Distributors, 570 Lexington Avenue, New York, NY 10022

Conclusion • A Meditation Upon Meditation

When there is peace and meditation, there is neither anxiety nor death.
— Francis of Assisi

A quiet limpid pool. A serene blue sky, empty of clouds.
A great tree, rising above all others in a dark forest.
A single uncomplicated breath. One eye, unblinking and clear.
The pulse of life. Silence in the midst of noise.
The stillpoint in a turning world.
Being in the flow, in the moment, beyond time.
Calmness. Serenity. Peace. Ecstasy. Union. Communion.

There are many ways to describe meditation, many images, many expressions, all too many words. But meditation will always ultimately be beyond description. No amount or quality of words, not even those that comprise this book, can truly convey what meditation is.

Like all truly religious experiences, meditation must be experienced to be understood. Thinking, observing, categorizing — none of these is meditation. One could read every book ever written on Zen and never experience sartori. One could think for years about the significance of the breath and never know a moment of unthinking focus. One could look at hundreds of videos of meditative movement, could become a scholar of the forms, could become an astute critic of others' performance, yet never once feel the unobstructed flow of cosmic energy.

Meditation is not an idea; it is an experience, a primal human experience that has been discovered and rediscovered in every era and on every continent. The multiplicity of forms is testimony to the ubiquity of the human need to achieve the state of focused grace we call meditation. That there are so many ways to meditate does not mean that all are variations on one primary form, nor that one is better than another. Those who argue that their variety or discipline is the one true way to meditate may hair-splittingly define meditation in such a way that their claims seem true. But cross a river, or a continent, or a few centuries, and a different form will appear just as true and effective. Each meditative tradition has its own history, its own spiritual flavor, but all can be effective and life-transforming if practiced over time.

Time is important in meditation, for despite the timeless state to which the meditator aspires, only through regular and frequent practice can benefits be achieved. Trying a meditation for a few weeks, then discarding it as unsuitable, too difficult, or ineffective is like being angry at a baby for not earning its rent. Every one of the meditations described in this book takes weeks, months, sometimes years to take effect.

Meditation is not the crash-diet of spirituality; you won't find yourself a new person at the end of a six-week course of once-weekly practice. What you will find is that, practiced regularly and with full attention of mind and body and spirit, meditation will change your life. You won't wake up one morning free of all bad habits and soaring on new spiritual wings. But wait: that's not quite true. You will one day discover that your bad habits have lost their grip and the world is fresh and new. But it will happen so subtly that you won't be at all surprised when it happens. Meditation changes lives the way water changes the landscape. Drop by tiny drop, the stream cuts into solid rock, the river carves a new canyon, the ocean makes sand out of boulders. Minute by minute, meditation creates a new person, more attuned to the spirit that suffuses this temporal world.

Start now. Place your feet on the path. One path, the other path, they will all lead to the same place, the one called by so many names: the still-point, the great silence, the void, the cloud of unknowing. Start now, and one day you will awaken to a new landscape, its features carved by the insistent tiny force of your practice. A new and better world. A new you.

Index

A

Aborigines, Australian, 280, 291
absorption, 77
acceptance, 301–2
Ackerman, Diane, 305, 306
adoration, 182
affirmations, 322, 326
aimlessness, 214
alchemical Taoism, 139
Alcoholics Anonymous (AA), 195
Allah, 161, 162, 165
alpha state, 322
altered states of consciousness, 2, 7,
    17, 33, 268
anger, 6, 303
anxiety, 142–43, 296
archaic hysteria, 40
archetypes. *See* symbols
art(s), 227, 228, 231, 232; spirituality
    and, 233, 234
ashtanga, 48

ashtanga yoga, 67
athletes, 265, 268, 326
attachment, 6, 94–95, 138
attention, 3; focused on inner state, 76;
    focusing, 76–77. *See also* concentra-
    tion; focus
aum. See Om/aum
authentic movement, 334, 336
autogenics, 63–64
aversion, 6
awareness, 95; development of, 105,
    138

B

balance, 142, 228, 288. *See also* yin and
    yang
balancing, 7
baqa, 162
barakah, 162
Basho, Matsuo, 246, 247
Bass Drum, The, 144–45

Benson, Herbert, xx, 84

Berra, Yogi, 268

bhakti yoga, 49

biofeedback, 221–24

bliss, 138. *See also* ecstasy

Bodhidharma, 121

bodily awareness, 333–36; losing, 78

bodily functioning, gaining control over. *See* biofeedback

body: increasing the spirit of the, 254; melting the boundary between self and, 335–36; paying attention to, 96; relaxing. *See* relaxation. *See also* posture(s); sensations

body-centered meditations. *See* Zen-in-action

body image, 253, 296

body intelligence, 332

body scan/body sweep, 62, 253–59

Body Scan Litany, 257–59

bodywork, meditative forms of, 332. *See also* kinesthetic meditations; movement meditation

books, learning meditation from, xxiii

boundaries, rigid personal, 35

brain: anatomy and physiology, 229–30; left vs. right. *See* right brain; reptilian, 229

brain states: art, meditation and, 230–32

brainwashing, 8

breathing, 67–70, 84, 96, 103; abdominal, 69–70; concentrating on, 118; conscious/voluntary, 68, 165; excretory function, 68–69; observing one's, 70–71; shallow, 68, 69; yoga, 67–73. *See also* yoga breathing

Buddha, 47, 105, 288

Buddhism, 89–90, 99, 199; Hinayana

and Theravada, 105; Indian, 199–200; walking meditations of, 143. *See also* metta; Zen

C

calmness. *See* relaxation

Calvinism, 205

candle meditation, 187–91

Catholicism, 183

Celtic pilgrimage, 281

centering prayer, 183, 184

Chang Tao-ling, 130

chanting, 201

chi (life force), 67, 132, 133, 142, 143, 147, 148, 151

children, meditating with, xxv

Choa-chou, 122

choice, xvii, 8

Christian meditation, 183

Christian pilgrimage, 280–81

Christian prayer, 181

Christianity, 83, 199, 205

Chung-li Ch'uan, 130

Clarke, Arthur C., 299

compassion, 99, 100, 102, 269, 292, 295, 300–302, 333

concentration, 3, 240; on all parts of experience at once, 118; becoming permanent, 77; defined, 76. *See also* attention; focus

consciousness: alteration of, 2, 7, 16, 17, 41, 268; increasing, 51

contemplation, 77, 213–14

contemplative prayer, 181–85

contrition, 182

control, letting go of the desire to, 248

Cooper, Andrew, 269–70

counting, 77

crafts, 227; needle, 239–44

creation, 321; as brain state alteration, 228–30

creative abilities, enhancing, 2, 4

creative act, 227

creativity, 229. *See also* "wild mind"

criticism, meditating following, 302–3

cross-legged postures, 59–60. *See also* *siddhasana*

crystal ball gazing, 187

cults, 8

D

dabao, 151

Dances of Universal Peace, 170–72

dancing, 19–22, 40, 335; as altering consciousness, 17; trance, 21–23

daydreaming, drifting into, 3

death, meditating on one's own, 301

defense mechanisms, giving up, 254

depression, 296, 303–4

desire(s), 6, 255. *See also* intention

Desouille, Robert, 321, 322

detachment, 94–95

dharana, 76

dharma yoga, 49

dhikr, 169

dhyana (contemplation), 77

Dina, Roman, 78

"direct pointing," 115

dis-ease. *See* illness

disabilities, physical, 4, 51

discipline to meditate, how to acquire the, xxiii

distractions, 3

divine force, 177–78, 181

drawing, 234–37; life, 234–35; and spirituality, 233

Dreamtime, 280

drug addictions, 16–17

drugs, mind-altering, 16

drum circles, 27, 31

drumming, 16, 17, 25–31, 35, 40, 42

drums, 25, 26, 28

dying, meditating with someone who is, 301–2

E

earth. *See* nature

Eastern *vs.* Western minds, 291

eating before yoga, 52

ecology, 288. *See also* nature

ecopsychology, 289

ecstasy, 15, 20, 137, 163; archaic techniques of, 40

ecstatic postures, 35–39

effort. *See* goal orientation; task-centered mode

ego, 102; unhooking consciousness from, 77

ego mind, emptying the, 317. *See also* mind, clearing/emptying the

ego purposes, use of meditation for, 194. *See also* meditation, as selfish

emergency, what to do in, 7–9

emotional disorders, 4, 222, 296. *See also specific disorders*

emotional states, dissolving of unresolved, 255

emotional suffering, 295

emotions, 298, 299; aroused by meditative practices, 210, 248–49; meditating on, 299–301; physical manifestations, 255, 298. *See* also psychosomatic disorders; tension; resolving, 299–301 energy. *See chi; kundalini*

energy body, 128–139

enlightenment, 127, 215, 265, 316;
    sudden, 114, 122

entrainment, 27

epilepsy, 4

equanimity, 300

equinoxes, 291

escape, meditation used as, 9

ethics, 5, 178, 269, 318

euphoria, 265. *See also* ecstasy

Eutony, 253

evasion, meditation used for, 9

exercise. *See* sports

"expire," xx, 67

F

fabric. *See* crafts, needle

faith, 299

fama, 162

families, 200

fana, 163

feng shui, 137, 139

flexibility, 49

floor, contact with, 55–56, 256

flow, 228, 270–71

focus, xxiii, 231, 270

forgiveness, 103, 300

Fox, George, 205

Freud, Sigmund, 288, 322

friends, groups of, 200

Friends, Society of. *See* Quakers

G

Gaia, 288–89

gardening, 273–77

gassho, 118

goal-orientation, 7, 113, 214, 243

God: names and titles of, 184; opening
    one's heart and mind to, 181. *See
    also* divine force

goddesses, 17, 20, 136, 189, 191, 240,
    335

Goldstein, Joseph, 101

Goodman, Felicitas, 34–37

grace, xxii, 182

greedy types, 6

grief, 295, 300–302

groups. *See* meditation groups; prayer
    groups

guided imagery, 322–23

guilt: about meditating, xxiv–xxv;
    changed into remorse, 103; loving-
    kindness and, 103

H

haiku, 245–50

handicaps, physical, 4

hands, 145

Happich, Carl, 321, 322

hara, 143

harmony, 288, 289. *See also* balance;
    relaxation

Harner, Michael, 40

Hart, William, 96, 266–67

hatha yoga, 49, 50, 52, 292

head, directing attention to, 58, 61

healing, xx, 189, 321, 334

healing center. *See* inner space

health benefits of meditation, 84,
    141–42, 321

healthy life, 132

hearing, 305–8

Hesychast prayer, 183, 184

Hinduism, 136

Houston, Jean, 322

hymns, 306
hysteria, archaic, 40

I

ignorance, 6
illness, 296; meditative techniques for, 40; psychic/visionary, 40. *See also* pain; *specific disorders*
illumination, 113–15, 117, 218, 269. *See also* satori
imagery, 58, 61, 68, 231, 249, 317, 318; guided, 322–23. *See also* visualization
images, types of, 328–29
imagination, 323; active, 313–14, 316, 317, 319, 332
in-the-body experience, 53
individuality, disappearance of, 78
individuation, 316
inner child, 64
inner search, psychological ramifications of, 4
inner self, hearing the voice of the, 317
inner space, 257; enhanced consciousness of one's, 254–55
insight, 293
inspirational reading, 193–97
"inspire," xx, 67
intention, 51, 106, 191; without, 113. *See also* desire
intuition, 269
Islam, 83, 157–62; Five Pillars, 161. *See also* Sufi

J

Jesus Christ, 83, 178, 181, 185
Jesus Prayer, 183, 184
jnani yoga, 49

John of the Cross, St., 182, 196
Johnson, Robert, 319
Johnson, Will, 108
journaling, 282–83
Jung, Carl Gustav, xx, 77–78, 99, 137, 289, 315, 316, 322, 332; and active imagination, 313, 314

K

karma yoga, 49
kath, 67
Keating, Thomas, 183
Khan, Pir Vilayat, 290
Khayyám, Omar, 163
ki, 67, 142. *See also* chi
kigo, 246
kinbin (walking), 123–24
kinesthetic body, 138–39
kinesthetic meditations, 331–37. *See also* movement meditation
Klein, Anne, 334
koan, 122, 246
Koran, 159–61
Kriyananda, 94
kundalini, 6–7, 127
kundalini awakening, 128

L

Labyrinth Project, 217
labyrinth walking, 143, 213–19
labyrinths and mazes, 215–16; mythical background, 216–17
language, 82
Lao-tze, 105, 129–31, 133, 141, 147
Lectio Divina meditation, 184–85
Levine, Stephen, 295, 301–2
Lewis, Samuel L., 170
life force. *See* chi

light, 210

listening, 305–8

literacy, 194

location. *See* meditation sites

longing. *See* desire

love, xvii, 77, 228; falling in, 77; *vs.*
      power, 99; Tantric Buddhist, 128

Lovelock, James, 288

lovemaking, 129–131

loving-kindness, 99–103

loving oneself, 100

lungs, 69. *See also* breathing

M

Macy, Joanna, 292

mantra, 81–85

marantha, 184

Margulis, Lynn, 288

martial arts, xix

Martin, Philip, 304

Mary, Virgin, 280–81

Masters, Robert, 322

material world, losing awareness of, 78

Mathieu, Alladin, 308

Mayan Empowerment, 35

medicine wheels, 214

meditation: as active process, xxi; as art
      of living in present, 283; assessing
      progress, xxiv; creative, 227–32;
      dangers and cautions, 7, 52, 53,
      193–94, 319; defensive uses, 9;
      definitions, 22, 35, 157; goals,
      xviii–xx, 303, 339; motives for,
      xxiv, 9; nature of, xvii–xviii,
      339–40; obstacles, 5–7; prerequi-
      sites, xxii, 5, 51, 84; reasons for,
      xviii, 2–4, 9; regular/daily *vs.* non-
      regular/nondaily, 3, 42–43, 195,

202, 283, 340; as selfish, xxiii–xxiv.
      See also specific topics

meditation groups, free-form,
      199–204. *See also* Quaker worship

meditation sites, 52; in nature, finding,
      291–92

meditation technique(s), 340; applying
      without understanding the funda-
      mentals, xxiii; selecting a, xxi–xxii,
      1–4. *See also specific techniques*

meditative disciplines, basis of, 15

meditative stance, melding with daily
      life, 123

Meeker, Joseph, 289, 292

menstruation, 53

mental disorders, 4, 222, 296. *See also
      specific disorders*

mental jumping, xxiii

merging of subject and object, 77

meridians, 148

Merton, Thomas, 181–83

metta, 99, 100

metta practice, traditional, 101–2

Mevlevi, 170

Miele, Philip, 322

mind: clearing/emptying the, 185,
      207–8, 317; filling the, 208; losing
      its identity, 78; not forcing it to
      stay focused, xxiii. *See also* focus;
      purifying one's, 102; relaxing the.
      See relaxation; stopping/holding it
      still, 76, 227; taming the, 76–77;
      wandering, 76. *See also* thought(s)

"mind games," 322–23

mindfulness, 93–97

Minos, 216–17

Mohammed, 157–62

"monkey mind," 118, 119, 247, 249,
      275

moon, watching the, 290

mountains, 54, 291, 328

movement meditation, 22, 267, 331. *See also* kinesthetic meditations

Mundy, Linus, 213

Murphy, Michael, 322

music, 305–8

mystics: works of great, 196. *See also specific mystics*

N

natural world, becoming more deeply conscious of, 2

nature, sketching from, 233–37

nature meditation, 287–93; cosmic ceremonies, 290–91

negativity, 300

Nei Dan, 149

neopagan groups, 188–90

Nhat Hanh, Thich, 84, 263

Nine Healing Arts, 133

nirvana, 114

O

object(s) of meditation, 324–25, 329; identification with, 78; preferred, 78

observation, 114–15; developing the ability of, 8

Om/aum, 75, 82

open mind and heart, 51, 181, 196, 218, 296

oral tradition, 193

orgasms, 129

orisha, 20, 21

P

Padoux, André, 83

paganism, 190. *See also* neopagan groups

pain, 6, 254, 255, 270, 296–97; chronic, 2, 222, 296; dealing with, 2, 222, 296–98

Pallaro, Patricia, 336

palms, 145

paradoxes, 7, 269

Pasiphaë, 216–17

passionate desire, 138

Patanjali, 47, 78

patience, 295

peacefulness. *See* relaxation

"people of the book," 193–94

"people of the word," 193

performance, enhanced by meditation, xix

permanence *vs.* impermanence, 47

personality types, 6

petition prayer, 182

phrases, repetition of, 101–2. *See also* affirmations

pilgrimage, 279–84

Plato, 177, 178

poetry. *See* haiku

posture-meditated trance, 34

posture(s), 33–37, 53, 108–9, 333; ecstatic, 33, 35, 36; in Zen, 117–19, 124. *See also* yoga asanas; *specific meditative techniques*

power, *vs.* love, 99

powwow dancing, 21

practice, the, xvii

prana, 67, 142. *See also* chi

pranayama, 67, 70

pratyahara, 75, 76

prayer, 181–85; contemplative, 181–85; *vs.* guided imagery/visualization, 323; *vs.* meditation, 181; repetition of, 183, 184; silent group, 199 prayer groups: nondenominational, 200. *See also* meditation groups

pregnancy, 53

present: being in the, 116, 197, 227, 283; choosing to be, xvii

"primary experience," 113

psychosomatic disorders, xx, 222

Puritans, 205, 206

purposefulness. *See* goal-orientation

Q

Qigong, 133, 142, 145, 147–52

Quaker worship, 205–11

Quakers, 199

questions, 94, 218

quiet: training the body to be, 334. *See also* silence

quiet heart, 51

"quiet prayer," 182, 184

quieting one's mind, 4, 93, 218, 317

R

raja yoga, 49

Ram Dass, 94

reading, inspirational, 193–97. *See also* scripture

relaxation, 50, 63–64, 143, 237, 240, 253, 257, 268–270, 297, 307; meditation *vs.*, xxi

relaxation exercise, "shower" of, 297–98

relaxation technique, 325–26

releasing, 333–34

religions: disapproving of meditation, 8. *See also specific religions*

religious affiliation, xxii, 3, 8, 115

renga, 245

repeating passage from scripture, 184–85

repetition: of phrases, 101–2. *See also* affirmations; of prayer, 183, 184

repetitive motions and activities, 231, 240

restlessness, 6, 37

retreats, 183–84

rhythm, 214–15, 231

right brain, 229–31, 235, 237, 323

right-brain activity, promoting, 50

Rilke, Rainer Maria, 270

ritual language, 82

ritual(s), 81–82, 283

Rohala, Walpola, 90

Rosenberg, Jack, 313, 331

roshi, 115–17

Rosicrucians, 188

Round the Platter, 143

Rumi, Jalaluddin, 169–70, 196

"runner's high," 265

S

sacred places, 290. *See also* pilgrimage

salat, 161

salvation, 178

Salzburg, Sharon, 101

samadhi, 77–78

samu (work practice), 122–23, 125

Sanskrit, 82

Satipatthana Sutta, 105

satori, 113–15, 122, 269

savasana (corpse pose/sponge), 62–65

scripture: silently repeating passage from, 184–85. *See also* reading, inspirational

self: boundary between not-self and, 289; dialogues with, 315–19

self-awareness, 304

self-hypnosis, *vs.* meditation, xxi

self-judgment, xxiv–xxv

self-realization, 316

self-transcendence, 269

Selver, Charlotte, 333

sensations, 7, 298; awareness of, 107, 265–66, 333. *See also* body scan

senses, withdrawal of attention from the, 75

setting. *See* meditation sites

sexual energy exchange, 139

sexual feelings aroused, 4

sexual techniques, 138

sexual union, 128–129

sexuality, transformed into religious experience, 129

shahadah, 161

Shaker movement, 170

shamanic dancing, 22

shamanic journey, 37–42; as meditative and healing technique, 37–38

shamanic techniques, 16–18, 40

shamanic world, levels of, 39–40

shamanism, 9, 39, 331; culture and, 14–15, 18, 37–38; trance and meditation in, 15–16; and women, 14–15

Shambhala warriors, 292–93

Shaw, Miranda, 130, 263

siddhasana, 59–62

silence, 210, 317. *See also* quiet

silent prayer and reading, 184–85, 199. *See also* reading

silent void, 185

Silva, José, 322

Silva Mind Control, 322

Sirhan Sirhan, 188

sitting postures, 54–61; practicing breathing in, 71–72; *vipassanā*, 107–8

sitting *za-zen*, 118

sketching from nature, 233–37

Skinner, Joan, 333

Skinner releasing, 333–34

sleep, drifting into, 3, 125

sleepiness, 6

Society of Friends. *See* Quakers

soft belly meditation, 301–2

solstices, 291

somatics, 334

sound, 305–8. *See also* drumming; *Om/aum*

spine, 59–62, 64

spirit, xx, 67

spiritual emergencies, 7–8

Spiritual Emergency Network, 7–8

spiritual essence of life, becoming better attuned to, 2

spiritual goals of meditation, xx

spiritual marriage, prayer of, 182

spiritual master, xxiii

spiritual materialism, xxii

spirituality, xx

spirotherapy, 68

sports, xix, 265–72

stillness, 50, 269, 334

stress, meditative techniques for dealing with, 2, 222, 327

stress-related diseases, xx. *See also* psychosomatic disorders

stretching, 50. *See also* yoga

striving, freedom from, 113, 114, 124

subtle body, 138

suffering, 100, 101, 295, 303. *See also* pain

Sufi breathing, 163–67; Five Purification Breaths, 165–66

Sufi dancing, 169–72; for non-Islamic

individuals, 171

Sufi movement, 161–62

Sufi tradition, 83, 159, 165

sunrise, watching the, 290

surrender and submission, 8, 157, 181

Sweigard, Lulu, 333

swimology, 266–67

symbols, 328–29

T

tadasana (mountain pose), 54

Tai Chi, 141–45

Tai Chi Chih, 143–45

tantien, 143

Tantric Buddhism, 127, 130

Tantric yoga, 130

Tantrism, 127–132, 263

Tao, 136

Tao Te Ching (Lao-tze), 105, 136–139, 147

Taoism, 135–139, 136; philosophical concepts of, 135–136; traditions of, 136–137. *See also* yin and yang

Taoist yoga. *See* Qigong

task-centered mode, 7, 269. *See also* goal-orientation

teachers/practitioners: learning meditation from, xxiii; selecting, 8, 41–42

technology, forms of meditation employing, 221

telepathy, 210

temperaments, 6

tension, 297. *See also* relaxation; stress

Teresa of ávila, St., 182, 196

terminally ill, meditating with, 301–2

Thamas, Katherine, 333

thanksgiving, 182

thinking, *vs.* meditating, xxi

Thoreau, Henry David, 289

thought(s): achieving state of no, 50; generating, 82; letting go of extraneous, 218; transcending one's, xxi. *See also* mind

time, 340; of day, 52

tonglen, 102

training, rules for, xxiii

trance, 16, 18, 33; attaining a light, 2, 240; *vs.* meditation, 33

trance dancing, 21–23

transformation, 335–36

"Try not to try," 7

trying. *See* goal orientation; task-centered mode

Twelve Step programs, 195

U

unconscious, 317–18; connecting to the, 2; enhanced awareness of the personal, xix–xx

union, 164, 218; prayer of incipient, 182

unity, 137, 138

unlearning, 147

V

vajrasana (hero pose), 59, 60

Vedic rituals, 81

Viereck, Eleanor G., 257–59

vipassanā , 93, 96, 105–9, 253

vipassanā centers, 110–11

Virabhadra, 65

Virabhadrasana pose, 66

virasana (thunderbolt pose), 59, 60

visual affirmations, 326

visualization, 265, 321–26, 329; and
    anxiety, 326–27; of biblical scenes,
    185. *See also* imagery
visualization exercises, 324–25
von Franz, Marie-Louise, 317
voudoun, 20, 21

W

Wai Dan, 149
walking meditation, 123–26, 214–15,
    291; discovery of, 213. *See also*
    labyrinth walking
warrior pose, 65–66
warriors, 292–93
water, 291, 328
well-being, promoted by meditation,
    xix–xx
Western mysticism, 178–79
Western tradition(s), 177–79; recent
    expansions, 179–80. *See also specific
    traditions*
Western *vs.* Eastern minds, 291
Whitehouse, Mary Starks, 336
wholeness, 316, 319
Wiccan groups, 188, 189
"wild mind," 118, 248, 249, 275
wilderness, 291–92. *See also* nature
wisdom, 51
Wisdom Tradition, 177
witness consciousness, xxi, 76, 255,
    317
witnessing with passive attention, 8
Wolf, Toni, 332
women: and Islam, 164; and shaman-
    ism, 14–15
World Community of Christian medi-
    tation, 183
writing. *See* haiku

Y

yin and yang, 135, 137, 138, 142, 148
yoga, 33; eight steps of, 48, 75. *See also
    Pratyahara*; goals, 49–51, 76; hatha,
    49, 50, 52, 292; origins, 47;
    Western version. *See* Eutony. *See also
    Qigong*
yoga asanas, 49, 51, 53–54; lying,
    62–65; sitting, 59–62; standing,
    54–58
yoga breathing, 67–73
yoga meditation, 75–79
yoga practice: hints and cautions
    regarding, 51–53; prerequisites, 51
Yoga Sutras, 136
Young, Shinzen, 271, 299

Z

za-zen, 113, 116–19, 124, 125
Zen, 7, 113–19, 121–26, 247–48,
    304; essence in daily life, 121, 125;
    goals, 113, 116, 118; haiku and,
    245–47
Zen-in-action, 122–25
Zen master, 114–17, 121–22
Zen walking, 123–24
zendo (Zen Buddhist monastery),
    115–17, 184, 199
zone, in the, 268–71

About the Authors

Patricia Monaghan, Ph.D., has been meditating for more than thirty years. A member of the Society of Friends (Quakers), she practices *za-zen* and qigong daily; she is also adept at many creative meditations. A member of the resident faculty of the School for New Learning at DePaul University, she teaches science and literature. She is the author of seven books of nonfiction and two of poetry. She lives in Chicago, Illinois.

Eleanor G. Viereck, Ph.D., is the author of *Alaska's Wilderness Medicine* and *Yoga: Skillful Means*. She is also the editor of *Daughters of Inanna*, a women's spirituality journal. Dr. Viereck frequently contributes articles on science, women, sports, and ecopsychology to popular magazines. She lives in Fairbanks, Alaska.

If you enjoyed *Meditation: The Complete Guide*, we recommend the following books from New World Library:

The Art of True Healing by Israel Regardie. Now in a stiking paperback edition, *The Art of True Healing* was first published in England in 1932. It centers around a very powerful meditation exercise — called the Middle Pillar — through which one can stimulate body, mind, and spirit. Through this technique, readers learn to focus energy in a variety of ways for improving their health, success, and ability to help others.

The Complete Book of Essential Oils and Aromatherapy by Valerie Ann Worwood. An encyclopedic book containing every conceivable use for essential oils and aromatherapy in everyday life. Now considered the "bible" on the subject, this book includes easy recipes for beauty products, health remedies, household cleaners, and more!

Essential Aromatherapy by Susan Worwood. This book is a lively A-to-Z reference on the preparation and use of essential oils as holistic healing agents. It reveals the secrets of the ancient art of aromatherapy, organized into accesible, alphabetical listings of applications and individual oil profiles.

Five Steps to Selecting the Best Alternative Medicine by Michael and Mary Morton. This easy-to-use guide alternative healing modalities and helps readers define find the best practitioner for their needs.

The Four Levels of Healing by Shakti Gawain. In this book, filled with deep insight and original thought, Shakti Gawain describes the four levels of human existence — spiritual, mental, emotional, and physical — and explains the importance of developing all four.

14 Days to Wellness by Donald Ardell, Ph.D. Drawn from author Donald Ardell's twenty years of experience promoting wellness worldwide, this two-week program features fourteen steps that take only twenty minutes each day to complete but make for a lifetime of physical, emotional, and mental well-being. Filled with humor, insights, a personal planning system, and proven tips and principles, it makes healthy living downright enjoyable.

The Fragrant Heavens by Valerie Ann Worwood. In this new volume, Valerie Ann Worwood explores the connection between fragrance and spirituality. She breaks new ground by exploring both the scientific and esoteric evidence of the spiritual dimension of essential oils. Worwood also examines the spiritual traditions that use aroma for ritual, prayer, and meditation.

The Fragrant Mind by Valerie Ann Worwood. This book paves a new way for the uses of aromatherypy, concentrating on the mood-changing effects of essential oils. This enormouse and fascinating work provides hundreds of applications.

The Handbook of Alternatives to Chemical Medicine by Mildred Jackson and Terri Teague. Renowned San Francisco Bay Area naturopath doctor Mildred Jackson and her student and colleague Terri Teague teach readers how to prepare remarkably simple and easy remedies from widely available fruits, vegetables, herbs, and medicinal plants. This book has become an alternative medicine classic.

Massage for Busy People by Dawn Groves. The easy-to-understand, how-to text and photographs provide a thorough description of the various types of self-massage techniques available to de-stress and relax.

Meditation for Busy People by Dawn Groves. Enjoy the peacefulness of meditation in just minutes a day! This concise, jargon-free guide introduces a simple method for fitting meditation into a complex and busy lifestyle. In a supportive, friendly style, the author shows us how even sporadic meditation can allow us to manage life's everyday demands with greater ease.

Miracles of Mind by Russell Targ and Jane Katra, Ph.D. A pioneering physicist and a renouned spiritual healer combine modern scientific evidence with ancient Eastern teachings to explain the existence of "nonlocal mind" and the process of spiritual healing. Along the way, they prove what metaphysicians have been teaching for thousands of years.

Scents & Scentuality by Valerie Ann Worwood. By the world's leading aromatherapist, this is the essential guide to aromatherpy to help you discover your true romantic self. *Scents & Scentuality* explores this little-known realm of fragrance and aroma, showing how the potent and pure essential oils of nature can heighten the pleasure of daily life or enrich a romantic evening.

The Tao of Healing by Haven Treviño. The profound, poetic wisdom of the *Tao te Ching* lends itself beautifully to the subject of healing. Haven Treviño's modern adaption of this ancient work captures the essence of the original in language accessible to all.

The 12 Stages of Healing by Donald Epstein. This breakthrough book identifies twelve basic rhythms, or states of consciousness, common to all humanity. Powerful exercises and personal declarations accompany each of the stages, helping us maximize our healing experience. *The 12 Stages of Healing* takes us beyond traditional healing books as it gently guides us through the lessons of each stage on a journey toward greater wholeness, spiritual awareness, and true healing in all areas of our life.

The Whole Mind edited by Lynette Bassman, Ph.D. *The Whole Mind* collects original writings on thirty-six alternative healing modalities — all by expert practitioners — that can help enhance emotional wellness and treat mental illness by addressing imbalances in the body.

Yoga for Busy People by Dawn Groves. Dawn Groves introduces the ancient art of yoga to the overworked bodies and stressed-out minds of busy people everywhere. She introduces a down-to-earth, practical, and easy-to-follow method for creating a yoga routine that provides maximum value in minimum time.